M000239282

Empires on the Waterfront

HARVARD EAST ASIAN MONOGRAPHS 373

Empires on the Waterfront

Japan's Ports and Power, 1858–1899

Catherine L. Phipps

Published by the Harvard University Asia Center
Distributed by Harvard University Press
Cambridge (Massachusetts) and London 2015

© 2015 by The President and Fellows of Harvard College
Printed in the United States of America

The Harvard University Asia Center publishes a monograph series and, in coordination
with the Fairbank Center for Chinese Studies, the Korea Institute, the Reischauer Institute
of Japanese Studies, and other facilities and institutes, administers research projects
designed to further scholarly understanding of China, Japan, Vietnam, Korea, and other
Asian countries. The Center also sponsors projects addressing multidisciplinary and
regional issues in Asia.

Library of Congress Cataloging-in-Publication Data

Phipps, Catherine Lynn, 1968–
    Empires on the waterfront : Japan's ports and power, 1858–1899 / Catherine L. Phipps.
        pages cm. — (Harvard East Asian monologues ; 373)
    Includes bibliographical references and index.
    ISBN 978-0-674-41716-8 (hardcover : alk. paper)   1. Free ports and zones—Japan—
History—19th century.   2. Japan—Commerce—History—19th century.   3. Japan—
Foreign relations—1868–1912.   4. Japan—History—Meiji period, 1868–1912.   I. Title.
II. Title: Japan's ports and power, 1858–1899.
    HF1418.3.J3P45 2014
    387.10952'09034—dc23

                                                                    2014011101

Index by the author

♾ Printed on acid-free paper
Last figure below indicates year of this printing
22   21   20   19   18   17   16   15

For Kären Wigen

Contents

Maps and Tables

Maps

Tables

Acknowledgments

All history contains a hidden record of lived experience that even foot-notes cannot convey. Beyond the historical actors whose stories form the overt subject of the manuscript sits the historian who has spent years gathering and analyzing documents and contextual evidence for the purpose of recreating some piece of those long-ago lives. For me, this book reads like a personal memoir, etching out a childhood guided by parents who focused on education, amazing teachers at Carleton College, adventurous years living in Japan, and the demanding journey to professional historian. These pages recount moments of archival discovery, extended discussions with colleagues and mentors, the kind patience of family and friends, and countless hours at the computer (some good, some not so good). It is my great pleasure to bring to light in these acknowledgments the numerous people who invisibly but unmistakably inspired and enabled the writing of this book.

When I entered graduate school at Duke University, little did I know that my adviser, Kären Wigen, would be a remarkable mentor and friend, whose endless support would sustain me across the many years that it has taken to publish this book. She has repeatedly gone above and beyond, all the while taking care to show me how to improve my work; her bettering influence appears throughout these pages. It is with much affection and great respect that I dedicate this book to her.

Several others shared freely their knowledge, opinions, and time as I first shaped this project in its early stages. My sincere thanks go to the late Jack Cell and to Sucheta Mazumdar, Simon Partner, Susan Thorne,

Gennifer Weisenfeld, and Tomiko Yoda. Special thanks go to David Ambaras, who believed in this project from the beginning, and to Kris Troost, for being there every step of the way. I am indebted to the kindred spirits whose friendship nourished me during graduate school, especially Jessica Harland-Jacobs, Matt Jacobs, Seonmin Kim, Gwenn Miller, Jeni Prough, and Linda Rupert. During this time, my research was generously supported by the History Department, Center for International Studies, and Asian/Pacific Studies Institute at Duke University as well as a Ford Foundation Seminar Travel Fellowship. I also appreciate later research and travel assistance from a Duke University East Asian Collection Travel Grant.

I am grateful to the Fulbright Foundation, which made possible the year I spent doing archival work in Japan. I would also like to thank the faculty, students, and staff at the Kyushu University's Coal Mining Research Center for teaching me about the coal industry and its archives. In particular, I am beholden to Professor Tōjō Nobumasa, who willingly took me under his wing and patiently shared his knowledge with me. Thanks also go to You Byonbu, Niikura Takuo, and Kusano Masaki for their help and friendship. I fondly remember the sunny day we had Gunkanjima to ourselves. Other scholars of the Chikuhō and Kitakyushu regions to whom I am indebted include Professors Tanaka Naoki and Mukai Yurio. I also thank Miwa Munehiro for his insights and for taking me on an unforgettable tour of Chikuhō. Michael Foster kindly introduced me to Ikeda Akihiko, whose hospitality and journalist's scrutiny were greatly appreciated. Imamura Motoichi, who unfortunately did not live to see this book in print, taught me a great deal about Moji and its history.

Special thanks go to Noell Howell Wilson, who from the time I met her on the Hakozaki Campus to the last time we had coffee together in Memphis, has been a great friend and constant sounding board as I worked through the minutiae of this book; the next mocha is on me. Barbara Brooks, whom I first met at the 2002 Social Science Research Council Dissertation Workshop in Monterey, CA, encouraged my work in the years afterward. I am grateful that she read the entire manuscript before she died much too young. I will always remember the fun we had trying to figure out who the anonymous readers were for this manuscript.

The University of Memphis has generously supported my research over the past several years. I thank the College of Arts and Sciences for travel funding at a key stage. My friends and colleagues in the History Department have provided a truly convivial working environment, especially Karen Bradley, Wendy Clark, Andy Daily, Courtney Luckhardt, Susan O'Donovan, Suzanne Onstine, Sarah Potter, Amanda Lee Savage, Kent Schull, Janann Sherman, and Steve Stein. Yuki Matsuda and Sachiko Matsushita have given unstintingly of their friendship and their help with translations. I would also like to thank the Interlibrary Loan staff at McWherter Library for their repeated assistance in obtaining the resources needed to complete this book.

Thank you to everyone who attended the November 2010 Midwest Japan Seminar for providing such valuable feedback on an early version of Chapter 1. Will Hammell, Bob Graham, and Deborah Del Gais at the Harvard University Asia Center have been great to work with while getting this book to print. I thank Scott Walker for generating the maps found herein. Readers Robert Hellyer and Steven J. Ericson provided constructive and detailed feedback, helping me see mistakes and hone my arguments.

Others who deserve my thanks for kindnesses large and small along the way include Kay Ariel, George Bourdaniotis, the Fransioli family, Peter Frost, Warren Gardner, Dick and Marti Gazley, Roy Hanashiro, the Kawakita family, Martin Lewis, Lee Makela, Cathy Maris and Dave Reiner, Kathi Matsuura, Louis Perez, Franziska Seraphim, Rob Sikorski, Bardwell Smith, Kathryn Sparling, Amy Strong and Dave VanHook, Yoshiko Todoroki, and Jun Uchida.

Finally, I cannot sufficiently thank the Owen, Phipps, and Mercer families for their love, encouragement, and support. I only wish that my father, Theodore Phipps, and my in-laws, Lois and Howard Mercer, were still here to celebrate with me. To Tom, Cabell, and Jane, your love and laughter sustain me always.

Note to the Reader

Japanese names are written with the surname first; an exception is made when an author publishes in English. Macrons are used to indicate long vowels in romanized Japanese; however, for common place names like Tokyo or Kyushu, the macrons have been omitted unless a Japanese publication is referenced.

Abbreviations

CSKK   Chikuhō Sekitan Kōgyō Kumiai

DNGBN   *Dai Nihon gaikoku bōeki nenpyō*

DR   Kokuritsu Kōbun Shokan Dijitaru Arkaibu, Dajō ruiten. http://www.digital.archives.go.jp.

FKS CSKK   Nishi Nihon Bunka Kyōkai, ed. *Fukuoka kenshi: Chikuhō sekitan kōgyō kumiai*. Vol. 2. Fukuoka: Fukuoka Prefecture, 1987.

FKS CKT   Nishi Nihon Bunka Kyōkai, ed. *Fukuoka kenshi: Kindai shiryōhen, Chikuhō kōgyō tetsudō*. Vol. 1. Fukuoka: Fukuoka Prefecture, 1990.

FKS TH   Nishi Nihon Bunka Kyōkai, ed. *Fukuoka kenshi: Tsūshi hen*. Vol. 1. Fukuoka: Nishi Nihon Bunka Kyōkai, 2003.

KGS   Proceedings of the Upper House of Japan's Diet (*Kizokuin giji sokkiroku*). http://teikokugikai-i.ndl.go.jp.

KKS   Kitakyūshūshi Kaikō Hyakunenshi Hensan Iinkai, ed. *Kitakyūshū no kōshi: Kitakyūshūkō kaikō hyakunen o kinen shite*. Kitakyūshū: Kitakyūshū-shi Kōwankai, 1990.

KKSGS   Kitakyūshūshi, ed. *Kitakyūshūshi sangyō shi*. Kitakyūshū: Kitakyūshūshi Sangyōshi, Kōgai Taisakushi, Dobokushi Hensan Iinkai Sangyōshi Bukai, 1998.

KKSS SK	Kitakyūshū Shishi Hensan Iinkai, ed. *Kitakyūshū shishi: kindai gendai, sangyō keizai.* Vols. 1–2. Kitakyūshū: Kitakyūshū-shi, 1991–1992.
KKSS KB	Kitakyūshū Shishi Hensan Iinkai, ed. *Kitakyūshū shishi: kindai gendai, kyōiku bunka.* Kitakyūshū: Kitakyūshū-shi, 1986.
KR	Kokuritsu Kōbun Shokan Dijitaru Arkaibu, Kōbun ruishū. http://www.digital.archives.go.jp.
KZ	Kokuritsu Kōbun Shokan Dijitaru. Arkaibu, Kōbun zassan. http://www.digital.archives.go.jp.
MKS	Kōnoe Kitarō. *Moji kōshi.* Moji: Kinkodō, 1897. Reprint, Tōkyō: Meicho Shuppan, 1973.
NYK	Nippon Yūsen Kaisha
NZE	Yokohama Zeikan, ed. *Nagasaki zeikan enkaku.* Vol. 3. Yokohama: Tōkyō Insatsu Kabushiki Gaisha, 1902.
OSK	Ōsaka Shōsen Kaisha
PRO FO	Public Record Office of the United Kingdom, Foreign Office. General Correspondence and Consular Court Records for Japan. 1888–1920.
SGS	Proceedings of the Lower House of Japan's Diet (*Shūgiin giji sokkiroku*). http://teikokugikai-i.ndl.go.jp.
ZH	Ōkurashō Kanzeikyoku, ed. *Zeikan hyakunenshi.* Tōkyō: Nippon Kanzei Kyōkai, 1972.

INTRODUCTION

O n July 12, 1899, at 4:30 PM, the offices of the *Moji shinpō* newspaper received an urgent telegram from Tokyo: an imperial edict had decreed that the twin ports of Moji and Shimonoseki (see Map 1), along with twenty other domestic ports, would soon open to international trade.[1] The Meiji government timed these openings to coincide with the enactment of the watershed 1894 Anglo-Japanese Treaty of Commerce and Navigation, a long-awaited event that put an end to half a century of national humiliation by eliminating foreign rights of extraterritoriality and largely restoring tariff autonomy. Signaling the return of Japan's sovereignty to the world at large, these twenty-two sites would become "open ports" (*kaikō* or *kaikōjō*) on a legal par with the soon-to-expire treaty ports.[2]

Over the next three weeks, word of Japan's anticipated opening hit newsstands around the globe. As the *New York Times* declared, "Changes in Rules Related to Foreigners Arouse Interest: Entire Country Open to

1. *Moji shinpō*, July 13, 1899. Moji and Shimonoseki together are known as Kanmon. They are located on opposite shores of the Kanmon Strait, or Strait of Shimonoseki, which links the Inland Sea to the Korea Strait, opening to the East China Sea and the Sea of Japan.

2. The revised treaties took effect on July 17, 1899, exactly a year and a day after the July 16, 1894 signing. The celebrations, however, were delayed for more than two weeks. Although July 17 was to be the date that all new treaties were enacted, the treaty with France mistakenly used August 4 and Austria-Hungary followed suit, pushing the final date to August 4 (*Times*, July 17, 1899). As per the terms of revision, Japan would not regain full tariff autonomy until August 1911.

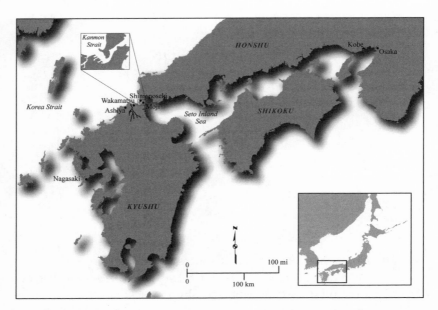

MAP 1 Moji and Its Environs.

All."[3] The *Times* of London pronounced: "Japan takes [its] place today as an equal amongst the civilized Powers of the world." And the *Moji shinpō*, true to its local interests, trumpeted "Treaties Enacted and Kanmon Opened" while chronicling the excitement and profound sense of achievement felt by residents in meeting the dual goals of revising the unequal treaties and opening their home ports.[4] A special municipal council organized the festivities for Moji's August 4 opening. Paper lanterns and national flags adorned doorways throughout the city as residents delighted in school ceremonies, banquets, live music, and fireworks at the city hall.[5]

In addition to highlighting the merriment and auspiciousness of the occasion, the paper's lead article asked readers to contemplate Japan's

3. *New York Times*, July 26, 1899. "Open" in this context means that foreigners gained access to the interior of the country as opposed to being limited to the physically circumscribed treaty ports.

4. *Moji shinpō*, August 4, 1899.

5. Ibid., August 1, 1899. Other cities with newly opened ports, including Hakata and Fushiki, held similar celebrations at the time (Fukuoka-shi Kōwankyoku, *Hakata kōshi*, 1–3, and Fushiki Kōshi Hensan Iinkai, *Fushiki kōshi*, 316).

history over the previous several decades. Since before the Meiji Restoration, the Japanese had suffered the great indignity of the unequal treaties as the Western powers had trampled Japan's rights to self-governance while taking "refuge beneath a stronghold of consular courts." Mojiites should be praised for their strenuous efforts in the national assembly— "writing until their brushes were worn and arguing until their voices were hoarse"—in winning this important milestone for their city. At the same time, there was hard work yet to be done and still higher aspirations to be met; this was but "the point of departure for the long-range plans of both ports" as they now embarked on their "natural" journey to become a center of international exchange in a free country.[6]

Despite the emphasis the *Moji shinpō* placed on this new beginning, 1899 does not, in fact, represent the start of the city's foreign trade. Moji had been exporting coal overseas and providing bunker coal to domestic and foreign ships in its harbor for a decade when the 1899 edict declared it an open port. In this short period, its inhabitants—from entrepreneurs and shopkeepers to stevedores, sailors, politicians, and journalists—had already made a name for their city as a key national and international transportation hub.[7] They had established commercial networks throughout East Asia and served on the front lines of Japan's first war with China. Moreover, as the newspaper proudly declared, of the country's twenty-two newly opened ports, Moji had enjoyed the top foreign trade earnings for the preceding two years. This rank was especially impressive since, unlike most of the others, it was authorized only to export goods.[8] Now granted permission to import as well, Moji's residents imagined a very bright future for their city.

Moji's story, and others like it, are barely known within Japan today, much less outside it. The history of Meiji globalization is usually narrated in reference to the five treaty ports of Hakodate, Kobe (Hyōgo), Nagasaki, Niigata, and Yokohama and the two open cities (*kaishi*) of Osaka and Tokyo.[9] Since the treaty ports became the physical

6. *Moji shinpō*, August 4, 1899.

7. With 30,000 residents, Moji had become large enough to be named a city just that April.

8. *Moji shinpō*, July 18, 1899.

9. Tokyo and Osaka received designation as open cities distinguishing them from the treaty ports. Nonetheless, Osaka quickly began functioning as a foreign trade port whereas Tokyo would not become an international port until 1941. On

manifestation of informal empire in Japan during the almost half-century of their existence, from 1854 to 1899, they are natural locations from which to discuss the country's international connections. Yet a framework that relies on the treaty ports alone misses the much more complex system of maritime relations that developed in East Asia during this pivotal era.

All but one of the ports that were "newly opened" in 1899 had already been functioning as restricted international trade ports prior to that year.[10] Although some had only recently begun operations, over half had been handling foreign trade for a decade or more. Classified broadly as "special trading ports," these sites already had, or were in the process of acquiring, the equipment necessary for modern global commerce: harbors capable of handling deep-draft steamships, lighthouses, storage sheds, loading docks, and more. All were administering customs and handling cargo as well as providing piloting services and connective land transportation. Some, including Moji, offered additional business opportunities as merchants sold wares and foodstuffs on smaller vessels in the offing and prostitutes found their way aboard foreign ships. In all these capacities, the special trading ports and their activities (legal or otherwise) operated under full Japanese jurisdiction.

The treaty port system looks very different with the inclusion of special trading ports. When the treaties ended in 1899, instead of six working international ports (including Osaka but not Tokyo), Japan had twenty-eight ports already appointed to handle overseas trade. The number rises to forty-one when we include the thirteen additional ports named in the recently acquired colonies of Taiwan and the Pescadores. Operating in the shadow of the treaty ports, the special trading ports proved to be a kind of foil to the overarching system, allowing Japan to establish its own foreign trade despite restrictions at the treaty ports. Still, the special trading ports and their role in building Japan's empire were contingent on the multinational treaty port system that developed across East Asia in the mid-nineteenth century. It was only within this broader set of networks that Japan was able to expand its global interactions at the height of the imperial age while tethering these vital connections to

---

the opening and function of these ports and cities, see Ōyama, *Kyūjōyakuka ni okeru.* In using "globalization," I mean a modern rather than postcolonial phase of this process, as A.G. Hopkins offers in his attempt to periodize this unwieldy term (*Globalization in World History*, 3–11).

10. The only exception was Taketoyo.

numerous local sites along the archipelago's shoreline and its growing periphery.

An examination of the special trading ports forces us to rethink Japan's speedy path from semicolony to empire.[11] Its course was not singular but entwined. Japan's ability to develop a geography of protected places at home that was linked to national, regional, and global networks reveals that the conditions of informal empire in East Asia created a framework that would enable Japan to become a modern imperial power. Within this shared space of commercial networks, shipping routes, and the dominance of Western law, we find a malleable spatial grid that allowed for Japan's international activities to increase as they began moving away from a small core of treaty ports to an extended number of coastal sites around the country before the enactment of the revised treaties in 1899.

Treaty Ports and Informal Imperialism

To understand the basic framework in which the special trading ports operated, a brief look at the conditions in East Asia during the late nineteenth century is warranted. The system of informal empire imposed upon Japan in 1858, first by the Americans and then in rapid succession by the British, Russians, Dutch, French, and others, is generally known as the treaty port system. Predicated on the tenets of free trade, the treaties in question aimed to secure foreign access to Japan's resources and markets with minimal protectionist intervention by its government. Since Japanese rulers did not wish to open their country to Western trade at the time, the initiation and implementation of the treaties took place under the threat of military force. The modern warships anchored near the capital made visible the "gunboat diplomacy" that encouraged Japan's acquiescence to the intruders' demands. Retaining power to negotiate, however, the Japanese importantly managed to limit the scope of treaty privileges to specified port locations, collectively labeled treaty ports.

As the oft-used phrase "unequal treaty" makes plain, the terms of these agreements were nonreciprocal, establishing a pattern of relations based on the compromised sovereignty of one country. The new laws

---

11. I use the term semicolony to mean that as a political entity, Japan did not have an "externally recognized right to exercise final authority over its affairs" (Biersteker and Weber, "Social Construction," 1–2).

specifically opened five Japanese ports to international trade while granting foreign signatories such rights as extraterritoriality, most favored
nation clauses, and fixed tariff rates, thus codifying an order of economic
and diplomatic imbalance in a single stroke. Japan would spend the next
fifty years maneuvering to free itself from these constraints, even while
partaking of its benefits, as it strived to be treated as an equal in the
comity of nations.

Japan was not alone in suffering the indignity of unequal treaties.
Constituting the leading eastward edge of the modern interstate system,
informal empire spread across the Ottoman territories and into Southeast
and Northeast Asia during the second quarter of the nineteenth century.[12]
The new relationships that came with this advance prescribed Western
standards of territorial sovereignty, trade, and international law as well
as an ideology of "civilization," compelling non-Western states and their
subjects to engage not only with foreign institutional practices related to
trade and diplomacy but also with new concepts of citizenship and
nationhood in a decidedly hierarchical world order based on military
power, wealth, and a shroud of Western superiority. Led by British efforts to establish Palmerstonian free trade around the world, the nonreciprocal treaties of informal empire would be negotiated by midcentury
with the Ottoman Turks, Burmese, Siamese, Chinese, and Japanese.[13]

Taking the modern system of interstate relations beyond Europe and
America meant that the terms of ingress had to be renegotiated with each
state. In every encounter, both sides drew on a growing body of legal and
experiential precedent that nonetheless resulted in unique variants each
time bilateral treaties were signed.[14] Western powerbrokers insisted on
stipulations that had proven effective in prior cases while local diplomats urged accommodations for indigenous circumstances.[15] Although

12. See Duus, "Japan's Informal Empire," xiv–xix; Gallagher and Robinson,
"Imperialism of Free Trade," 1–14. Additionally, Alan Knight contends that informal imperialism existed in Latin America even though it was not marked by unequal treaties ("Britain and Latin America").

13. Horowitz, "International Law," 445–48; Lynn, "British Policy, Trade, and Informal Empire," 104–6.

14. Horowitz, "International Law," esp. 446. On Japan, see Matsukata, "King
Willem," regarding Dutch interpretations of and influence on Japan's diplomatic
situation.

15. The Chinese, for instance, introduced the most favored nation clause in an
attempt to guard against having any one nation gain undue power over their country.

such basic tools of informal empire as tariff restrictions and extraterritoriality were applied universally, the use of treaty ports was more limited.

The opening of select ports for trade and residence by Westerners in China and Japan, and then later by the Japanese in Korea, became the hallmark of informal empire in Northeast Asia.[16] Here the Western advance breached long-standing restrictions confining foreign trade to designated ports. The treaty port system was rooted in this earlier pattern of geographically limited exchange while it expanded the existing port structures and networks first developed by local groups.[17]

In China, Westerners had been allowed to trade at the southern port of Canton (now Guangzhou) since the 1750s. Nearly a century later, the British were pushing the boundaries of legal trade to increase their profits from the sale of opium. When met with determined Chinese resistance, Great Britain used military force to ensure their commercial interests in the First Opium War of 1839–42. As a result, China ceded Hong Kong and opened five ports (Shanghai, Ningpo [Ningbo], Foochow [Fuzhou], Amoy [Xiamen], and Canton) to foreign residence and trade in a succession of treaties with foreign powers starting with the 1842 Treaty of Nanking (Nanjing).[18]

Whereas the Chinese initially succeeded in confining the foreigners to this handful of sites, they would steadily have to yield more ground, literally and figuratively, over the next half-century. After ratification of the 1858 Treaty of Tientsin (Tianjin), signed during the Second Opium War (1856–1860), the first treaty ports were joined by eleven more, for a total of sixteen, some along interior riverine routes. The restriction of foreigners to the treaty ports, as agreed to in China's first set of treaties, meant that the transport and sale of merchandise beyond these sites

---

Unfortunately, they did not foresee how it would be employed to multiply concessions against them (Fletcher, "Heyday of the Ch'ing Order," 383).

16. Kasaba suggests that the Sublime Porte unsuccessfully tried to limit treaty privileges to specific ports in the 1840s ("Treaties and Friendships," 222).

17. On the importance of local populations and longer-term perspectives on port development, see Broeze, "Introduction," 4–9.

18. Jürgen Osterhammel states that Chinese historians counted 1,182 unequal agreements signed in that country alone by the end of the century, giving the treaty port system "an almost impenetrable complexity" ("Britain and China," 153).

depended on indigenous merchants and their networks. The second set of treaties, however, allowed trade, travel, and missionary activity in China's interior, significantly increasing the level of foreign penetration into that country.[19] By the early twentieth century, a series of lost battles led China to grant further territorial concessions and to open a staggering total of ninety-two treaty ports.[20]

By contrast, Japan never had to concede to opening more ports beyond those agreed upon in the 1858 Ansei Treaties. The difference in the trajectories of the treaty port system in the two countries is striking.[21] As the Japanese managed, through acuity, persistence, and luck, to keep Western encroachment in check, they began consolidating national boundaries and increasing their own presence on the continent by making effective use of the treaty port system's complex, porous infrastructure and its evolving matrix of imperial relationships.[22] Redefining ties with its neighbors was a first step toward building a competitive modern nation-state. Following the Meiji Restoration, the Japanese began incorporating Hokkaido (known as Ezo before 1869) and the Ryukyu Islands into the polity.[23] The Meiji leaders signed a treaty with China in 1871 enabling the two countries to trade with each other on an equal basis until an increasingly antagonistic relationship led to war. The subsequent 1895 Treaty of Shimonoseki gave Japan the same privileges as the Western powers in China as a most favored nation. Meanwhile, in 1876, the Japanese used their own version of gunboat diplomacy to open the first three treaty ports in Korea, which were followed by five more by century's end. In 1899, on the eve of the treaty revision in Japan, Northeast Asia had fifty active treaty ports (see Map 2). After that pivotal date, revisions eliminated treaty ports in the archipelago even as Japan maintained privileged access to all of the others, thus ensuring a sharp

19. See Moulder, *Japan, China, and the Modern World Economy*, 124–27, 140–43.

20. Cassel, *Grounds of Judgment*, 5.

21. On differences between China and Japan, see, for example, Duus, *Abacus and the Sword*, 21; Moulder, *Japan, China, and the Modern World Economy*; and Osterhammel, "Semi-Colonialism," 299–302.

22. On the porous nature of British control over its empire, see Benton, *A Search for Sovereignty*.

23. The degree to which Japan's absorption of Hokkaido in 1869 and the Ryukyu Islands in 1879 constituted imperialism is an open debate. See, for example, Caprio, *Japanese Assimilation*, ch. 2; Morris-Suzuki, "Lines in the Snow"; Oguma, *"Nihonjin" no kyōkai*, chs. 1–3; Sawada, *Okinawa to Ainu*.

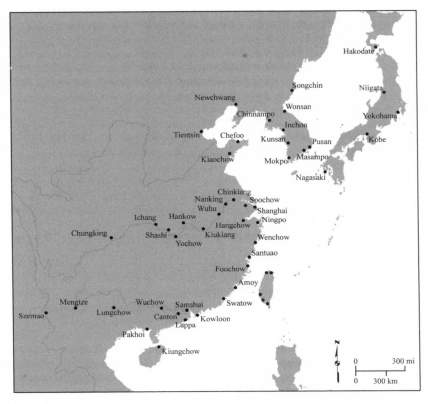

MAP 2 East Asian Treaty Ports, 1899.

divergence in legal positions and economic privileges across the region at the start of the twentieth century.

Special Trading Ports

Although the treaty port system necessarily serves as the main frame of reference here, an assessment of Japan's modern maritime networks needs to consider what the unequal treaties did *not* do. For our purposes, one thing in particular stands out: they did not forbid Japan from opening additional ports on its own. From the Western perspective, such a stipulation would not have been in the interests of the many foreign diplomats and merchants who repeatedly asserted that additional treaty ports should be named. On the Japanese side, although the government proceeded

with caution, politicians, prominent businessmen, and local citizens
eyeing their own economic gain tempered Tokyo's reluctance with their
frequent calls for opening the country.[24]

The Meiji oligarchs responded to these calls by designating a score
of special trading ports, at different points in time, to aid in bringing international trade revenues to hinterlands throughout Japan. Surprisingly,
these ports have largely gone unnoticed as a set of active international
ports, but they offer important new information about how Japan was
able to advance economically and militarily at the end of the nineteenth
century. It would, after all, only make sense that the Japanese people and
government would feel the limitations of five international trade ports,
especially ones dominated by foreigners, and would seek alternative ways
to ensure their commercial and military well-being. Although the treaty
port system purposefully favored Western merchants, it did not by any
means shut down native commercial networks or inhibit their evolution.
The special trading ports provided a way for Japan to minimize its vul-
nerability while maximizing its opportunities. Moreover, they became
places where Japanese merchants could use international trade and shipping networks yet remain free of foreign competition in what amounted
to a kind of "reverse liberalization of trade."[25]

By actively tapping into the larger matrix of informal empire, these
sites developed and extended their own tendrils of capitalist enterprise
and imperialistic advance into other parts of Asia. These sprouts grew
on the durable mesh that had been tightened by the dominant Western
(and Western-employed) diplomats, merchants, compradors, shippers, and
sailors in the region whose activities were reinforced by distant home governments, militaries, and powerful financial interests. By the time Japan
regained its sovereignty at the end of the century, it had already woven
its own sturdy fibers into the warp and woof of East Asian transport and
exchange, allowing it to sustain an increasing, independent level of

24. Not everyone felt this way. For example, some foreign merchants feared
greater opening would detract from existing trade and dilute their efforts across
too many sites. See Hoare, *Japan's Treaty Ports*, 139. As late as 1898, arguments
against the persistent idea that opening more ports would automatically take trade
from existing ports were still being made in Japan. See, for example, Ishii, *Nihon no
kōwan*, 38–42.

25. I am indebted to Steven J. Ericson for this formulation.

participation in the global economy. The special trading ports provided a mechanism for locales across Japan to directly join this spatial grid.

Transmarine East Asia

The principal geographical space considered here is transmarine East Asia.[26] This term is fairly straightforward, incorporating the seas and coastal zones of Northeast and Southeast Asia, and describing a shared site—one with "layered sovereignties"—where people from around the world interacted with one another.[27] More specifically, it designates the primary arena where the Japanese engaged with Western and Asian powers, established independent nodes of commerce, and launched military initiatives in the late nineteenth and early twentieth centuries. Whereas Japan's diplomatic concerns within transmarine East Asia centered on China and Korea, its trade patterns followed Western, especially British, shipping networks, which cut a wider swath of commerce that reached treaty ports and colonized coasts from Bombay (Mumbai) and Rangoon (Yangon) to Singapore, Hong Kong, and Shanghai. These networks, and Japan's creation of new ones, had a global reach where Japan found important markets.

Using transmarine East Asia to designate a specific region of interaction incorporates four of Takeshi Hamashita's "Maritime Zones of Asia."[28] From north to south, then, transmarine East Asia covers the Sea of Japan and the Yellow Sea, as well as the East China and South China Seas (see Map 3). This region covers both the treaty port system and the primary locations linked to the special trading ports. Under the mantle of formal and informal imperialisms that spanned this region in the nineteenth century, sites with varying degrees of territorial occupation and mixed shades of economic dependence coexisted in patchwork fashion.

Within this varied space, Japan's relative freedom to pursue modernization was inexorably bound to its own international status. Even as Japan advanced its economy, it nonetheless faced an international society of

26. Mimi Hall Yiengpruksawan uses the phrase "transmarine Northeast Asia" in *Hiraizumi*, 17.

27. Benton, *A Search for Sovereignty*, 31–32.

28. See map 3, "Maritime Zones of Asia," in Grove and Sugiyama, "Introduction," 4. See also Hamashita, "Tribute and Treaties."

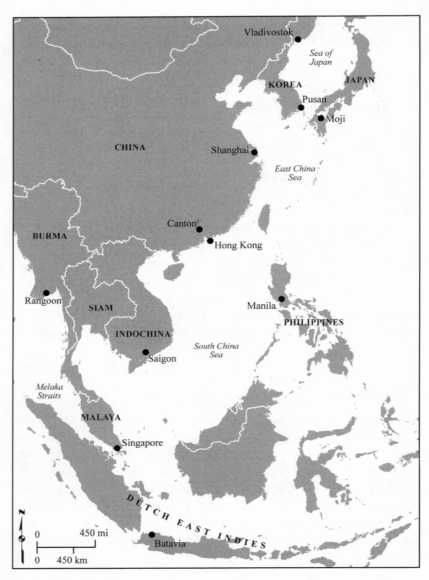

MAP 3 Transmarine East Asia.

states that viewed it as inferior.[29] Through the unequal treaties, the Western powers delivered a vague but loaded charge for Japan to earn back its full sovereignty. Like China and other countries subjected to informal empire, Japan was pushed into a normative order prescribing that it modernize or be overtaken.[30] Japan's activities in the nineteenth century must be viewed in this environment. The Japanese desire to be recognized as a sovereign nation and revise the unequal treaties, which was a constant refrain at state and local levels throughout the second half of the nineteenth century, guided how the central government approached both modernization and the country's infrastructural development.

Viewing Japan as a state seeking the rights and privileges of the world's leading powers focuses attention on the international relationships that contextualized and contributed to Japanese decision making.[31] Recent studies of imperialism that employ a more global perspective have been moving away from once-predominant linear models that view Japan as an anomaly, latecomer, or imitator, and end up placing the country temporally—and spatially—at odds with the Western powers as well as with its colonies.[32] This historiographical turn instead allows us to see more clearly that Japanese imperialism developed in direct relation to other contemporaneous empires and the pressures, possibilities, and conventions accompanying them. In practice, all empires learn, borrow, and even rely on those that precede them or compete against them.[33] Japan was no exception. In fact, Japan's ability to make effective use of the Western presence in East Asia, especially through Western shipping and markets (which in turn relied on indigenous networks), is key to understanding Japan's growing power during this era.

Once Japan signed an unequal treaty in Korea in 1876, the country began participating as an aggressor within East Asia's structure of informal imperialism even while it remained subordinate to the Western

29. Biersteker and Weber, "Social Construction," 11–14.

30. Hong, "Stranger within the Gates," 329–30; Horowitz, "International Law," esp. 449. See also Barlow, "History and the Border," 24–25.

31. Biersteker and Weber, "Social Construction," 6, 11.

32. On newer trends in the field, see Caprio, *Japanese Assimilation*; Cassel, *Grounds of Judgment*; Dusinberre, "Janus and the Japanese Empire"; and Schmid, "Colonialism and the 'Korea Problem.'"

33. Benton, *A Search for Sovereignty*, esp. 2–7; Burbank and Cooper, *Empires in World History*, 3; Kamen, *Empire*, xxiv–xxv; and Kramer, "Power and Connection," 1350.

treaty powers. Two decades later, however, Japan's victory over Qing China in the Sino-Japanese War of 1894–95 signified three important shifts in Japan's bid to be recognized as a sovereign nation-state: an unprecedented change in East Asian power relations, the acquisition of new colonial territory, and a major step toward parity with the Western empires. The trade and transportation infrastructures established after decades of work at home proved to be a constituent part of these changes.

Although the special trading ports initially sprang from the need to establish trade in more locations across Japan, they came to support the country's economic and military endeavors in ways unforeseen at their naming. By the turn of the twentieth century, it was clear that Japan's international ports were central to the material functioning of Japan's empire. The treaty ports and special trading ports embodied the layers of sovereignty and power at work in East Asia, and the perils and opportunities located therein, as they unequivocally shaped intra-Asian relationships. Japan's rise as an expansive nation-state and the development of its port system must be understood in this context for the Japanese were acutely aware of the double-edged nature of the empires on their waterfront.

Connecting Japan at Multiple Spatial Scales

Examining the ways the treaty port system and the special trading ports functioned together reveals the multiplicity of connections that both challenged and empowered Japan as it joined the late nineteenth-century world order. Yet Japan's emergence as a modern nation-state was not solely the result of high-level diplomacy and elite economic leadership for this process took place across multiple scales. The dismantling of the unequal treaties, the establishment of regional networks, and the creation of an infrastructure that would support an empire hinged on initiatives undertaken at the local level. Japan's international ports functioned as spaces of activity where denizens established and maintained networks vital to their own well-being so that even as they operated within the broader set of imperial relationships underpinning all Asian port cities, they accommodated local, regional, and national ambitions.

As the most successful of the special trading ports, Moji exemplifies the sustained development of maritime networks that directly linked local sites to commercial and military operations spanning East Asia. Since activities taking place in Moji often depended on key legislative decisions and recognition from Tokyo, this narrative must necessarily acknowledge the role of the central government. At the same time, focusing on Moji's maritime and local histories allows us to decenter Tokyo as the prime creator of Japanese industrialization and commercial expansion.

Shifting the view away from Tokyo to focus on how the "local" interacted directly with the "global" also makes room for a discussion of how the people of Moji strategically positioned their port city to gain advantage, not merely within Japan, but in East Asia and beyond. As the people of Moji concerned themselves with domestic coal supplies, competing ports, and overseas markets, we can map how they defined their city in relation to these larger geographies. Moreover, since Moji functioned as a principal military depot and information hub during the Sino-Japanese War of 1894–95, its newspaper reveals how the Japanese nation and its fledgling empire galvanized the city's own identity.

The present study is structured to highlight the three dominant geographical scales of place-making in mid-nineteenth-century Japan: global, national, and local. The region of transmarine East Asia serves to help locate the global in space and serves as a consistent backdrop against which these scales shift. The intent is to create a nested history of Japan in three parts. Part I covers the large-scale, top-down processes that set the framework for Japan's port systems under the consequential Ansei Treaties. Part II shows how ports like Moji were key to the modernization of the nation's infrastructure and its military operations. Lastly, Part III hones in on the locally based actors who engaged these global and national forces in their home ports.

While this work crosses spatial scales, it proceeds in a generally chronological fashion. Chapter 1 delineates five distinct phases in the opening of the country, explaining how the treaty ports and special trading ports became Japan's chief sites of foreign interchange. Chapter 2 examines the economic turmoil that resulted from opening the country to foreign exchange and the measures the Meiji oligarchs took to stabilize national finances. Central to this discussion is the way the nation's leaders targeted rice and coal exports to ship overseas from an extended number of locations in order to facilitate the flow of revenues into Japan. In so doing, they unwittingly laid a foundation for the special ports of export (*tokubetsu yushutsukō*), which partly rested upon older patterns of domestic transportation and production.

Part II looks at the development of national infrastructures in relation to the special trading ports. Since ports formed the links between water- and land-based transportation routes, the third chapter examines harbor improvements, shipping lanes, and railroad networks together with news and markets, to consider how these elements came together in the creation of a thriving port. Chapter 4 moves beyond economic imperatives to look at Japan's commercial and naval vulnerabilities. Close inspection of the special ports of export reveals the ways in which the Japanese used Western shipping networks and fleets in strategic ways to enhance their own commercial profiles. Additionally, incidents with foreigners at the ports highlight Japan's limited control over the waterways immediately surrounding the archipelago.

Finally, Part III zooms in on the port of Moji to detail how its boosters, politicians, and businessmen created an identity for the port in relation to the nation-state and its rising empire. Chapter 5 examines the port's functions during the Sino-Japanese War through the *Moji shinpō*'s reportage of the conflict. More broadly, the chapter asks how the war became part of people's daily lives and contributed to the developing identity of this port city. The final chapter takes up the prolonged campaign to have Moji named an open port. Through nationwide collaboration and competition, the port finally secured its spot as a principal hub in transmarine East Asia. The enactment of the revised treaties in 1899 heralded the end of the treaty port system in Japan and the recovery of Japanese sovereignty. This moment also, however, signaled a new level of opening to international trade, a long-term transition that was eased considerably by the special trading ports. Now with the hard-won status of open ports, these locales remained core places of exchange where Japanese citizens engaged the world during peace and war well into the twentieth century.

PART I

Japan in the World

ONE

Special Trading Ports

A New Framework for the Opening of Japan

Japan's modern international history is essentially a maritime story, for the only way to engage with other countries was by sea.[1] Ports and their networks were vitally important for trade and communications, as well as military advance and defense. Certainly Japan's position as an island nation surrounded by waterways made it vulnerable. But the setting also afforded the country great opportunity to participate in the expanding global commerce that came to the shores of an early modern polity characterized by heavy restrictions on overseas travel and trade.

Starting in the late eighteenth century, as Western interest in Asia and its trade potential grew, foreign ships sailing in nearby waters began coming ashore at unsanctioned ports along Japan's coast. Some attempted to gain the right to provisions and fair treatment for distressed ships while others more directly sought the establishment of formal commercial relationships. Although these vessels were successfully turned away for decades, such early incursions presaged the convergence of forces that would soon envelop the region. The new dynamic in East Asia required, and already commanded, Japan's engagement.[2]

---

1. On using oceanic perspectives in historical inquiry, see Bentley, "Sea and Ocean Basins"; Braudel, *The Mediterranean*; and Wigen, "Introduction," 1–18.

2. See Hellyer, *Defining Engagement,* and Wilson, *Defensive Positions,* on how domains and the *bakufu* responded to the growing numbers of foreign ships passing Japan's coasts and stopping at its ports.

Limits of the Treaty Port System in Japan

When the Ansei Treaties were signed in 1858, shogunal officials were famously reluctant to increase the number of permitted trading partners, allow unknown ships to anchor in Japan's harbors, or welcome new foreigners to their shores.[3] It was in large part this reluctance that drove the Western powers to demand the opening of ports. In an important sense, the grudging opening of the treaty ports ultimately represented a compromise between armed encounter and willing participation in a world order defined by other, more powerful, entities. It was primarily in these circumscribed locations that people in Japan would interact with the rest of the world—treaty signatories and East Asian neighbors alike—for most of the Meiji era (1868–1912).

To assume that the treaty ports were the only international trade ports operating in Japan until their abrogation in 1899, however, would be a mistake. Over time, the Meiji leaders recognized their country's increasing need for a larger number of functioning deepwater harbors in an era when national power derived from commercial, industrial, and military modernization. Five scattered ports simply could not provide satisfactory access to the heartlands of production and consumption, especially as the volume of trade rose.[4] Traditional ground, riverine, and coastal transportation links to these designated ports would soon prove insufficient. Such limitations were even more problematic before the building of extensive railroad networks, an undertaking that posed logistical problems of its own. The relatively small number of treaty ports would hamper development unless they could be supplemented by additional facilities able to accommodate modern steamship traffic.

Certainly, when the unequal treaties were signed, the Tokugawa government's main concern was its own survival.[5] Even the most forward-thinking people would not have been able to predict how the treaty ports might serve a commercial, industrial, and imperialistic Japan in the long

3. See Mitani, *Escape from Impasse*, for details of the *bakufu*'s internal deliberations about opening the country.

4. Moreover, they had widely varying levels of success. Niigata, in particular, has often been regarded as a complete failure. Isabella Bird, for example, on visiting Japan in 1878, referred to Niigata as "a [t]reaty port without foreign trade" (quoted in Cortazzi, *Victorians in Japan*, 173). See also Hoare, *Japan's Treaty Ports,* 19.

5. See Mitani, *Escape from Impasse*, e.g., 115, 185–86.

term. But as the country's geopolitical circumstances evolved over five decades to the end of the nineteenth century, the Meiji government strategically—and with great caution—did allow a number of nontreaty ports to handle limited international trade. The number of these supplementary ports increased geometrically in the second half of the century to reach twenty-two at home plus an additional eight special trading ports in Japan's colonies of Taiwan and the Pescadores by 1899 (see Map 4). As the treaty revision negotiations progressed along with Japan's economic growth through the Meiji era, the central government became more and more willing to unlock points of entry. The oligarchs in Tokyo were effectively trying to solve a puzzle with three different, yet interrelated, sets of demands. Negotiators had to quell foreign and domestic calls for further opening, meet the structural and financial demands of development, and preserve the keystone in the treaty revision process: using the promise of opening the country fully to foreign trade as leverage to secure the return of full sovereignty.[6] If greater access was granted too early, the treaty powers would have what they wanted without rescinding objectionable inequities.

Chief among those inequities were two concessions: fixed tariffs and extraterritoriality. Fixed tariff rates signaled the dangers inherent in allowing trade to be conducted on an unequal basis, especially for an economy already reeling from an influx of cheap goods at the treaty ports. Japan's inability to set protective tariffs on imported goods not only hurt native industries but also cost coveted revenues that would have helped to mitigate the exorbitant costs of political and material change. Meanwhile, the notoriously demeaning privileges of extraterritoriality required strict boundaries to control the foreign presence. The original treaties had been drawn up on the assumption that foreign interaction would remain confined to the treaty ports, each of which had a set radius for lawful foreign settlement and activity. Opening special trading ports, which existed outside treaty port legislation, compelled the Japanese government to issue new regulations to prevent any geographic extension of extraterritorial privileges.

Finally, expanding the reach of international trade while Japan was still struggling to build its own ocean-going commercial fleet created secondary complications. To open additional ports to commercial traffic

6. Perez, *Japan Comes of Age*, 61.

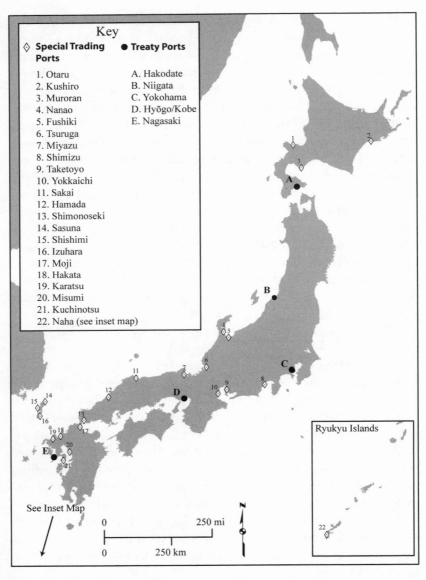

Key

◇ **Special Trading Ports** ● **Treaty Ports**

1. Otaru	A. Hakodate
2. Kushiro	B. Niigata
3. Muroran	C. Yokohama
4. Nanao	D. Hyōgo/Kobe
5. Fushiki	E. Nagasaki

6. Tsuruga
7. Miyazu
8. Shimizu
9. Taketoyo
10. Yokkaichi
11. Sakai
12. Hamada
13. Shimonoseki
14. Sasuna
15. Shishimi
16. Izuhara
17. Moji
18. Hakata
19. Karatsu
20. Misumi
21. Kuchinotsu
22. Naha (see inset map)

Ryukyu Islands

See Inset Map

0   250 mi

0   250 km

N

MAP 4 Japan's Open Ports, 1899.

before the country's own fleet could accommodate that cargo meant chartering foreign, especially British, ships. Chartered ships in turn brought Western pilots and their crews to areas of Japan not formally regulated by the treaties. Permitting the anchorage of foreign vessels in nontreaty locations thus became a hotly debated topic, necessitating protective legislation and enforcement as well as the appropriate management of customs procedures.

Special trading ports constituted a viable answer to many of these thorny issues. Placing strict limits on what could be traded where and with whom allowed the regime to open more points of access while minimizing the risk of Western penetration into the country. The timing was strategic, for the growing Western presence in Asia offered new commercial opportunities for Japan. Merchants in the treaty ports were already using and building on transportation and business networks created by Western interests across Asia, giving them ready access to markets across transmarine East Asia and beyond. By extending limited trade privileges to another score of ports, Japanese officials effectively allowed local merchants throughout the country to avail themselves of these same markets by chartering foreign vessels to carry Japanese cargoes.

Greater access to markets was not the sole advantage that Western shippers provided the Japanese. Equally important was their voracious demand for fuel coal, the commodity that fully half the special trading ports were established to handle. Designated ports like Moji were regularly used as coaling stations for steamships—domestic and foreign, commercial and military—plying neighboring seas. The benefits to be found at these nontreaty ports flowed in both directions. The rewards to Western traders included revenues to shipping companies, expanded access to coal supplies, and greater commercial involvement in Japan. Apparently, these were enough to prevent objection to an arrangement that, in effect, allowed Japan to bypass the restraints of the treaty port system, legal though it may have been.

Naturally, even as the Japanese tapped into Western commercial enterprises, they also developed their own trading capacities and pursued their own distinct commercial and geopolitical interests in the region. In the case of several ports that were permitted to conduct trade with Korea, Russia, and China, the government limited their activities to Japanese ships, establishing clear control over both commercial transactions and transportation. Such stipulations reflect efforts to empower Japanese merchants and shippers to conduct business without Western intermediaries as well as to develop new maritime routes not already dominated by foreign shipping concerns. The decision to restrict trade to domestic ships demonstrates that attention was given to developing independent avenues of commerce as well as creating hubs capable of serving Japan's own modern maritime networks. In time, these sites would facilitate the country's ability to compete with the Western imperial powers across East Asia.

The special trading ports become most important to our understanding of modern East Asia at this intersection between Japan's integration into the system of global capitalism and its own economic and military advances on the continent. These sites reveal the dialectical processes at work as Japan moved from semicolony to formal empire. Through a combination of mutually advantageous, interimperial ties with the Western powers and their networks, on the one hand, and a related but more autonomous infrastructure for maritime trade and transportation, on the other hand, Japan's commercial and military activities with its nearest neighbors intensified considerably by the end of the century. It is to this extended transition that we now turn.

Opening Japan: A Story in Five Acts

During the late nineteenth century, the composition of Japan's ports was dynamic; their locations and restrictions were adjusted as commercial, diplomatic, and military needs changed and new opportunities emerged. The Japanese created some flexibility in their international relationships by combining treaty ports with special trading ports to form a hybrid maritime system that would help satisfy their own needs and ambitions. The rest of this chapter traces the development of the special trading ports within a primarily diplomatic framework and identifies five key junctures when the central government sanctioned opening more ports between 1854 and 1899 (see Table 1). Each set of openings expressed its own logic in answering unique combinations of internal and external imperatives and involved trial and error, successes and failures, and negotiation at every stage.

The initial reconfiguration of Japan's foreign trade system, in what amounted to a shift from "gates" to treaty ports, was an extended and not particularly smooth process. Although the catalyst for this shift was provoked from the outside, the Japanese state retained some leverage—often

Table 1
Types of Special Trading Ports and Their Opening Dates

Port Name (in alphabetical order)	Korea	Korea & Russia	China	Special Export	World
Fushiki		1894		1889	
Hakata	1883			1889	1896
Hamada					1896
Izuhara	1883				
Karatsu				1889	1896
Kuchinotsu				1889	1896
Kushiro				1890	
Misumi				1889	1898
Miyazu		1893			
Moji				1889	
Muroran				1894	
Naha			1894		
Nanao					1897
Otaru		1894		1889	
Sakai					1896
Sasuna	1888				
Shimizu					1897
Shimonoseki	1883			1889	
Shishimi	1889				
Tsuruga					1896
Yokkaichi				1889	1897

SOURCE: Adapted from *Moji shinpō*, October 9, 1896, *NZE*, and PRO, FO 881/8741x.

using it to great effect—in determining where openings might offer advantage without creating undue disruption. First the Tokugawa *bakufu* and then the Meiji government guarded and oversaw the country's opening in the five acts described here.

ACT 1—RECONFIGURING THE TOKUGAWA GATES,1858–1879

Throughout the Tokugawa era, Japan maintained restricted foreign trade and diplomatic relations by using a system of "selective opening," which deliberately channeled all transactions to a small number of specified locations.[7] This means of containing foreign relationships was used across East

---

7. The term "selective opening" is from Hamashita (quoted in Lee, "Trade and Economy," 7).

Asia during the early modern era and can be seen in three well-known sites: Pusan Korea's *Waegwan* (Japan House), which controlled Japanese trade beginning in 1611; Dejima Island in Nagasaki, which became a trading post for the Dutch in 1634; and the Canton factories in southeastern China, which were established in 1757 to exclusively manage a growing trade with Western merchants.[8] These instances of deliberately circumscribed interchange hold important clues for understanding the creation of both the treaty port and special trading port systems in Japan. Despite the critical transformations that occurred with the signing of the unequal treaties, continuities in approach to managing foreign relations can be found in general method if not detailed substance across the two eras.

The Tokugawa shogunate maintained a well-ordered set of foreign connections that either came directly under its own aegis or were parceled out to appropriate domains. Together with key feudal lords (*daimyō*), it engaged in skillfully crafted diplomatic and commercial relationships, relegating interaction with named foreign partners to four designated locations, or "gates," at a distance from the political center—Matsumae, Tsushima, Nagasaki, and Satsuma.[9] Once faced with Western demands to open new sites convenient to their own needs, the shogunate applied this same kind of selective approach by resolutely limiting the spaces where additional dealings would occur. Officials worked determinedly to shepherd treaty port locations to areas that they judged would be least disruptive to the country, its security, and its existing patterns of commerce.[10]

As trade opened to the treaty powers at these negotiated locations, the "four gates" (*yottsu no kuchi*) with special commercial, diplomatic, and

8. On the *Waegwan* in Pusan, see Lewis, *Frontier Contact*. Kazui Tashiro says the type of settlement at Pusan has roots in customs offices active in Song, Yüan, and Ming China (Tashiro, "Foreign Relations," 292). George H. Kerr states that a Ryukyuan "trading depot" for confined trade and diplomacy existed for over four hundred years (1439–1875) at Chuangzhou in Fujian Province (*Okinawa*, 93). Basil Hall Chamberlain explains that there was a medieval concession for Chinese traders in Naha at the castle of Omono-Gusuku, which he likens to the later Dutch site at Dejima ("The Luchu Islands and Their Inhabitants," 309). Also see Larsen, *Tradition, Treaties, and Trade*, 49–50, esp. his notes, for more examples and evidence of practices circumscribing foreign trade.

9. Studies on Tokugawa foreign relations include Arano, "The Entrenchment of the Concept"; E. Katō, "Research Trends"; H. Katō, "The Significance of the Period"; Tashiro, "Foreign Relations"; Toby, *State and Diplomacy*.

10. Recent works detailing the negotiation process are Auslin, *Negotiating with Imperialism*, and Mitani, *Escape from Impasse*.

defense functions did not remain the same as before. The revolutionary changes that came with signing the treaties and the subsequent Meiji Restoration (1868) dramatically altered the contours of the country's foreign trade between 1854, when the Treaty of Kanagawa opened the first ports, and 1879, when Japan formally colonized the Ryukyu Kingdom and, with it, effectively brought the early modern gate system to an end.[11] Within this fifteen-year period, three of the treaty ports— Yokohama, Niigata, and Kobe—were newly opened to foreign trade. Two gates essentially shifted to nearby locations in becoming treaty ports (Matsumae to Hakodate and Satsuma to Nagasaki) in a process that more broadly entailed the central government's colonization of Hokkaido to the north and Ryukyu to the south. The last two gates remained open but were transformed: Nagasaki was remodeled as a treaty port, while Tsushima continued to trade with Korea—outside the treaty port system—until Japan itself forced the opening of treaty ports on its neighbor in 1876 and channeled its own commerce through special trading ports.

Matsumae and Hakodate With regard to the north, the port of Matsumae conclusively lost its status to Hakodate under the first unequal treaties. The town and port of Matsumae, ruled by the feudal lords of the same name, served as the authorized point of passage between the Ainu people of Hokkaido and the Japanese in Honshu for most of the Tokugawa period. Initially, American Commodore Matthew Perry, during negotiations with shogunal officials, sought the right for American whaling vessels to land at Matsumae for shelter, provisions, and fuel.[12] Because the Tokugawa government's chief envoy, Hayashi Akira, did not want Perry to negotiate separately with domain leaders in Matsumae who were nominally in control of that territory, he instead offered to open Hakodate.[13] Perry agreed to the substitution, and the Treaty of Kanagawa, signed by the United States and Japan on March 31, 1854, designated Hakodate as one of two ports (along with Shimoda) open to Americans.

11. Even though the first ports were named in the 1854 Treaty of Kanagawa, these were not technically part of the treaty port system since this was not a commercial treaty. I use the dates 1858 to 1899 to specifically indicate the era of treaty ports in Japan.

12. His first two requested sites were Matsumae and Naha.

13. Mitani, *Escape from Impasse*, 190–91. Hakodate sits 30 miles northeast of Matsumae on the Tsugaru Strait.

In turn, this arrangement meant that the shogunate had to requisition Hakodate from the Matsumae clan in order to fulfill its part of the bargain.[14]

The shogunate's primary concern in the north lay with Russia, which had been steadily moving into portions of the southern Kuril Islands, southern Sakhalin, and the island of Hokkaido for more than half a century.[15] It is within this longer span that the shift from Matsumae to Hakodate took place. Russian advances in the region led a nervous shogunate to take direct control over Hokkaido temporarily, from 1779 to 1821. During this period, Hakodate was singled out for development; the shogunate established a Hakodate magistracy (bugyō), made improvements to its naturally favorable harbor, and built a road from Hakodate to Nemuro (700 miles to the northeast).[16] After fears had subsided and responsibilities were handed back to the Matsumae clan, Hakodate continued to thrive as a port.

The Tokugawa government's apprehension over Russian objectives in the north would again come to the fore by midcentury in the sustained discussions between Russian vice admiral Evfimii Vasil'evich Putiatin and Japanese magistrate Kawaji Toshiakira. Even when the Treaty of Kanagawa was being concluded with the United States, these negotiations between Russia and Japan were ongoing. In early 1855, the two sides reached a partial agreement to settle the northern border and signed the Treaty of Shimoda. This first Russo-Japanese pact split the Kuril Islands between the two countries and allowed the Russians to trade in Hakodate and establish a consulate there.[17]

14. Shimoda, on the Izu Peninsula southwest of Tokyo, was chosen for its convenience and proximity to the Tokugawa centers of commerce and power. See Auslin, *Negotiating with Imperialism*, 41. Shimoda closed when Yokohama opened. Uraga and Kanagawa were also in contention as Shimoda was hard to access by land, see Mitani, *Escape from Impasse*, 191. The idea that Matsumae was "requisitioned" comes from an English-language timeline of historical events found at Hokkaidō Ainu Kyōkai (http://www.ainu-assn.or.jp, accessed March 22, 2014).

15. Howell, *Geographies of Identity*, 221, n1. It was also in the north that the first Russian ships began to call in Japanese harbors in the late eighteenth century, stoking fears around the country.

16. Irish, *Hokkaido*, 53.

17. Mitani, *Escape from Impasse*, ch. 9. The territorial borders would be more fully demarcated in the Treaty of St. Petersburg (1875), which gave all the Kuril Islands to Japan and gave Sakhalin (which had been left open to both Japanese and

The selection of Hakodate as a "wood and water" provisioning port cannot be divorced from Japan's broader geopolitical concerns. In line with the Russian treaty, the shogunate once again took direct control over Hokkaido and its foreign relations rather than leave them in the hands of the Matsumae clan. This move served to recast the roles of the shogunate and the domain as well as the ports of Matsumae and Hakodate in the late Tokugawa era. The gradual displacement of the older power center would be further solidified in the Ansei Treaties of 1858, which opened Hakodate to commerce with five treaty powers, and then in 1869, by the establishment of the Hokkaido Development Agency (Kaitakushi). The Meiji government's interests in developing Hokkaido proved decisive for altering the trade and production patterns of the native population. During the second half of the nineteenth century, officials in Tokyo sent teams to survey the island's natural resources. Its coal and sulfur reserves, in particular, were readily exploitable in the service of an industrializing Japan, to which Hokkaido was now unequivocally joined. As Hokkaido became an integral part of the Japanese state, the port of Hakodate together with the later-named special trading ports on the island (Kushiro, Muroran, and Otaru) would function as key nodes in Japan's modern commercial and strategic networks.[18]

Satsuma and the Ryukyu Islands (Naha) The keeper of the southernmost gate, the domain of Satsuma, would help usher in the modern era, its lower samurai playing a principal role in overthrowing the Tokugawa regime and providing leaders to fill the ranks of the Meiji oligarchy. Leading up to that time, Satsuma had garnered wealth and power from its long-term exploitation of the Ryukyu Kingdom as well as through active trade ventures that its leaders pursued with other domains. For two and a half centuries, Satsuma's Shimazu clan in Kagoshima had subordinated Ryukyu as a vassal state while allowing it to simultaneously remain a tributary state to Qing China.[19] In this way, Satsuma was able to take advantage of Ryukyu's dual tributary ties, without provoking the

---

Russian influence in the 1855 treaty) to Russia. The 1855 treaty also opened Nagasaki as a third port of refuge.

18. See Howell, *Geographies of Identity,* and Walker, *Conquest of Ainu Lands,* for very different methodological approaches to the incorporation of Hokkaido into Japan.

19. Kerr, *Okinawa,* 183–227.

Nagasaki The case of Nagasaki was sui generis. Unlike either the Matsu-mae or Satsuma/Ryukyu gates, Nagasaki officially remained open to foreign trade during the political shifts of the mid-nineteenth century. Moreover, it would continue to accommodate Japan's trade with both Asian and Western entities. As Japan's only centrally administered gate during the early modern era, Nagasaki became the "official port of reception" and a first line of defense when Western ships appeared in coastal waters starting in the late eighteenth century.[27] Nagasaki, therefore, was where local officials sent those commercial vessels and warships that sparked distrust, and at times panic, when they dropped anchor elsewhere along the archipelago's extensive shoreline.

Although historical precedent supports Nagasaki's selection as a treaty port, the choice was not automatic. This southern harbor had been formally charged with overseeing foreign exchange with the Chinese and the Dutch since the early seventeenth century, providing Japanese officials there with valuable experience managing defense and foreign trade. These relationships had long been carefully circumscribed; the Chinese were allowed to reside in a concession area within the city while the Dutch were confined to an offshore "factory" on Dejima Island. With such a background in successfully managing foreign contact, Nagasaki was a good choice for a treaty port to the Japanese but proved problematic for the Americans. During negotiations with Hayashi in 1854, Perry rejected using Nagasaki as a treaty port, stating that he did not wish to be subordinated there as he believed the Chinese and Dutch had been. Instead, he agreed to the two ports of Hakodate and Shimoda.[28] Evaluating the situation differently, the Russians and the British readily accepted Nagasaki, along with Hakodate and Shimoda, thus gaining access to all three ports.[29] Perry may have been dismayed by this turn of events, but the Americans did not miss out for long. Nagasaki would subsequently open to all treaty signatories through the 1858 commercial Ansei Treaties and remain a key node in East Asia's modern maritime networks.

27. Mitani, *Escape from Impasse*, 158; also see Wilson, *Defensive Positions*.

28. Hawks, *Narrative*, 424–25.

29. Mitani suggests Japan may have avoided opening a third port, but mistranslations and assumptions made in the context of the Crimean War meant the British and Russian treaties each specified Japan provide three ports for their vessels (*Escape from Impasse*, 226–29).

After it became a treaty port, however, Nagasaki did not function exactly as it had before. The addition of several new trading partners brought in foreign merchants who enjoyed relative freedom of movement in the vicinity of the port as well as extraterritorial privileges and beneficial terms of trade. Moreover, long-standing relations with the Chinese and the Dutch were modified both in law and in practice. Following a series of preliminary agreements, Holland secured the second of the five Ansei Treaties and, in doing so, effectively remade the nature of its relationship with Japan.[30] Whereas earlier ties had been based on reciprocal interest, the modern ones hewed to the "cooperative imperialism" and threat of force that Western powers leveraged to gain Japanese acquiescence.[31] To be sure, men like Philipp Franz von Siebold, the Dutch minister of colonies, and Janus Henricus Donker Curtius, the superintendent of the Dejima factory, acted faithfully as intermediaries in assisting Japan through this difficult era.[32] Ultimately, however, they too extracted unequal privileges from Japan, and just as the factory at Dejima became a vestige of their bygone relationship, the Dutch themselves soon blended without distinction into Nagasaki's multinational foreign settlement.[33]

The China trade at Nagasaki also changed. Even before the significant move to modern diplomatic relations that came with the signing of the 1871 Sino-Japanese Treaty of Amity, Chinese traders, interpreters, and sailors began to play a vital role as go-betweens in Japan's trade with the West. Their numbers in Nagasaki increased rapidly as they helped to facilitate the operation of the treaty port system during its translation from China to Japan. Importantly, however, the majority of these agents would be directly involved in Qing China's own growing trade with Japan.[34] Although Nagasaki's Chinatown would soon be overshadowed

30. The 1858 Ansei Treaties were signed, in chronological order, with the United States, Holland, Russia, Great Britain, and France.

31. The term "cooperative imperialism" comes from Beasley, *Japanese Imperialism*, 17.

32. Chaiklin, "Monopolists to Middlemen," esp. 260–61.

33. See the Nagasaki City website, "Yomigaeru Dejima," on the restoration of Dejima, http://www.city.nagasaki.lg.jp/dejima/ (accessed September 27, 2013). The island itself was submerged as a result of later harbor engineering projects, but tourists can visit a nearby site to see a replicated version of the bygone factory.

34. Hoare, "The Chinese in the Japanese Treaty Ports," 20, 28.

by those of Yokohama and Kobe, both located nearer Japan's major urban centers of Osaka and Tokyo, this port would continue to serve a significant role in Kyushu until the end of the nineteenth century.[35]

Yokohama, Kobe, and Niigata In contrast to the shuffling of residential and trade patterns in Nagasaki and the more complex territorial dislocations in the north and south, the opening of Yokohama, Kobe, and Niigata were relatively straightforward. None of the three functioned as gates during the Tokugawa era. All were selected in negotiations leading up to the Ansei Treaties based on their location: close enough to urban centers or key shipping routes to satisfy Western negotiators, yet distant enough from essential sites (commercial, cultural, or military) to afford some measure of protection for the Japanese. Shogunal officials involved in the Ansei treaty discussions, such as Inoue Kiyonao and Iwase Tadanari, fought hard to maneuver the concessions away from areas considered critical to the country's welfare. For example, in allowing the opening of Kobe (together with the city of Osaka), they purposefully avoided opening Kyoto, Japan's oldest cultural center.[36] Further, in delineating the foreign settlement at Kobe, negotiators rejected placing it in either the bustling town of Sakai or Kobe proper and instead moved it two miles away, to an area that foreign residents disdainfully called a "swamp."[37]

The Japanese similarly managed to unilaterally push the foreign concession in Edo Bay from Kanagawa, which sat directly on the vital overland Tōkaidō route (the country's main transportation artery to the capital), to the fishing village of Yokohama, 5 miles away. The Americans and the British, who wished to be close to the road and its markets, were pleased when, because of miscommunication with U.S. Consul Townsend Harris, they believed that Kanagawa had been agreed upon as the treaty port location. The Japanese, however, found Kanagawa too important to open and expected the concession to be at Yokohama. After the misunderstanding was discovered, *bakufu* officials deliberately obfuscated subsequent discussions. Meanwhile, echoing the successful

35. Ibid., 20.

36. Auslin, *Negotiating with Imperialism*, 64.

37. Western residents also complained about the distance from the port as an inconvenience (Cortazzi, *Victorians in Japan*, 160–61).

isolation of the Dutch at Dejima, the *bakufu* had speedily erected docks and a customs house at Yokohama before redirecting the first arriving merchants to this site.[38] After their merchants began to establish themselves, the Americans and British recognized that they could not have Kanagawa.[39]

In the case of Niigata, its location along the Japan Sea coast weighed heavily in its selection as a treaty port. Although it had long been a key node in Japan's *nishi mawari* (western sea circuit) for transporting the region's abundance of rice to market in Osaka, it was also quite removed from the country's major urban centers.[40] The British minister to Japan, Harry Parkes, never liked the site, which was prone to heavy silting from nearby rivers and faced strong winds and seas. The port of Nanao (then named Tokorokuchi) to Niigata's southwest was briefly considered as an alternative and would be designated a special trading port in 1896, but officials in Kaga domain strongly opposed this idea because the region was already weary from preparing to defend against the foreign ships that had been making unwelcome stops along the coast.[41] To keep the negotiation process moving forward, Niigata was named in the treaty with a caveat to later change the site to one more suitable to foreign steamship traffic. The move never happened, and Niigata officially remained the fifth treaty port.[42]

Unofficially, however, the nearby port of Ebisuminato, located on Sado Island, served at times as a proxy for Niigata, especially for ships needing shelter in rough weather. Despite this reinforcement, Niigata never generated much Western trade during the early Meiji era because it remained off the beaten track for regular steamship traffic. Along with nearby Fushiki, Nanao, and Tsuruga (all three of which would later be named special trading ports), Niigata would grow in prominence for

38. Auslin, *Negotiating with Imperialism*, 43, 50–54; Cortazzi, *Victorians in Japan*, 54.

39. Auslin, *Negotiating with Imperialism*, 57.

40. Flershem, "Some Aspects of the Japan Sea Trade," 407.

41. Ibid., 415; *Yomiuri shinbun*, November 27, 1895. Nanao was under consideration to serve as a military port for the Sino-Japanese War and was designated a special trading port in 1896.

42. Hoare says the idea was dropped when Parkes left Japan in 1883 since he was really the only one who cared ("The Chinese in the Japanese Treaty Ports," 19).

foreign exchange starting with the establishment of navigation and trade routes to Korea and the Russian Maritime Province in the mid-1890s.

Tokyo and Osaka Two other sites that are sometimes counted among the treaty ports are Tokyo and Osaka. Both were opened to foreigners through the Ansei Treaties as "open cities" but not technically as "open ports." The *bakufu* had intended to keep open ports in more remote areas and thus away from the country's two largest cities.[43] During the 1854 negotiations over which ports to select, the *bakufu* specified that Osaka was not to be considered.[44] Tokyo, then named Edo, was not under consideration either until Harris arrived in late 1867 and presented the Japanese with a commercial treaty proposal. Among other things, he demanded the opening of Edo and Osaka to trade and American residence, and despite ongoing opposition, Hotta Masayoshi, who was an adviser to the shogun (*rōjū*), agreed.[45] After the Meiji government took power, it quickly sent foreign surveyors to four of the country's most important ports—Osaka, Yokohama, Niigata, and Tokyo—to evaluate prospects for modern construction projects at these sites. The central government, however, did not pursue construction at any of these locations at that time, diverting attention to what would end up being a misguided project at Nobiru instead.[46] Despite fraught efforts to turn Tokyo's harbor into a site for foreign trade, most notably in the mid-1890s, it would not become an international port until 1941. By contrast, the port of Osaka had begun handling foreign trade after the city opened in 1868.[47] Thus it would be reasonable to count Osaka but not Tokyo among the treaty ports.

Tsushima (Izuhara) Tsushima alone was a gate that remained open outside the treaty port system in the Meiji era. The island occupied an ambiguous position between Japan and Korea, and its ruling Sō family had long functioned as intermediaries between the two countries. Its people

43. Mitani, *Escape from Impasse*, 243.
44. Ibid., 217.
45. Ibid., 191, 271–73.
46. Kokubu, *Shittemoraitai Nihon no minato*, 35.
47. Yokohama Zeikan, *Ōsaka zeikan enkakushi*, 27–29.

had strong economic ties to Korea and traded regulary at Pusan. Located centrally within transmarine East Asia, Tsushima did not escape being changed by the shifting international circumstances. After withstanding the 1861 Tsushima Incident, when a Russian captain unsuccessfully attempted to turn the island into a warm water anchorage for Russian vessels, and weathering the upheaval of the Meiji Restoration, Tsushima's economic, but not diplomatic, ties to Korea survived intact.[48] In 1872, the Meiji government decided to bring Tsushima under its direct jurisdiction. By making it part of Nagasaki Prefecture, the government aided the island financially, taking over the domain's longstanding debt with Korea, and established military garrisons there.

Centralized efforts to bring Tsushima more fully into the Japanese polity were driven by two convictions by the oligarchs. First, Tsushima provided a significant but vulnerable line of defense for Japan, hence the immediate move to fortify this outpost. Second, this agriculturally poor island needed to maintain its trade with Pusan in order to feed its population. Thus, Izuhara (previously Fuchū), the former castle town and main port of Tsushima, was allowed to continue trade with Pusan and would remain open during the gradual reorderings that would take place in East Asian relations over the next few decades. The additional Tsushima ports of Sasuna and Shishimi would open as special trading ports, in 1888 and 1889 respectively, to further support trade with Korea.[49]

In each of these cases of port openings and closings in the late Tokugawa era, the shogunal officials charged with negotiating the unequal treaties maneuvered as best they could to contain foreign trespasses, the repercussions of which were unknowable at the time. They appraised each gate and treaty port individually and with studied attention, consolidating newly open sites with the former gates where possible. Ultimately, they were able to check foreign encroachment by winnowing down the locations where foreigners could live and do business and by

48. See Deuchler, *Confucian Gentlemen*, on the changes in 1876, and Hellyer, *Defining Engagement*, 240–44, on the late Tokugawa and early Meiji years.

49. Izuhara's status would shift in 1883, when it received special trade designation, and again in 1899, when it was fully opened with the enactment of treaty revision.

demarcating clear physical boundaries around those activities, a practice that had long proven successful at the gates.[50]

ACT 2—THE KOREAN INTERIM, 1876–1889

The second phase in Japan's modern opening was directly related to the establishment of informal empire in Korea. In the 1875 Kanghwa Incident, the Japanese staged a contrived military encounter inspired, in technique but not necessarily substance, by Western gunboat diplomacy.[51] Japan exacted unequal terms of trade with Korea through the resulting 1876 Treaty of Kanghwa, which called for continuing trade at Pusan and opening trade at two additional ports (Inchon and Wonsan) while giving Japan privileges for settlement and extraterritoriality. The same treaty declared Korean independence from the Qing empire.[52] Although not successful in removing Chinese authority from Korea, in fact inversely serving to harden Chinese resolve, the treaty marked a sea-change in the nature of East Asian relationships. It began the process of "relocating Japan's place in the world and redefining power in Asia" by using Western legal and military methods to assert Japanese influence on the continent.[53]

After signing this landmark agreement, Tokyo decided to permit an unlimited number of Japanese citizens to travel to Pusan, as yet the only treaty port open for trade. The regime also declared that trade with Korea was henceforth to be treated "just like domestic trade."[54] In other words, imports from and exports to Korea could be handled anywhere in Japan at any time according to the same regulations and procedures governing trade at home. Additionally, the trade was duty-free and to be carried only by Japanese ships. These legislative efforts encouraging Japanese citizens to conduct direct trade with Korea were animated by business leaders like Ōkura Kihachirō, who personally called on mer-

50. Auslin, *Negotiating with Imperialism*, 46, 54.

51. Duus, *Abacus and the Sword*, 47.

52. On this incident and how this treaty differed from those signed with Japan earlier, see Larsen, *Tradition, Treaties, and Trade*, 63.

53. Dudden, *Japan's Colonization of Korea*, 27. Regarding the significance of the Chinese World Order that came before, see, e.g., Key-Hiuk Kim, *Last Phase*; Conroy, *Japanese Seizure of Korea*.

54. DR, vol. 2 (1871–1877), no. 278: Sozei 8, "Chōsenkoku bōekihin yushutsu wo yurusu," October 14, 1876. See also Shimonoseki-shi, *Shimonoseki shishi*, 269. Minkyu Kim offers strong evidence for why the 1876 agreement at Kanghwa should not be considered a Western-style treaty ("Revolutions," 148).

chants to participate.[55] As the only foreign country with treaty rights to trade on the peninsula, Japan risked little in allowing its citizens new freedoms to capitalize on this opportunity. This combination of high-level diplomacy and expanded commercial activity was a clear attempt by Japan's leaders to stake a unique claim on Korea.

The new arrangements did give Japan a privileged position between 1878 and 1883, allowing the fledgling trade to produce some tangible results. The combined trade at Pusan and Wonsan, which opened in 1880, drew between 200 and 250 merchants, many from Tsushima, to these ports. Korean-Japanese trade increased during this short period, with Korea's share of Japan's total trade growing from less than 1 percent in 1877 to nearly 5 percent in 1883. The bulk of what Japan exported to Korea in these early years was textiles, much of which were re-exported via Japan from Great Britain, but also included dyes, copper, silk, matches, and watches. By contrast, Korea sent mainly agricultural products and raw materials to Japan, including rice, ginseng, medicines, gold dust, and gold ore.[56] The spell of free trade with Korea, however, lasted only about five years. In 1882, a series of watershed events brought new sets of relationships to Korea and further shifted diplomatic and commercial dynamics there.

Swelling tensions in foreign and domestic matters culminated in significant changes for the peninsula. At the urging of Qing China, Korea signed an unequal treaty with the United States in May 1882 to help counter Japan's growing power in Korea. Other Western countries, including Great Britain, Germany, Italy, and Russia, soon followed with treaties of their own. By July, strong discontent with corruption in the Chosŏn government and poor living conditions for the people erupted in the soldier-led Imo uprising, which also expressed anger at the Japanese, who were exporting precious rice. Korean soldiers led attacks on the national palace, rice granaries, and military barracks and burned down the Japanese legation in Seoul. The Qing government, protective of its tributary state, responded quickly to suppress the revolt, kidnap the implicated Grand Prince (Taewon'gun), and prevent a Japanese military response.[57]

55. Deuchler, *Confucian Gentlemen*, 71–72. On early settler merchants, see Uchida, *Brokers of Empire*, 36–44.

56. See Deuchler, *Confucian Gentlemen*, 80–83, and Uchida, *Brokers of Empire*, 35–44, on the composition of traders, trade amounts, and commodities exchanged.

57. See Larsen for a detailed account of the Imo Incident and its meanings (*Tradition, Treaties, and Trade*, 80–88).

In another show of dismay with Japan's interference in Korea affairs, the Qing statesman and general Li Hongzhang initiated a new
agreement with Korea that October. The "Sino-Korean Regulations for
Maritime and Overland Trade" served to redefine the nature of the bilateral relationship, positioning China to interfere directly in Korean
affairs and reap some of the benefits found in the world of modern international law. The agreement also promoted commerce, containing
some of the same features, such as extraterritoriality and set tariffs, as
Korea's other unequal treaties. But even as these regulations altered the
bilateral relationship however, it aimed to increase Chinese influence
on the peninsula and reinforce the tributary bond connecting the two
countries.[58]

As important as these changes were for Korea and China, they were
also momentous for Japan and challenged the influence that its leaders
were trying to create in East Asia. Now that Western countries had also
secured unequal treaties with Korea and Japan's rivalry with China was intensifying, the short-lived era of treating Korea as a domestic trading partner had to end. Accordingly, the Dajōkan (Grand Council of State) issued
new rules governing the trade with Korea on December 7, 1883. Because this trade, like all other foreign trade, now had to be restricted, the
edict opened three special trading ports on Japan's southwestern coast.
The Dajōkan authorized Izuhara, Shimonoseki, and Hakata to conduct
trade with Korea, but the goods could be carried only on Japanese-owned
ships.[59]

Theoretically, Japan could have resumed funneling trade through just
the five treaty ports and Tsushima. The main rationale provided for naming additional trading ports was the inconvenience of the treaty ports for
trade with Korea. Shimonoseki and Hakata were considerably closer to
Korea than Niigata, Kobe, or Nagasaki. The choice of these three ports
in 1883 reflected both their geographical positions and their preparedness
to begin handling even relatively small amounts of foreign trade. With

58. M. Kim, "Revolutions," 186–94; Larsen, *Tradition, Treaties, and Trade*, 88–91.
See also Lin, "Li Hung-chang's Suzerain Policy," 180–82.

59. KR, vol. 7 (1883), no. 51: Sozei, "Chōsenkoku bōekihin yushutsunyū rikuage
kokoroekata . . . ," December 7, 1883. The following year, a branch of Nagasaki
Customs was established in each location, with corresponding military installations
to ensure their protection (ibid., vol. 7 [1883], no. 2: Kanshoku 2, "Chōsenkoku
bōeki no tame . . . ," December 19, 1883).

respect to maritime geography, all three are clustered together in Japan's southwest and offered functioning harbors able to provide ready and proximate access to Pusan, Wonsan, and Inchon (the last opened in 1883). Izuhara's Pusan networks were long-standing by 1882, and Hakata and Shimonoseki, both important hubs in domestic trade routes, had concentrated populations of merchants and local officials who supported opening to trade with Korea.[60]

Maintaining Tsushima's Korea trade at only one port, however, proved difficult. Because the port of Izuhara sits on the southeastern side of the island, it was costly and time-consuming for merchants and suppliers on the western coast to have to ship their goods east to Izuhara and then go back across the island to reach Korea. Accordingly, Sasuna (1888) and Shishimi (1889) were soon opened and equipped with a branch office of the Nagasaki Custom House.[61] Both ports were already linked to interior networks and directly faced Korea, allowing for faster and easier navigation. The port of Shishimi accommodated the loading of commodities like wood, coal, and fish from the island's central regions for export. Sasuna could better handle the various goods of Tsushima's western villages, including Inazaki and Saosaki, which could not themselves be effective special ports, as they had to contend with harsh winds and tides. Opening these additional ports was not only a response to the needs of Tsushima's population but also reflected the central government's desire to suppress smuggling by removing some of the barriers to sanctioned trade while placing still more regulatory control over the island.[62] All three of Tsushima's special trading ports would continue to conduct trade with Korea even after they became open ports at century's end.

As for the other two newly designated ports, Shimonoseki fared better than Hakata from the start. The first year that Shimonoseki recorded exports, their value totaled 28,000 yen, with rice topping the list of roughly 50 commodities, which also included sake, salt, and tobacco. The value of imports reached 70,000 yen, with beans, or

60. Fukuoka-shi Kōwankyoku, *Hakata kōshi*, 23–27.

61. KR, vol. 8 (1884), no. 8: Bunsho, "Chōsenkoku bōeki ni zoku suru kamotsu . . . ," April 2, 1884. Sasuna had been permitted to conduct some import and export trade with Korea as early as 1884.

62. Ibid., vol.14 (1890), no. 62: Un'yu 4, "Nagasaki ka Tsushima-no-kuni Sasuna Shishimi nikō ni oite . . . ," March 27, 1890.

mamerui, leading 29 import goods, which also included dried sardines, raw cowhide, rice, and seaweed (*funori*).[63] By contrast, Hakata tallied a grand total of less than 9,000 yen for imports and exports combined.[64] Starting in 1889, in addition to retaining their special functions with regard to Korea, both ports would expand their foreign trade as special ports of export, a designation that allowed them to handle the five approved commodities of rice, coal, wheat, wheat flour, and sulfur for export on either Japanese-owned or chartered foreign ships.

Long a key site in Japan's coastal trade circuits, Shimonoseki's strategic position—in relation to both the continent and Japan's own commercial, military, and transportation systems—held both promise and peril for its development as a foreign trade port. It was considered for designation as a treaty port on two occasions, but it was not to be. By the time that Shimonoseki was selected for exchange with Korea, it had already garnered substantial attention at home and abroad. As part of the "revere the Emperor, expel the barbarians" (*sonnō jōi*) movement leading up to the Meiji Restoration, the domain of Chōshū used shore-based cannon and recently purchased warships to block foreign vessels from passing through the Strait of Shimonoseki. Because this narrow chokepoint links the Korea Strait (conduit to the East China Sea and Sea of Japan as well as travel south to Nagasaki) to the Inland Sea (with access to Kobe and Osaka as well as Yokohama and Edo/Tokyo), the blockade succeeded in impeding the movements of foreign ships.

After staging a retaliatory bombardment of Chōshū, the victorious British, led by Harry Parkes, offered to waive a stiff indemnity of $3 million in exchange for securing Shimonoseki as a sixth treaty port. The Japanese rejected the offer. Two decades later, Shimonoseki nearly became a treaty port once again when a new commercial treaty was signed between Japan and the United States on July 25, 1878, but it was never fully ratified. The whole effort fell apart the next year, when other powers, effectively bound together in negotiations by their most

63. Shimonoseki-shi, *Shimonoseki shishi*, 269.
64. Fukuoka-shi Kōwankyoku, *Hakata kōshi*, 24.

favored nation clauses, failed to agree to the same terms.[65] Nonetheless, the attempt shows that the Japanese thought that greater sovereignty outweighed the risks of opening this additional treaty port.

Meanwhile, the importance of the port's location to Japan's own fledgling sea routes was reinforced in 1875, when the Mitsubishi company made Shimonoseki its port of call for a new mail service to Shanghai. Equipped with a customs agency the next year, Shimonoseki administered Mitsubishi ships carrying passengers, mail, and domestic cargo.[66] Its subsequent designation as a special port for Korea in 1883 and then a special port of export in 1889 were thus part of a long series of attempts to make use of this key spot. When war between Japan and China broke out over Korea in 1894, Shimonoseki, along with Moji, would play an important military role and serve as the negotiating site for the peace settlement bearing its name.[67] Local and national debates about Shimonoseki's commercial and military roles continued until it became an open port in 1899.

It was through Japan's own network of ports, including Shimonoseki, Hakata, and the three Tsushima ports, that Japan's trade with Korea would increase, accompanied by growing tensions on the continent, from 1883 onward. The Meiji government continued to encourage and channel this trade in response to changing needs and opportunities and would add more special trading ports to bolster commercial ventures in Korea in the mid-1890s. The oligarchs' use of selective opening was not limited to the Korea trade but was applied to advance Japan's commercial and financial interests in other directions as well.

ACT 3—THE PUSH TO EXPORT, 1889–1894

On July 30, 1889, the Ministry of Finance (Ōkurashō) created a new class of ports, the "special ports of export." Numbering nine in all, these ports—Shimonoseki, Hakata, Kuchinotsu, Otaru, Yokkaichi, Moji,

65. On the signing of the revised treaty in July 1878 and the reasons why it never came into effect, see *New York Times*, 1878–80, esp. February 24, 1879, May 22, 1879, and January 1, 1880.

66. The port of Fukue in Hizen gained similar mail call privileges to Korea in 1884, but it did not otherwise become a special trading port (*NZE*, 4; *ZH*, 148–49).

67. In 1891, Shimonoseki's total trade with Korea alone reached nearly 1.5 million yen. By comparison, its overseas export of rice and coal, excluding Korea, was nearly 3 million yen (Shimonoseki-shi, *Shimonoseki shishi*, 270).

Karatsu, Misumi, and Fushiki—were authorized to directly export five duty-free items: coal, rice, sulfur, wheat, and wheat flour. The chosen sites, the designated export commodities, and the new rules of trade were all specific to this type of port. Intended to create new opportunities for exports despite the limited number of international trading ports, these locales would assist Japanese merchants situated near important production sites to sell some of the country's key products. The announcement of these partially open ports came as new agreements were being reached with the Western powers and treaty revision seemed imminent.

During the previous month, Japan had just ratified its first equal treaty with a non-Asian state the previous month. Signed with Mexico, a country that had few dealings with Japan and remained outside the imperialist competition in East Asia, this treaty represented a symbolic victory for the Japanese who were increasingly intolerant of their semi-colonial status. Japan's foreign minister, Ōkuma Shigenobu, who took office in 1888, purposefully redirected the treaty powers away from joint discussions, insisting on negotiating separately with each signatory in order to give Japan more room to maneuver. And Mexico, which did not yet have a treaty with Japan, seemed to Ōkuma a good place to begin changing the terms of Japan's foreign relationships.

Negotiated between Mutsu Munemitsu, minister to Washington, and Mexican envoy Matias Romero, the 1889 treaty provided Mexican citizens with unprecedented privileges for Westerners in Japan. It stated, "His Majesty the Emperor of Japan . . . hereby grants to Mexican citizens resorting to Japan . . . the privilege of coming, remaining, and residing in all parts of His Territories and Possessions; . . . of there trading by wholesale or retail in all kinds of products, manufactures, and merchandize of lawful commerce."[68] But there was a crucial trade-off. In order to obtain these privileges, Mexico agreed to "unconditionally recognize the independent autonomy of Japan" and forgo extraterritoriality and fixed customs duties.[69] Although Mexican citizens were not expected to come to Japan in great numbers, Ōkuma had established a precedent for equality that could be used in future negotiations with other Western countries. Mexico had little to lose in signing; the treaty could be

68. The English text of this article is in Jones, *Extraterritoriality in Japan*, 208.
69. *New York Times*, June 7, 1889.

nullified if other countries did not agree to the same terms. But, Japan could benefit if the treaty encouraged others to agree to the same terms.[70] Ultimately, Ōkuma gambled that the treaty powers wanted access to the interior enough to give up their other privileges.

Ōkuma got part of the bet right and did, in fact, sign new treaties with the United States, Germany, and Russia soon thereafter. He did not, however, anticipate that the introduction of other requirements would generate division among government leaders and backlash from the public. As expected, the proposed treaties eliminated most provisions of extraterritoriality, providing that "foreigners will be freely permitted to travel, trade, reside, or own real property, in all parts of the empire outside the limits of the present treaty settlements."[71] Although these foreigners would be subject to Japanese law, there was a catch. Because Western diplomats did not have confidence that the Japanese legal system would handle cases involving their citizens fairly, they insisted that foreign judges be allowed, for a transitional period of twelve years, to sit on mixed courts up to the level of Japan's Supreme Court, a stipulation that Ōkuma had conceded.[72]

The public's violently negative reaction to Ōkuma's concession came as a surprise. For a population buoyed by its own recent victory for people's rights in the promulgation of a constitution (itself a prerequisite for treaty revision) and increasingly convinced of Japan's inherent equality, this provision was unacceptable. The *North China Herald* reported that "up to the end of September 120 memorials with 6,754 signatures had been presented to the Senate in favour of revision, and 185 memorials, with 56,837 signatures, against it."[73] The majority of an increasingly vociferous public demanded nothing less than full sovereignty for Japan. Its outrage stalled the revision process and reached a crescendo in October, when a radical member of the ultranationalist Genyōsha society, Tsuneki Kurushima, threw a bomb into Ōkuma's carriage. The statesman survived, but his badly injured right leg had to be amputated. Treaty revision was now just as irreparably damaged, and by year's end,

70. Perez, *Japan Comes of Age*, 83 and 204, n74.

71. *Times*, April 19, 1889.

72. For a detailed account of the 1888–89 negotiations, draft treaties, and public opposition, see Jones, *Extraterritoriality in Japan*, 113–27.

73. *North China Herald*, November 1, 1889.

Ōkuma had resigned along with the rest of the Kuroda Cabinet, bringing the latest round of treaty negotiations to a close without any ratified agreements.

Amid the "treaty drama in Japan," as a headline in *The Times* described the intense revision process, the opening of the nine special ports of export proceeded in relative quiet.[74] The first four of these ports—Shimonoseki, Hakata, Kuchinotsu, and Otaru—were already equipped with customs branches and would open on August 15, 1889; the remaining five—Yokkaichi, Moji, Karatsu, Misumi, and Fushiki—required more preparation, and their openings would follow three months later. For Shimonoseki and Hakata, this additional designation did not override or change their status as ports handling the Korea trade; instead, it created supplemental and expanding functions for them.

The law designating the new openings was issued when Tokyo was still optimistic that treaty revisions would soon come to fruition. The special ports of export were designed to bring in needed revenues, but they also reflected a keen awareness that treaty revision would bring fresh fiscal and operational challenges, especially in opening the country to foreign merchants and residents. It would, therefore, be important to encourage and protect the development of Japanese businesses around the country, in part by creating avenues of exchange that could be run by the Japanese rather than foreigners. Opening a number of ports under Japanese jurisdiction in advance of granting foreigners access to the interior was certainly preferable to being unprepared when the time came.

In this way, the special ports of export served an intermediary function ahead of Japan's full opening. Because the first goal was to build a stronger export trade and bring in needed revenue, the ports were not at this time allowed to import commodities of any kind. Moreover, exports were restricted to the five goods of rice, coal, sulfur, wheat, and wheat flour, the last two of which were added only at the final stage of deliberations. All five were deemed key resources that would fare well in overseas markets and could be supplied in sufficient quantities. Each of the selected ports required transportation networks to key hinterlands and tended to specialize in either the coal trade (Karatsu, Kuchinotsu, Misumi, Moji, Otaru) or the rice trade (Fushiki, Hakata, Shimonoseki,

74. *Times*, April 19, 1889.

and Yokkaichi). In 1898, just before the system was terminated, five more targeted goods were added to the approved list of exports: charcoal, cement, manganese ore, sulfuric acid, and bleaching powder.

A crucial stipulation for these chosen sites was that exports could be handled either by Japanese ships or by chartered foreign ships. This meant that the Japanese government was now willing, whereas earlier in the decade it was not, to allow foreign pilots and crews to anchor in nontreaty harbors, thus opening a door to possible interaction with local populations even in the absence of permission to disembark. Some clear protections were put in place to minimize abuses. For example, each port was managed by a branch of one of the treaty port customs houses, which was charged with administering and policing the flow of people and goods. Importantly, ships carrying export goods were not permitted to simultaneously conduct domestic coastal trade, a clause intended to minimize Western dominance in shipping while curbing new chances for smuggling.

The choice of each port was based in part on its suitability to handle international trade. All nine ports had already been opened to foreign export in some capacity prior to 1889. For example, Kuchinotsu had been profitably exporting Miike coal overseas by special permission since April 1878. In addition to these nine, Hokkaido officials had petitioned the central government to open two more ports on the northern island. Kushiro and Muroran were added in 1890 and 1894, respectively, thus bringing the total number of special ports of export to eleven. The *Yomiuri shinbun* reported that Hokkaido's port of Akkeshi (northeast of Kushiro) would open in addition to Otaru, and although it may have been under consideration, it was never designated. Other Japanese ports, including Taketoyo, began petition campaigns to gain special trading status as early as 1891.[75] Taketoyo was not at this time successful in its attempts to become a special trading port but would become the only port without special trading status to open in 1899.

The special ports of export managed varying levels of trade by 1894, with Shimonoseki, Kuchinotsu, and Moji tallying the highest amounts. Although they still fell well below the top treaty ports of Yokohama, Kobe, and Nagasaki, many already exceeded Niigata, and

75. *Yomiuri shinbun*, November 24, 1889.

some bested Hakodate.[76] Boosters in the special ports believed that they could do even better and began extended rounds of petitions for greater privileges. These petitions went through their elected officials to the capital to be deliberated in the Lower House of the Diet. Most commonly, petitioners asked for greater opening, legitimately claiming that their inability to import products curtailed the amount that they could export. Local populations would fight hard to gain permission to import as "world trade ports" before all became open ports in 1899.

Unlike the 1883 special trading ports, which had been designated specifically to handle trade with Korea, these ports did not have a similar geographical target. The focus was on exporting key products and earning revenue wherever possible. These openings were based more closely on domestic needs, with the sites chosen for their foreign trade capacity as well as their convenience to productive hinterlands. The next sets of special trading ports encompassed both impulses, targeted trade partners and hinterland service, as new trade routes, primarily along the Sea of Japan, opened to Russia, Korea, and Taiwan.

ACT 4—REGIONAL POWER SHIFTS, 1893–1899

Within a decade of naming the first special trading ports, Japan's international trade sites expanded well beyond the treaty ports. In the final years of the nineteenth century, six more ports—Miyazu, Hamada, Nanao, Sakai, Shimizu, and Tsuruga—were added to the growing list of those with permission to function as special trading ports, while seven with earlier designations—Fushiki, Hakata, Karatsu, Kuchinotsu, Misumi, Otaru, and Yokkaichi—gained additional privileges. Beyond these domestic locations, five ports in Japan's newly claimed colony of Taiwan became special trading ports in 1896.

Three interrelated changes in the broader international climate helped spur the latest set of openings: Russia's eastward progression, Great Britain's change of heart over treaty revision, and Japan's ambivalent relationship with Russia. First, the 1891 announcement that Russia would build the Trans-Siberian Railway contributed heavily to shifting the balance of power in East Asia, moving it away from the tenuous equilibrium maintained by British-dominated Western interests. Russia had been

76. *Moji shinpō*, October 10, 1895.

gradually increasing its presence in the East after the Crimean War deprived the growing empire of its naval base on the Black Sea, and building the railway signaled a new level of commitment to continental expansion.

Second, on the heels of these Russian advances, Great Britain, the intractable power that had long held the keys to Japan's treaty revision, shifted its diplomatic posture and finally granted Japan sovereign rights on July 16, 1894 (effective July 1899). The other Western powers soon followed suit, and Japan gained the return of full sovereignty and the legal equality that it had sought for nearly half a century. Although British reasons for signing the new treaty may have been related to the progress Japan demonstrated in modernizing and Westernizing their country, changes in the international climate were equally critical. Never before had it been so clearly in British interests to let Japan stand on its own.

The degree to which the first two changes encouraged Japan's next actions are unclear, but the timing of the treaty revision is suggestive. On July 23, less than a week after signing the new treaty, the Japanese took Korea's King Kojong captive and installed a pro-Japanese government in Seoul, forcefully launching the events that would lead China and Japan to declare war on each other. Japan's easy wins throughout the war meant that Japan's victory was expected long before the peace was signed on April 17, 1895. The Treaty of Shimonoseki ceded Taiwan, the Pescadores, and the Liaodong Peninsula to Japan. With this turn of events, Russia redoubled efforts to muscle its way into East Asian politics. By helping China pay off its indemnity to Japan, and engineering the Triple Intervention (forcing Japan to return the Liaodong Peninsula to China—which Russia subsequently leased in 1898), Russian officials were able to use the postwar settlement to advance their own designs on the region. Within just a few years, tensions in East Asia shifted from Japan and China to instead focus on a growing rivalry between the two expansive powers of Japan and Russia, each of which possessed a significant territorial stake in the region.

Despite the geopolitical tensions between Japan and Russia, however, the new relationship brought economic opportunity. Japan's new port openings reflect the increased proximity of these neighbors' activities. Most of Japan's newly designated ports were concentrated along the Sea of Japan in order to facilitate trade with the developing Russian territories of Vladivostok, the Russian Maritime Province, and Sakhalin. Residents of these ports in Ura Nihon (the back of Japan) lobbied the central government heavily through the early 1890s, eager to avail themselves of the chance to bring foreign trade to a part of the country that had been largely bypassed in the modern era.

Sea of Japan Ports The first ports granted new status with an eye toward trade with Russia and Korea were Miyazu, Fushiki, and Otaru. Miyazu's boosters were apparently able to make a compelling case, arguing that its favorable location, excellent topography, railroad access, and overall convenience for transportation, would allow the port to outperform its nearest competitors, especially Tsuruga, in conducting trade in the Sea of Japan.[77] In March 1893, both houses of the Diet approved a bill to open Miyazu as a special trading port, permitting both export and import trade with Vladivostok and Korea.

Fushiki and Otaru had already been operating as special export ports with their own customs agencies for several years prior to gaining additional privileges in May 1894. Both now had permission to trade with the Russian Maritime Province, Sakhalin, and Korea. Otaru in particular had a special incentive for expanding its trade. Greater numbers of people, including former samurai seeking work, moved to western Hokkaido as the northern island continued to be integrated more fully into Japan. As a result, the fishing grounds were unable to sustain these greater numbers of fishers, and many were asking to be allowed to "work away from home" (*dekasegi*) in the Russian Maritime Province and Sakhalin to fish and harvest *kombu* (kelp) as well as trade there.[78]

"World Trade Ports" Yet another round of openings took place less than two years later, in October 1896, when Hamada, Tsuruga, and Sakai on the Sea of Japan, together with Hakata, Kuchinotsu, and Karatsu in Kyushu, were all granted permission to export and import goods. The

---

77. Konishi, *Miyazu-kō*.

78. KR, vol. 17 (1893), no. 24: Kōtsū, "Iburi-no-kuni Muroran-kō wo tokubetsu yushutsukō ni tsuika . . . ," December 16, 1893; ibid., vol. 18 (1894), no. 38: Kōtsūmonshi, "Iburi-no-kuni Muroran-kō wo tokubetsu yushutsukō ni tsuika . . . ," December 16, 1893.

three Sea of Japan ports were all named for the first time that year, while the Kyushu ports had been partially opened before.[79]

These ports were selected, as the Yokohama Customs House later documented, "for the purpose of foreign trade (except for trade with enemies) outside the open ports. The comings and goings of ships owned by imperial subjects and the import and export of general cargo is allowed. The difference with open ports is simply that foreign ships are forbidden."[80] Overall, the newly designated sites were less restricted than any of the previous types. In 1896, the *Moji shinpō* published its own description of these ports, calling them "world trade ports" (*taisekai tokubetsu yushutsunyūkō*, more commonly referred to as *tokubetsu yushutsunyūkō*) and explaining that they would allow imperial subjects to freely import and export any cargo they wished, without any geographical restrictions, to or from any country in the world.[81] This depiction, however, comes with the observation that the geographic location of the world trade ports, especially Tsuruga, Sakai, and Hamada along the Sea of Japan, pointed them clearly toward the East Asian "Tōyō" trade.[82]

In 1897 one more Sea of Japan port, Nanao, was named to handle the Tōyō trade in addition to the others designated the year before. Yet not all world trade ports targeted East Asia. Shimizu and Yokkaichi, respectively located on the Pacific Coast between Kobe and Yokohama on Suruga Bay and on Ise Bay, were also added as "world trade" ports. Merchants in Shimizu, backed by the Shizuoka Prefecture Tea Industry Association, had petitioned as early as 1890 for special export privileges. The central authorities encouraged the development of tea plantations in the prefecture in order to help the former samurai, and by the early 1880s, Shizuoka became central to the country's tea production, shipping considerable amounts to Yokohama for export even before Shimizu

79. *Yomiuri shinbun*, December 15, 1891, and November 9, 1893. Sakai's representatives applied again in 1895, and the port was designated in 1896 before opening that November. Sakai had been previously considered a couple of times during the early 1890s.

80. *NZE*, 63. The enemy reference is unclear but could mean the recently defeated China or serve as a catchall for a decidedly fluid diplomatic environment.

81. Many documents refer to them as "special ports of export and import" (*tokubetsu yushutsunyū-kō*), but they are called "world trade ports" here for ease of use.

82. *Moji shinpō*, October 9, 1896.

opened as a special port in 1889. After its 1896 petition gained approval, the port soon became a major overseas exporter of green tea. As a world trade port, Shimizu was not restricted to any specific commodities, and its tea trade came to rival Yokohama's by 1910.[83] Yokkaichi's enhanced designation also increased the range of commodities it could handle. Although originally named a special port to ship mainly rice, it could now trade other potentially lucrative local products, including tea and pottery, which it primarily exported to the United States.[84]

The special trading ports designated in the mid-1890s represented two general trends in Japan's trade. One trend behind these designations was the development of trade with Russia as that country quickened its eastern advance by building the Trans-Siberian Railway. Of six ports newly opened to international trade in 1896 and 1897, five were on the Sea of Japan coast and were expected to trade mainly with Russian territories, although Korea was also in their purview. Prior to this time, Fushiki and Otaru were the only two ports on the Sea of Japan with trading privileges. The additional designations were intended to increase the economic profile of Ura Nihon by developing the hinterland and engaging more heavily in markets across the sea.

The other trend was the government's willingness to allow export ports to begin handling imports, as seen in the naming of Hakata, Karatsu, Kuchinotsu, Misumi, and Yokkaichi as world trade ports. Neither Moji nor Shimonoseki gained import status at this juncture even though they had been in the running when six others were named in 1896. They were deemed too important for military defense to gain additional privileges but, after strenuous lobbying, would be named open ports in 1899. The decisions behind these openings were related to Japan's internal political and economic situation, as more locales called for greater opening, petitioned the government, and through its elected bodies, pushed their own agendas for greater development. Augmenting their trade capacity required gaining the ability to import as well as export, which would enable ships to fill with cargo on all runs and grant merchants more freedom to deal in a greater variety of commodities. The

83. Moritake, *Sekai ni Shizuoka-ken*, 166–68, 172; Sugiyama, *Japan's Industrialization*, 155–56.

84. Kōno, *Yokkaichi chikkō*, 13–19.

Meiji oligarchs' allowance of additional privileges came as they prepared for the enactment of the revised treaties at the end of the century.

Taiwan When the Japanese colonized the island in 1895, Taiwan (then called Formosa) was a newly independent province of China and home to a large aboriginal population. This strategically located island had been variously under Dutch, Spanish, and Chinese rule since the seventeenth century and competing powers continued to show an interest in Taiwan. The island also produced highly desired camphor, sugar, and tea. Two decades earlier, the Meiji oligarchs had sent a military expedition there in what was both a challenge to China and a failed grab for power.[85]

When Japan invaded the island during the First Sino-Japanese War, it already had four functioning treaty ports: Kelung (Keelung), Tainan (Taiwanfu), Takao (Kaohsiung), and Tamsui (see Map 5). Of them, Tamsui was the largest and was home to a British consulate.[86] Together with An-ping (Anping) the Japanese designated them treaty ports, keeping them "open to the subjects of Powers having Commercial Treaties with Japan for residence and trade."[87] As a result, after 1896, Taiwan was "as free to foreign trade as any portion of Japan" at the time, except that no rights of extraterritorial jurisdiction were extended there.[88]

Colonization demanded that the Japanese first squelch military resistance to its takeover while also reducing China's ties and limiting its trade there. In order to redirect Chinese interactions in Taiwan, Tokyo issued new regulations. Chinese citizens, for example, were to reside only in the treaty ports, where they would be regarded as any other foreigners.[89] And to ensure that China and its citizens were considered foreign entities from that point forward, "Chinese-style vessels" (*Shina-gata*

85. On rationales for and transnational discourses concerning this expedition, see Eskildsen, "Of Civilization and Savages."

86. After the British opened treaty ports in Qing China in 1842, they opened them in Taiwan (which the Qing had annexed in the seventeeth century) as well.

87. Tainan was the only exception, allowing for foreign vessels and cargo but not foreign residence (PRO FO881/8741x, 1904, "Treaty Ports, Ports of Call, and Places Open to Foreign Trade in the Far East").

88. *New York Times*, February 2, 1896.

89. KR, vol. 21 (1897), no. 16: Gaiji 2, "Taiwan zairyū Shinkokujin toriatsukai-kata," May 5, 1897.

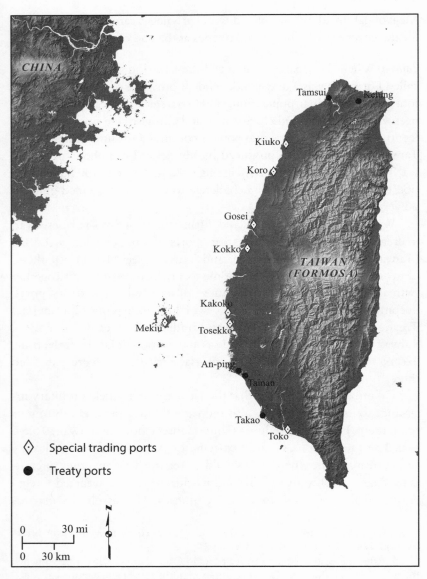

CHINA

Tamsui · Kelung

Kiuko ◇

Koro ◇

Gosei ◇

Kokko ◇

TAIWAN
(FORMOSA)

Kakoko ◇

Mekiu ◇   Tosekko ◇

An-ping ●
Tainan

Takao ●

Toko ◇

◇ Special trading ports

● Treaty ports

0   30 mi

0   30 km

N

MAP 5 Taiwan's Treaty Ports and Special Trading Ports.

senpaku) could trade only at the treaty ports and would now have to pay port entry and exit fees.[90] Additionally, the ubiquitous Chinese junks were no longer allowed to navigate the coastal waters while making stops freely along the way. The Japanese were not entirely successful in controlling the situation, at least early on; they issued new legislation a couple of years later to try to end the smuggling taking place between Taiwan and China.[91]

Another step toward shifting Taiwan's trade away from China and toward Japan came in December 1896, when Home Minister Matsukata Masayoshi, together with the new colonial affairs minister Takashima Tomonosuke and Governor-General Katsura Tarō, outlined the need for special ports for export and import in Taiwan. These were designed, in part, to restrict the Chinese trade to the treaty ports. Importantly, however, these special ports were also designed to function as they did at home, providing what was, in effect, privileged space for Japanese merchants. The stipulations, however, confined this trade to Japanese vessels and specified that the ports would remain open only as long as the governor-general deemed necessary.[92]

The initial proposal listed five promising ports for special export and import status: Su'ao, Karen (Hualien), Beinan, Kōshun (Hengchun), and Kokko (Lugang). In the end, three of these would not be designated, but still others would be added. The final list, issued on January 12, 1897, named the eight ports of Su'ao, Kiuko, Kōrō (Houlong), Gosei (Wuchi), Kokko, Tōsekko (Dongshi), Tōkō (Donggang), and Mekiu (Magong), the last located in the Pescadores.[93] When the treaty revisions took effect less than three years later, all but one of these special trading ports (Su'ao) would open, and another, Kakoko, would replace it.[94] All became key nodes of the East Asian maritime network that Japan

90. Ibid., vol. 20 (1896), no. 24: Kōtsū 2, "Taiwan kaikōjō ni deiri suru Shinagata senpaku ni taisuru kitei wo sadamu," December 2, 1896.

91. Ibid., vol. 23 (1899), no. 25: Zaisei 7, "Taiwan ni okeru kanzei oyobi senbai kisoku . . . ," December 16, 1899.

92. Ibid., vol. 20 (1896), no. 24: Kōtsū 2, "Taiwan tokubetsu yushutsunyūkō ni kansuru ken wo sadamu," December 14, 1896.

93. Taiwan Jimukyoku, *Taiwan jijō ippan*, 35–36.

94. PRO FO, 881/8741x, 1904, "Treaty Ports, Ports of Call, and Places Open to Foreign Trade in the Far East."

would continue to develop as it reclaimed its sovereignty while strengthening and expanding its empire.

ACT 5—THE OPEN PORTS, POST-1899

When Moji celebrated the auspicious occasion of becoming a fully open trade port in July 1899, its stevedores, shopkeepers, merchants, and others had already trod a long and winding path to receive this designation. Residents in all the ports discussed in this chapter had also been party to the considerable changes taking place in Japan and across transmarine East Asia during the second half of the nineteenth century. At the time that the revised treaties were enacted, Japan had a total of forty-one international ports. This high number of ports presents a much richer and more active picture of Japan's trade capacity and overseas networks at the turn of the twentieth century than does the one implied by five treaty ports.

The five original treaty ports at home (Hakodate, Kobe, Nagasaki, Niigata, and Yokohama) together with Osaka comprise six of the forty-one open ports. Another five had been treaty ports in Taiwan (Anping, Kelung, Takao, Tamsui, and Tainan). Twenty-two were special trading ports in Japan, and eight had recently been designated special trading ports in Taiwan and the Pescadores. The only port that opened to foreign trade in 1899 for the first time was Taketoyo in Aichi Prefecture.

Taketoyo's boosters had lobbied hard to have their naval port gain commercial functions by emphasizing its naturally favorable harbor, branch access to the Tōkai Railway, convenience to the country's centers of production, including Aichi, Mie, Gifu, Shiga, Nagoya, and Shizuoka, and the ability to accommodate mixed residence.[95] Soon after Japan regained full sovereignty, the ports of Itozaki (1900) and Wakamatsu (1904) opened to foreign trade as well. These are not the only ports that applied, or would later apply, for permission to open after 1899. Even though special trading ports originally developed to contend with the treaty port system imposed on Japan, the state continued to use this designation, and the control it afforded, for a handful of ports even after the treaties were revised. The system of special trading ports proved highly effective in helping Japan with its half-century of opening. Some of the special trading ports would never meet expectations, but most of them

95. *Yomiuri shinbun*, January 6, 1899.

would go on to function as Japan's major trade and transportation hubs at least until World War II.

Conclusion

The opening of Japan's doors between 1854 and 1899 was a gradual and strategic process. The signing of the unequal treaties, along with the subsequent Meiji Restoration, unequivocally transformed the matrix in which Japan's foreign trade and international relations operated. Yet the new patterns and networks of interaction that emerged afterward reveal that the treaty port system was not so hegemonic as to exclude other kinds of overseas trade. Rather, within the interstices of this mandated system, the Japanese government was able to create additional outlets for trade—with Asian countries as well as Western ones—that operated under full Japanese jurisdiction.

A close reading of the story of the special trading ports suggests that the opening of Japan in the nineteenth century took place in a significantly more gradual fashion than has been generally understood. Over time, the Japanese government created space for its citizens to establish their own trade networks, which were connected to, but not entirely bound by, the treaty port system. These openings come at five significant junctures in Japan's domestic and international history. The first set of ports opened with the signing of the 1854 Kanagawa and 1858 Ansei treaties. These were followed nearly three decades later by sites named for the Korea trade in 1883 as Japan increased its economic penetration of the peninsula. The special ports of export were designated in 1889 as Japan's economy stabilized and Tokyo permitted the export of five key commodities in non-treaty-port locations. The fourth set of ports opened in conjunction with changes at home and abroad. Local merchants and politicians around the archipelago used the new national Diet to gain international trading rights at their home ports. At the same time, Asia's diplomatic, strategic, and commercial environments were shifting as construction began on the Trans-Siberian Railway, bringing new threats and opportunities to the Sea of Japan coast, and as Japan signed a revised treaty with Great Britain. Finally, the last set of ports—the open ports—were named as Japan gained its first formal colony and as the treaty port era in Japan ended with the enactment of the revised treaties in 1899. Using these five main periods of opening, we can draw three main conclusions.

First, the special trading ports show that even under the treaty port system, Japan maintained some measure of freedom to determine how its people engaged in international trade. The Japanese were able both to use the treaty port system and to get around it to put more trade in the hands of domestic merchants. Importantly, this was not a top-down effort, and, especially after the creation of a national assembly, local groups joined forces with one another to gain more privileges for their home ports. Further, these openings reflect carefulness on the part of the oligarchs. The special trading ports balanced a need for trade liberalization with concerns over protecting the country's commercial and strategic interests even as the day approached when Japan would become a fully sovereign country.

Second, during the last decade of the nineteenth century, government edicts decreeing the locations and parameters of the special trading ports demonstrate that concerted preparations were being made in advance of the anticipated treaty revisions. Taken together, these openings can help explain the country's dramatic rise—industrial, economic, and military—at the end of the century. Japan's seemingly sudden progress at the end of the century resulted from a longer trajectory of change in opening the country and promoting regional development than has typically been understood. Crucially, Japan had a more comprehensive commercial infrastructure and more extensive networks in place before the end of the century than evidenced by the treaty ports alone, and these contributed to its rapid late nineteenth-century gains.

Finally, the special trading ports offer traction when assessing the rise of Japanese imperialism, which can be quite slippery historical terrain. Ironically, the semicolonialism forced upon Japan in 1858 helped establish conditions that would allow Japan to increase its presence on the Asian continent through the treaty port system. Two Meiji-era projects—revising the unequal treaties and developing the infrastructure to support overseas commerce—came together in the special trading ports. Japan successfully used the treaty port system to its own advantage not just by relying on the Western networks to connect to East Asian ones or using Western law to legitimate the country's imperialist advances but also by steadily developing its own subsystem of ports for international trade. These ports became carefully protected domestic spaces that allowed Japan to build new areas of exchange on its own terms and begin establishing its own independent networks first in Korea and later in Taiwan.

Although these openings—in all but the first of the five acts—were ultimately legislated by Japan's central government, the wider context of informal imperialism in East Asia greatly informed decision-making. In building their own expansive nation, the Japanese made effective use of the other empires in East Asia, including the precedents, infrastructure, and markets that they provided. In the three decades between the signing of the 1858 Harris Treaty and the opening of the special ports of export in 1889, the dynamics of informal imperialism helped shape transmarine East Asia's geography of trade as Japan struggled to modernize its transportation infrastructure and stabilize finances through its unplanned and tumultuous, but ultimately successful, integration into the world economy.

TWO

Geographies of Direct Export

Rice and Coal, 1858–1889

When Japan made its headlong plunge into the churning waters of global trade in 1858, its rather ungainly entry sent ripples across the country. Since it had long maintained an independent economy based on its own operational, though hardly uniform, currency structure, trading internationally across different monetary systems posed an immediate challenge.[1] Problems that arose while trying to standardize and revalue home currencies were compounded by disproportionate exchange rates at the outset of trade, which swiftly led to the hemorrhaging of bullion, inflation, and continual adjustments to the monetary system.[2]

Underlying the story of the *bakumatsu* monetary crisis is the more fundamental saga of shogunal attempts to gain control over the new foreign trade and to check the destabilizing effects that it had unleashed. Loss of faith in the Tokugawa regime's ability to manage the situation quickly exacerbated existing tensions. The opening of Japan and resulting financial problems focused the battle between the *bakufu* and the

1. Metzler, *Lever of Empire*, 15. Metzler makes the important argument that one of the primary reasons behind the Tokugawa government's curtailment of foreign trade in the eighteenth century was concern over the country's precious metals irredeemably leaving the country.

2. Frost, *The Bakumatsu Currency Crisis*, 35–45; Huber, "Effect on Prices." For ongoing problems in the Meiji era, see Patrick, "External Equilibrium." Metzler states that as a direct result of the 1858 U.S.-Japan Treaty of Amity and Commerce "every available ship was pressed into service for the Yokohama-to-Shanghai run," as foreigners rapidly took gold out of Japan (*Lever of Empire*, 17).

domains on control over foreign trade.[3] Although the *bakufu* lost this battle, the Meiji regime that took its place would also face an extended fight to gain mastery over the unequal treaties and the accompanying treaty port system it had inherited. Within the treaty port framework, issues of foreign trade would remain central, but not immutable, concerns for the rest of the century.

Viewing the special trading ports in the broad strokes of Meiji economic and financial history, we find that Japan increased the pace of its slow but progressive trade liberalization during the treaty port era. The central government's highly cautious stance toward trade after the country opened was symptomatic of the need to balance restraint with opportunity in coping with a highly volatile economy. But as the economy rested on a more stable foundation with the pivotal Matsukata deflation (1881–1884), a greater range of action became available to the oligarchy. The special ports of export are a manifestation of this shift toward greater control over the country's economic situation, representing a strategic bid to generate additional revenue for Japan's modernization. The oligarchs found a way to abide by the strictures of the treaty port system and prevent further Western encroachment while also taking advantage of the growing commercial networks linking Japan to the world economy.

In opening the special ports of export, the central government had to balance three different yet interrelated sets of imperatives. First, it had to contend with the economic turmoil the country faced after it opened to foreign trade. Japan, operating at a disadvantage within a tough diplomatic and economic climate, was unable to establish protective tariffs. Second, it had to modernize the country's administrative systems and its infrastructure. The treaties effectively demanded that Japan become modern, and thus more like the Western powers, if it wanted to become an equal member in the comity of nations. Third, the central government faced pressure from domestic voices calling for the liberalization of trade and greater opportunities to market their products abroad. The special ports of export responded to all these needs. Importantly, they did so without raising the ire of the treaty powers. The special ports were beneficial to all sides; they represented greater economic stability for Japan, increased engagement with the world economy, opportunity for Western

3. Crawcour, "Economic Change," 600.

steamship lines and merchants, and greater access to key products without sacrificing trade at the treaty ports.

The special ports of export signify a protectionist effort to increase Japanese-controlled trade at locations outside the treaty ports. These ports, which mark the third act of Japan's gradual opening, were established by imperial decree in July 1889 with the specific aim of facilitating the direct overseas export of five "key products" (*jūyōhin*): rice, coal, sulfur, wheat, and wheat flour. The Ministry of Finance, under Matsukata Masayoshi, in consultation with the Foreign Ministry and the Cabinet, declared that the treaty ports were not "convenient" to domestic production zones. As such, they presented an obstacle to exporting these five goods at higher volumes, which was necessary to bring in greater revenues.

This seemingly straightforward explanation offers a plausible reason why additional ports were needed. What it does not reveal are the longer-term processes that paved the way for these designations. Since the start of foreign trade, the central government's policies continually shifted. Creating special ports to promote key exports was thus a logical policy step in 1889, one in keeping with a series of legislative acts, trading activities, and infrastructural improvements that started decades earlier. It is in this deeper history that we can find answers to other significant questions, such as why these particular goods were being targeted for export, why these particular ports were chosen, and why this need for revenue was being addressed in 1889.

To answer these questions, the present chapter traces the export of rice and coal, and the selection of ports to handle them, from the signing of unequal treaties in 1858 to the naming of the special ports of export in 1889.[4] Each of these products was vital, in its own way, to enabling the country's transition from a relatively closed and self-sufficient economy to one participating autonomously in the global arena of late nineteenth-century capitalism. Each was originally exported in a fairly ad hoc fashion before developing more regular rhythms of exchange, and each took a distinct path before the two were named side by side as items for special export in 1889. Along the way, each developed its own distinct transportation geography in reaching unopened ports for legal ex-

4. Takeuchi, *Dai Nihon bōekiron*, 73–105.

port. The circuits of production and distribution that they inscribed during these earlier transactions had a direct bearing on which ports would be named in 1889.[5]

Rice and coal were the most important of the five commodities exported, both in terms of revenue and in the roles that they played in Japan's economy prior to these designations. The other three commodities—sulfur, wheat, and wheat flour—were not exported at anywhere near the totals of these two. Sulfur, which was used in the making of gunpowder, matches, sulfuric acid, and so on, was excavated mostly in Hokkaido. Before the special trading ports opened, this resource was exported primarily through the treaty ports of Yokohama and Hakodate. The great majority of sulfur exports went to the United States, and through the 1890s, it was also exported regularly to Australia, Hong Kong, China, Korea, and a handful of others that received small amounts. A few of the special trading ports did begin handling sulfur in the 1890s, particularly Shimonoseki, but they exported only small amounts at infrequent intervals.

Wheat is a category that includes *komugi* (wheat), *ōmugi* (barley), and *hadakamugi* (naked barley). These varieties of wheat, along with wheat flour, were added at the eleventh hour of discussions. As a winter crop, wheat may have been used to supplement the rice trade in some cases. This grain was exported in small amounts to markets in Korea, China, and the East Indies prior to the designation of key products.[6] Even after being named for special export, however, wheat was not exported in great quantity via either the special trading ports or the treaty ports through 1899. In 1892, a rare year when national statistics list wheat (combined here with entries for barley), Nagasaki shipped 7 tons of wheat while the majority was sent from special trading ports. Shimonoseki

5. The ports named for special export in 1889 can roughly be divided into those primarily designated to handle rice (Fushiki, Hakata, Shimonoseki, and Yokkaichi) and those to handle coal (Karatsu, Kuchinotsu, Misumi, Moji, and Otaru). For rice, this chapter discusses Fushiki, Shimonoseki, and Yokkaichi. It also discusses ports in the Tōhoku region that did not work for this purpose. Hakata did not handle these pre-1889 direct exports; it was only active in this period with regard to its designation for the Korea trade from 1883. For coal, this chapter discusses Karatsu, Kuchinotsu, and Misumi. Moji and Otaru will be covered in Chapter 3.

6. Takeuchi, *Dai Nihon bōekiron*, 94–100.

exported roughly 36.5 tons and Shishimi exported approximately 4 tons to Korea out of a nationwide total of about 55 tons. Another 2 tons went to Hong Kong, and the remainder went to unspecified destinations.[7] Nonetheless, wheat appears to have remained an afterthought, trading at much lower volumes than the other three key products.

The rest of this chapter focuses on rice and coal. Next, it considers the ways in which the unequal treaties and opening of Japanese trade disrupted the national economy from the time of the Meiji Restoration to the mid-1880s. Additionally, it shows that the central government deliberately pursued a gradual liberalization of trade and initially promoted the direct export of rice and coal as a means to bring in much needed revenue. The periodization offered here parallels the opening of the special trading ports and contextualizes them in relation to national financial policy.

The second section looks specifically at why rice became a targeted export and discusses the legislative changes necessary for this to happen. It also shows the ways in which the government drew on a combination of older circuits and new foreign steamship routes to transport rice so it could be exported overseas. Exploring why certain ports worked for this task (Fushiki, Shimonoseki, and Yokkaichi—all to become special ports of export in 1889) while others initially did not (many in the Tōhoku region), this section reveals that linking modern modes of land- and sea-based transportation was fundamental to success. Rice continued to follow older transportation circuits, but only some of these could be reconfigured to accommodate overseas export.

The third section examines the export of coal from the start of the treaty port era to the end of the 1880s. During these decades, major changes in the legislation and regulation of coal mining and sales aimed to have this commodity meet a suddenly heavy demand. The export of coal also necessitated the creation of new networks, which were located primarily near important mines in western Kyushu. Although the naming of special ports of export in the region was generally straightforward, some potential sites for export met with difficulties in developing effective transportation.

Overall, this chapter considers the decades that preceded the naming of special ports of export in order to show three things. First, it

7. *DNGBN*, 1892.

reveals how the situation of informal empire prior to 1889 shaped these strategic openings. Second, it examines how the geography of pre-Meiji and modern transportation networks influenced which ports would succeed. Finally, this chapter explains early attempts to export rice and coal overseas from non-treaty-port locations, setting the stage for the unprecedented port openings of 1889.

A Cautious Liberalization of Foreign Trade

Japan's import and export tariffs were integrally tied to the unequal treaties and the more theoretical underpinnings of the treaty port system. As a direct outgrowth of free trade imperialism, the unequal treaties opened the country to Western commerce on disadvantageous legal terms.[8] The basic idea of "free trade," as put forth by the British in the mid-nineteenth century, was to develop trade relationships among foreign countries that minimized, and ideally eliminated, government restrictions and protectionist tariffs on trade in order to encourage exchange at mutually beneficial prices. The catch, however, was that Great Britain would have immediate advantage over others because it was the world's most industrially advanced country: one with a long reach and a state-of-the-art commercial fleet.[9] Although some Western states had experimented with reducing or eliminating tariffs, implementation of free trade among them continued to be limited, and the standard international tariff rate at midcentury stood at roughly 10 percent.[10]

In the case of Japan, the Western powers demanded free trade under threat of force at a time when the shogunate had no independent intention of modifying the existing system of restricted foreign exchange through the four gates. By the time regent Ii Naosuke signed

8. Gallagher and Robinson, "Imperialism of Free Trade"; Lynn, "Policy, Trade, and Informal Empire," 103–6.

9. Bayly makes a compelling argument for the convergence of multiple positive factors that allowed for the "temporary and qualified" rise of western European nations (*Birth of the Modern World*, 71). On the strength of Britain's Royal Navy, see Black, *British Seaborne Empire*, ch. 6. Further, in the mid-nineteenth century one-quarter of all international trade passed through British ports (Sugiyama, *Japan's Industrialization*, 14–15). Benton cautions that the British empire was located in diverse legal environments with varied levels of sovereignty in maritime spaces (*A Search for Sovereignty*, esp. 106).

10. Perez, *Japan Comes of Age*, 56.

the country's first commercial treaty with Townsend Harris in July 1858, he saw no alternative to ceding some of Japan's sovereign rights in order to avoid going to war.[11] Within days of this signing, Harris and Iwase Tadanari, Japan's diplomatic representative, negotiated the new tariff schedules and, item by item, detailed the surrender of Japan's tariff autonomy. At this point, the newly fixed tariff rates ranged within a fairly moderate scale. The duty on most imports of 20 percent, for example, was higher than contemporary international standards.[12] Had the tariffs remained that high and thus been able to more fully protect domestic industries and generate greater revenues, Japan might have recovered from the shock of entering the world economy sooner than it did.[13] Regardless of the exact tariff amounts, however, the expansion of Japan's overseas trade through coerced participation in a global system of industrial capitalism had immediate economic ramifications. The economic shocks, in turn, reverberated powerfully across the political terrain and helped topple the Tokugawa regime within a decade.

Despite painstaking attempts to revise them over the next three and a half decades, the Ansei Treaties of 1858 continued to govern Japan's international trade until a new set of treaties took force in 1899.[14] A series of amendments, however, pushed the contracts closer to "free trade" between 1858 and 1899. The first and most serious such amendment was the result of the punitive and ultimately very costly Tariff Convention of 1866.[15] The convention established two significant changes to the terms of Japan's foreign trade. The first was an across-the-board reduction of fixed tariff rates to 5 percent *ad valorem* for both imports and exports, bringing import tariffs well below the earlier

11. The three main pillars of the treaties are widely recognized to be the loss of tariff autonomy, as well as the loss of privileges for extraterritoriality and most favored nation status. None of the three was reciprocated, which in turn compounded Japan's inequality vis-à-vis those powers that held such privileges.

12. Mitani, *Escape from Impasse*, 290.

13. Huber argues Japan's opening led overall to economic gain and an increased national income within a decade or so of opening the country ("Effect on Prices," 615). Between 1860 and 1867, exports increased approximately 2.5-fold and imports increased close to 13-fold (*ZH*, 9).

14. Once Japan regained tariff autonomy the Meiji government did, in fact, raise tariffs on several items.

15. The Tariff Convention of 1866 was legislated as a partial reparation for losses incurred during the 1863–64 Shimonoseki Incident.

terms of 20 percent and below the approximate international norm of 10 percent.[16] This would significantly decrease customs revenues for the next half-century. Moreover, it would serve as a deterrent to reducing export tariffs, a right that the Japanese effectively held in the absence of either legislation against it or foreign opposition to doing so, since any further loss of revenues could not be balanced by raising import tariffs.

The convention also ended the *bakufu*'s monopoly over foreign trade at the treaty ports.[17] It "granted freedom to all merchants, *daimyō*, and *daimyō* retainers to trade or associate with foreigners without government interference at the treaty ports; to employ foreign shipping in trade with the open ports or abroad; . . . to travel abroad for study or trade, and to be employed on foreign ships."[18] In the long run, these demands would have far-reaching consequences, but these practices could not all be implemented at once nor would results manifest overnight. Accommodation would first require major changes in domestic law, practice, and economic thought during the turmoil of the Meiji Restoration and beyond.[19] The new leaders would gradually liberalize trade one step at a time, proceeding in stages that roughly hew to the phases of opening the special trading ports. The same broad circumstances that allowed for measured tariff liberalization would also allow for an expansion of commercial privileges that were increasingly designed to create new trade outside the treaty ports, putting it into the hands of Japanese merchants across the archipelago.

When the Meiji regime came to power in 1868, some loosening of foreign trade proved consistent with the newly articulated strategies of *fukoku kyōhei* ("enrich the nation, strengthen the military") and *shokusan*

16. See Mitani, *Escape from Impasse*, 290. Commissioner of Finance Oguri Tadamasa suggested in vain that Japan would eliminate all export taxes in exchange for keeping 1858 import rates, but both were reset at 5 percent (Fox, *Britain and Japan*, 182–83).

17. Two important ways the *bakufu* held control was over the domestic circulation of export items and in dictating which Japanese merchant houses were allowed to handle foreign negotiations regarding these items (Wigen, *Making of a Japanese Periphery*, 166–67).

18. These freedoms started at Yokohama on July 1, 1866, and at Hakodate and Nagasaki on August 1, 1866 (Fox, *Britain and Japan*, 182–85).

19. *ZH*, 103.

kōgyō ("increase production, promote industrial enterprise").[20] In particular, the building of Japan's modern infrastructure required importing
goods from abroad that could not yet be produced at home, including
military essentials like modern ships and armaments, industrial materials
like iron and steel, and communications equipment for telegraphs.[21] Acquiring these items was a centralized effort as the new oligarchs worked
to strengthen the nation and maintain their still-tenuous hold on power.

The commodities traded through the treaty ports, however, were
only partly decided by Tokyo, which never had full control over exchange
either within the country or in dealing with foreign entities. From the
start, Japanese and foreign merchants selling goods and the consumers
purchasing them also influenced which commodities would be exchanged.
As a result, early imports consisted of many nonessential, luxury items
such as woolen goods, cotton textiles, sugar, and even kerosene. The primary Japanese goods sought by the foreign powers were raw silk, tea,
coal, copper, and pottery, even though Japanese producers and merchants
attempted to sell a wide variety of other items as well.[22] The successful
products were in many cases the same as those sought in China, especially raw silk and tea. Japan and China would, in fact, compete against
each other for decades in supplying these items to the Western treaty
powers.[23] At local and national levels, it soon became clear which products could be put up effectively for sale—in the 1870s, raw silk and tea
together made up two-thirds of export totals, but both rice and coal were
also among the top exports. Aware of these trends, the central government invested in the production of raw silk, tea, and coal.[24]

20. For an extended discussion of these twin ideologies in the Meiji period, see
Samuels, *Rich Nation, Strong Army*, 35–44.

21. Crawcour says that the "major imports were woolen and cotton textiles,
with arms and vessels becoming important (20 percent) as the Restoration approached" ("Economic Change," 602). Also see *ZH*, 32–33.

22. When Yokohama opened in 1859, local entrepreneurs from Iida immediately sent their goods to the treaty port in order to sell their local specialties, such as
lacquered bowls, dried persimmons, rice wine, paper umbrellas, and hair-dress ties,
but to no avail (Wigen, *Making of a Japanese Periphery*, 141). For statistics on imports
and exports for the first fifteen years of the Meiji era, see *ZH*, 23–33.

23. Iwakura Tomomi, for example, proclaimed that "the very existence of our nation is in peril" (quoted in Smith, *Political Change*, 24–26).

24. Despite longer-term efforts to channel trade of these goods into Japanese hands,
direct export was only successful for coal (Sugiyama, *Japan's Industrialization*, 160).

Whether the Meiji oligarchs personally favored or merely acquiesced in expanding foreign trade, however, they were not at this time actively working to promote free trade through their policies.[25] Rather, they were using trade more pointedly as a means to a desired end—recovering economic stability while industrializing to become more competitive in the modern world. The combined shocks of economic opening and political revolution mandated that the highest priority be given to regaining economic stability. Foreign trade at once proved a leading cause of the problem and offered an opportunity for solving it. Despite an initial surge of exports, opening the country to trade rapidly led to an imbalance of imports over exports.[26] At the same time, the foreign exchange earned by selling export goods became a significant source of funds for offsetting the monumental costs of development efforts, especially in a period when Tokyo was short on cash and had no power to set import tariffs. During this time, the oligarchs adjusted the existing export tariffs with the utmost care.

As domestic industry developed and exports grew, export taxes stood in the way of potentially beneficial and lucrative commerce. Yet Tokyo had to be careful not to do away with these revenues unless necessary. The Ministry of Finance's *Customs History* delineates four periods when tariff reduction occurred. The first came between 1869 and 1874, when the Meiji oligarchs ended trade prohibitions on five goods, including coal, rice, wheat, and wheat flour (all of which would be targeted for special export in 1889).[27] The next, between 1876 and 1881, saw the lifting of export tariffs on twenty-eight more goods, constituting a first era of export promotion. It is important to note that many of these items were ones that had so far generated little income, and so eliminating tariffs

25. Hoare, for one, argues the government remained officially hostile to trade "and did nothing to encourage its development" (*Japan's Treaty Ports*, 12).

26. Howe, *Origins of Japanese Trade Supremacy*, 80, 91.

27. *ZH*, 99–102. The *Zeikan hyakunenshi* also includes rice flour here, which did not become a special export. The main concern was in allowing originally prohibited goods to be traded, which included rice flour along with rice, wheat, and wheat flour. Coal is listed only as a fuel, not as an export (and its export tax would remain in place until 1888). The fifth item, copper coins, was not included in the 1858 tariff schedule. By contrast, the precious metals of silver and gold were made duty-free in the Ansei Treaties. Although the ban on the export of copper coins was lifted in 1869, it would gain and lose duty-free status over the next few years in fluctuation with inflation and government revenues.

on them did not present a high chance of losing significant revenues. In part, eliminating tariffs in this period and the next were concessions to foreign and domestic voices calling for greater liberalization.

The third period—from 1887 to 1891—is known as the second era of export promotion. The elimination of tariffs on 113 goods during this four-year span expresses less a frantic measure to avert crisis than a deliberate attempt to promote exports while remaining cautious in the face of still-weak revenues and some opposing domestic voices.[28] There was also a growing awareness that after the treaties were revised, Japan would have the ability to increase import tariffs (which it did). In 1899, after three years of strong agitation at home (between 1894 and 1896), the Ministry of Finance removed the export tariffs on the 147 goods remaining. The final abolition of export tariffs was deliberately planned to take effect with the enactment of the revised treaties and the changeover from special trading to open ports; all three were fully intertwined in the handling of foreign trade and the return of tariff autonomy.

In the scheme presented here, the third period of liberalization, centered on 1889, coincides with the start of the third phase of Japan's gradual opening. We find that 1889 marks a shift from a period of direct government intervention in the export of rice and coal (from 1878 to 1889) to a period when the government decreased its role as an exporter, relaxed oversight, and placed more transactions in the hands of the Japanese. Until Finance Minister Matsukata Masayoshi effectively brought inflation under control, the Meiji government's general economic policy was to use overseas trade in the service of industrialization. At first, the main objective was simply to earn revenues and stabilize prices, but by 1889, it became increasingly important to the country's modernization efforts to further expand revenue channels by encouraging Japanese merchants in their efforts to export directly overseas.[29]

The rest of this chapter focuses on the central government's efforts to get key goods to market. Japan was able to overcome semicolonization partly by taking advantage of global commercial markets and transportation systems in order to secure the economic and industrial

---

28. Retaining export tariffs provided the central government with both a safety valve at home and a bargaining chip to use with the treaty powers. Domestic voices for tariff elimination included both the pro-free trade group led by Taguchi Ukichi and advocates of protectionism, such as Inukai Tsuyoshi (*ZH*, 103–4).

29. Sumiya and Taira, *Outline of Japanese Economic History,* 312–13.

modernization that would help lead to treaty revision. Before special ports of export were designated in 1889, the central government exported some goods through outlets that bypassed the treaty ports. Grounds for this included the high cost of transshipment to treaty ports, the added cost of using Western intermediaries, and an inability for private Japanese entities to raise enough capital on their own. At the same time, Japan relied on the treaty port system for these exports for two main reasons: Westerners were the main consumers for their products, and Japanese overseas trade was dependent on Western, mostly British, steamship service and routes.

The special trading ports show that Japan was able to simultaneously use the treaty port system and steer around it, establishing alternative ports and channels of exchange at home to put trade in Japanese hands, avoid unfair tariff restrictions, and maximize revenues coming into the country. One valuable way in which the central government responded effectively to Japan's global economic integration was by ensuring that the country's physical infrastructures could accommodate the direct export of targeted commodities. Examining the liberalization of foreign trade and government measures to improve trade infrastructures by tracking the two most heavily exported products reveals the logic of the special ports of export as they emerged within the broader treaty port system. Doing so shows how the export geographies of rice and coal are both "artifact and agent" of Japan's incorporation into the modern world economy.[30]

Creating a New Geography of Overseas Rice Exports

Changes in the handling of rice during the first decade of Meiji rule exemplify the Gordian knot presented by the terms and conditions of foreign trade set by the Ansei Treaties. In order to protect food staples and Japan's key source of government tax revenue, Article 3 of the 1858 Harris Treaty clearly stated: "No rice or wheat shall be exported from Japan as cargo."[31] Despite this protection, the central function that rice

30. Wigen, *Making of a Japanese Periphery*, 2–3.
31. This ban did not include rice for consumption: "Americans resident in Japan, and ships, for their crews and passengers, shall be furnished with sufficient supplies of the same" (Beasley, *Select Documents*, 185).

held in Japan's agricultural economy as well as in government finances, which were based on a rice tribute-tax system, meant that the price of rice would be linked to the new foreign trade. Soon after the Meiji Restoration, inflation from the excessive issuance of paper currency coupled with a poor harvest in 1869 led to high rice prices and a compensatory turn toward importing rice, against which there were no legal restrictions. After a better harvest in 1871 brought prices down sharply, the sudden drop created hardship for many farmers. The ban on rice exports hampered the government's ability to do more in responding to this harmful cycle.

Thus, in January 1872, Finance Minister Ōkubo Toshimichi lifted the barrier to exporting rice in an attempt to both stabilize prices and earn specie for the government. Rather than a general lifting of the ban, it meant that the central government itself was the exporter, buying up and exporting 400,000 *koku* of surplus rice via British merchants in Yokohama.[32] The next year, with the start of comprehensive Land Tax Reforms (1873–81), the government again played a pivotal role in exporting surplus rice. Under the new system, success in turning tax payments from rice to money required that farmers themselves be able to sell their rice crops for cash. In order to prevent rice prices from falling when the anticipated surge of rice hit the market that first year, the government enlisted the Mitsui-gumi, Ono-gumi, and other conglomerates to purchase rice and sell it abroad through Yokohama. This rice was then sold in "trial sales" to numerous places in Asia—like Hong Kong, Amoy, Shanghai, and Swatow (Shantou)—and beyond, including Sydney, Melbourne, London, and San Francisco.[33] The amount exported in 1873 was more than double that of the previous year, for a total of 860,000 *koku*. Despite earning nearly 5 million yen in specie in these early export attempts, however, after factoring in the costs of purchasing the rice and other expenses, the government lost over 1.5 million yen in the transactions.[34] Nonetheless, it learned that it could sell this product in multiple markets.

After briefly reinstating the ban, the government again exported rice three years in a row (1875–77) after establishing new rules for

32. Ōwaki, *Beikokuron*, 80; Sakurai, *Kome*, 18–21; KR, vol. 13 (1889), no. 28: Zaisei 3, "Ōkurashō oite beikoku kaigai yushutsu wo haishi su." February 5, 1889. One *koku* equals 5.1 bushels.

33. Ōwaki, *Beikokuron*, 80–81.

34. Sakurai, *Kome*, 20.

maintaining stock rice. During this span, it exported over 1 million *koku* of rice. The main aim was again to acquire specie, but a second objective was to have overseas exports play a role in modulating the price of rice at home. This deliberate commodification of rice required the establishment of proper channels to regulate supplies, sales, and prices in domestic markets. Given the importance of rice to the national economy, Tokyo deliberately pursued a policy of direct intervention and continued to maintain a heavy hand in this trade over the course of the next decade.[35]

Regulating the country's rice markets was congruent with the renewed demands of building a modern industry and strong national infrastructure. In the wake of the 1877 Satsuma Rebellion, the last major domestic uprising to challenge the Meiji regime's legitimacy, the oligarchs redoubled their efforts to strengthen the nation both financially and militarily. Promoting industrialization was key to both objectives. Ōkubo, now head of the newly created Home Ministry (Naimushō), launched his extensive Industrial Development Plan in 1878.[36] He held that it was the role of the central government to guide economic development, and although his main goal was strengthening Japan's industrial base, he necessarily made agricultural production an essential piece of the project.[37] The improvement and expansion of agricultural crops and products would help fulfill a second goal, namely, generating revenue by reducing imports to Japan while promoting exports to help pay for industrialization.[38]

Both retooled and newly established institutions were placed in the service of stabilizing and developing the rice market. The famous Tokugawa-era Dōjima Rice Exchange in Ōsaka, for example, had been

35. Ibid., 21–23. The quality of the rice was important, helping determine a crop's suitability for overseas export to Western buyers. Through this period Japan would sell its higher quality rice to generate income but then buy cheaper (and lower quality) rice from nearby Asian countries to help feed its own population.

36. Another important component of this plan was to help settle the disestablished samurai and provide them with gainful employment.

37. Maeda Masana demonstrated an interest in promoting agriculture as well as local economies in his 1884 *Kōgyō Iken* (Advice for the Encouragement of Industry). See Crawcour, *Kōgyō Iken: Maeda Masana*; Fletcher, "The Japan Spinners Association," 51; Inukai and Tussing, *Kōgyō Iken*.

38. Brown, "Ōkubo Toshimichi," 195. This central attention to agriculture was especially, but not solely, seen in the silk industry.

dismantled in 1869, revived by an Osaka merchant in 1871, and given a new set of trade rules in 1878 to accommodate new national circumstances.[39] That same year, along with the Department for the Regulation of Rice Supply and Demand (Kome jukyū chōsetsu tantō bukyoku), Finance Minister Ōkuma Shigenobu's Grain Reserve Bureau (Jōhei kyoku) began operations. Designed to implement the Rice Storage Ordinance of 1875 (Chochiku mai jōrei), which detailed rules for storage and exchange, the Grain Reserve Bureau exclusively focused on regulating the price of rice.[40] Creating such oversight was a significant step. It would be for naught, however, if it did not also improve transportation systems to enable rice to reach and be loaded onto foreign steamships for export.

The next two sections examine how nontreaty ports were used during the country's economic transformation of the 1880s. First, looking at Yokkaichi and Shimonoseki allows us to see how channeling exports at key moments from convenient nontreaty ports eased the transition from an economic system based on tribute rice to one that collected monetary land taxes. Doing so appears to have been both expedient and experimental, garnering revenues while laying the foundation for what would soon become the third wave of special ports, those geared for designated exports. The second section considers seaports along the Tōhoku coast, with particular emphasis on Ishinomaki, Nobiru, Tsuchizaki, and Aomori. Focused less on the economics of the rice trade (a key commodity for most of these locations), this section concentrates more on the creation of a transportation infrastructure capable of accommodating new commerce.

YOKKAICHI AND SHIMONOSEKI

As the central government scrambled to rein in the economy and use foreign trade to its advantage, a few Honshu ports emerged as possibilities for the overseas export of rice. Between 1876 and 1889, on multiple occasions, the Dajōkan approved special arrangements for rice exports to be transported on foreign ships at unopened ports. In 1880, the Tokyo Chamber of Commerce discussed a government white paper proposal that suggested opening Ishinomaki, Fushiki, and Shimonoseki as "new

39. See Tsugawa, *Ōsaka Dōjima komeshōkaijo*, 3–14, on early Meiji rice policies.
40. Sakurai, *Kome*, 25. Masuda, *Japan's Industrial Development Policy*, 7.

open ports" (*shin kaikō*) to handle overseas rice exports, in anticipation of rising trade volumes in coming years.[41] Although this particular project did not go forward, Shimonoseki and Yokkaichi would soon emerge as nontreaty ports where rice (*beikoku*) and brown rice (*genmai*) were exported overseas by special arrangement. Fushiki, on the Sea of Japan, was also named, and although it did not dispatch anywhere near the same volume as the other two, all three would subsequently be named special ports of export in 1889.[42]

Yokkaichi, like the three ports of Shimonoseki, Ishinomaki, and Fushiki, had a deep history as a center of commerce. An active port along the Tōkai coastline, Yokkaichi was noted for both its commerce and its role as the forty-third of the Tōkaidō's fifty-three post stations.[43] Yokkaichi also held a key location at the crossroads to the Ise Sangū Kaidō, or Pilgrimage Road, leading to the famous Ise Shrine. Although it played a relatively minor role in Tokugawa rice circuits, it did regularly ship tribute rice to Edo.[44] Following the Meiji Restoration, locals established the Kaisō Gyōsha transportation company, and a steamship entered Yokkaichi's harbor for the first time in 1870.[45] As early as 1873, one of the region's most important boosters, Inaba Sanemon, led efforts to begin construction of a proper harbor. The port would soon boast a regular shipping route to Tokyo and become a collection and distribution site for a variety of commodities.[46]

41. Fushiki Kōshi Hensan Iinkai, *Fushiki kōshi*. This is the only place I have seen mention of *shin kaikō*, but it could be an intellectual precursor to the 1883 special trading ports, which did allow for both imports and exports.

42. Fushiki appears to have only handled one shipment of rice, loading 21,500 *koku* of *genmai* on a German steamship in late 1888 (KZ, vol. 8 [1889]: Ōkurashō 1, "Nagato-no-kuni Akamagaseki narabi Etchū-no-kuni Fushiki-kō e . . . ," January 8, 1889). Shinagawa also comes up a handful of times as a possible site for early restricted export of both rice and coal but does not appear to develop any further in this capacity. See, for example, DR, vol. 3 (1878–79): Gaikoku kōsai, "Yushutsu beikoku tsumitori no tame . . . ," January 14, 1878.

43. Vaporis, *Breaking Barriers*, 23.

44. Dohi, *Kinsei beikoku ryūtsūshi*, 83.

45. Hiroi, *Nihon chikkōshi*, 275.

46. During the Russo-Japanese War, Yokkaichi would serve a fixed shipping route to Manchuria and Korea in the maintenance of Japan's war effort (Yokkaichishi Kyōikukai, *Yokkaichi kōshi*, 10–13).

Although it would not be opened to handle foreign exports officially until 1889, foreign steamships got special authorization from the Foreign Ministry in 1878 to stop at Yokkaichi to load grains that had been purchased by the Ministry of Finance. The port had some key advantages that made it an attractive choice: established routes to a rice hinterland, local transportation services, a good harbor with functioning port facilities that were in the process of receiving upgrades, and a location convenient to ships traveling between Kobe and Yokohama.

Just a few years later, in 1882, the Ministry of Agriculture and Commerce (Nōshōmushō) then headed by Saigō Tsugumichi, submitted a petition to the Dajōkan proposing that the country's reserve fund be used to purchase rice. This rice was to be directly exported overseas in a concerted effort to bring in specie to help offset high military costs. By the next year, as government funds were depleted in the face of enormous expenses, the allowance for exports at unopened ports would be expanded. The Ministry of Finance announced that it would, with imperial sanction, direct foreign ships to the ports of Shimonoseki, Yokkaichi, and Shinagawa, in order to export rice. The decree provided for a one-year trial period when foreign ships could apply to obtain licenses from the Foreign Ministry in order to drop anchor at these locations. The government was able to sell this rice because it was of higher quality and thus would be purchased by the treaty powers and fetch a decent price. Since rice was a dietary staple, however, the lost amount would be made up by purchasing cheaper, lower-quality rice from neighboring Asian countries, like Korea.[47]

On five different occasions during 1884, German and British steamships stopped at Yokkaichi expressly to load Ministry of Finance rice for export. These ships stayed in port for a range of six to twelve days to load 916,000 *koku* of rice each time, a quantity perhaps deliberately set by the ministry.[48] Again, from 1886 to 1888, at least eight British steamships stopped at Yokkaichi to load *genmai*, though in much smaller quantities than in 1884.[49] The shipments ranged from as little as 716

47. Fujimura, Matsukata, and Okubo, *Matsukata Masayoshi*, 2, 146–48, 240. Shinagawa does not appear to have exported rice at this time.

48. The only exception was one British ship that loaded 7,700 *koku* that September.

49. It is unclear whether this *genmai* had first been purchased by the government or if the government's Finance and Home ministers (Matsukata Masayoshi

tons to more than 3,380 tons, for an average of just under 2,088 tons. The ships loading this *genmai* also stayed in port for about the same intervals as in 1884, averaging roughly eight days.

Similarly, Shimonoseki handled several loads of export rice and *genmai* in 1883 and 1889, prior to being named a special trading port. Throughout the Tokugawa era, Shimonoseki (then known as Akamagaseki) was a primary rice exchange and collection center, handling rice coming from Kyushu and the Sea of Japan coast via the *nishi mawari* circuit and heading to Osaka. It was one of the country's five major relay markets (*dai-go chūkeichi ichiba*), linking regional to central rice markets and thus placing it high in the rice tribute system hierarchy.[50] Even after the port was opened for special export, a new Akamagaseki Rice Exchange would be established in 1893. But Shimonoseki also gained new functions in the modern era since its prime location placed it on Western steamer routes as ships made their way from China to Nagasaki or eastward to Kobe and Yokohama via the Inland Sea.

In the mid-1880s, as Shimonoseki was being named a special trade port for Korea, at least four British commercial steamships received special licenses to drop anchor to load rice purchased by the Ministry of Finance and export it overseas.[51] And again, from 1886 to 1888, British steamships stopped at Shimonoseki to load an average amount of almost 2,386 tons of *genmai* on at least ten occasions. The ships stayed in the harbor for as little as two days and as long as eleven days. In terms of the number of ships entering the harbor, the average amounts loaded per ship, and lengths of stay, there are only minor differences

---

and Itō Hirobumi, respectively) oversaw these transactions in the absence of a customs agency.

50. The other four were Kobe, Tsuruga, Onomichi (Bingo-no-kuni), and Chōshi (Shimousa-no-kuni) (Dohi, *Kinsei beikoku ryūtsūshi*, 70–73; Shimonoseki, *Shimonoseki shishi*, 283–84).

51. KR, vol. 6 (1882), no. 13: Gaikō 3, "Dōkoku shōsen *Harutoru*-gō Ōkurashō kaiire mai yushutsu no tame . . . ," February 22, 1882; ibid., "Eikoku shōsen *Hanama*-gō Ōkurashō kaiire mai yushutsu no tame . . . ," July 17, 1882; ibid., vol. 7 (1883), no. 13: Gaikō 2, "Ōkurashō chochikumai Nagato Shimonoseki yori kaigai e yushutsu ni yori . . . ," May 5, 1883. Amounts of rice loaded are not given for these stops (ibid., vol. 8 [1884], no. 44: Un'yu, "Eikoku kisen Ōkurashō yushutsumai wo tōsai shi Nagato Shimonoseki batsubyō," May 30, 1884). In this last instance, 16,000 *koku* of rice was loaded but the ship's length of stay in port is unclear.

between transactions at Shimonoseki and Yokkaichi.[52] Together, these snapshots indicate that Japan's central government was taking experimental steps toward stabilizing the economy by increasing revenue-generating exports. They also reveal some preliminary measures that would lead to the creation of a new infrastructure for exporting overseas.

With the 1889 naming of the special ports of export, exceptional government arrangements to load export rice at ports like Yokkaichi and Shimonoseki were, in effect, made permanent. Customs agency branches established at each designated port would regulate the flow of foreign ships and the goods that they carried. Importantly, the special ports of export also enabled the central government to adopt a non-interference policy in rice markets. After 1890, it began to leave prices largely to the forces of supply and demand.[53]

The special ports of export were an important mechanism in efforts to maximize profits from this shift, but they were not the fundamental reason for them. Tokyo's willingness to curtail its involvement in the rice trade stems from much more gradual changes. By 1889, land tax reforms had at last been fully implemented; the rice tax system was abolished as a period of leniency ended and all payments had to be made in cash.[54] The changing place of rice in the national economy coincides with the naming of the special ports of export. A reduction in the government's central oversight of rice markets came at the same time as its willingness to allow specified sites and their local merchants to handle more transactions on their own.

The situations at Yokkaichi and Shimonoseki reflect three interrelated changes in state policy. The first is the shift to a monetary tax, based

52. Shimonoseki had two more visits, loaded on average about 1,500 more *koku* per ship, and the ships stayed in port roughly two days less than they did in Yokkaichi. Shimonoseki additionally handled approximately twelve shipments of export *genmai* in early 1889, loading them onto British steamships for overseas export. The smallest amount loaded was just over 4,500 *koku* and the largest was more than 21,500 *koku* for an average of roughly 11,500 *koku* per shipment. These ships stayed in port for an average of five days for loading (KZ [1889], no. 8: Ōkurashō, "Nagato-no-kuni Akamagaseki narabi Etchū-no-kuni Fushiki-kō e . . . ," January 8, 1889).

53. Sakurai, *Kome*, 27–28. This period of *laissez-faire* rice policies would last until the end of the Meiji period in 1912, when the government would reevaluate regulating rice prices.

54. Ibid., 23.

on land values rather than more volatile harvest levels, to ensure steady revenues for ambitious programs of modernization. The second is government efforts to regulate the price of rice, which began in 1873 and only fully ended in 1889. The third key policy change was the Ministry of Finance's decision to generate income through rice exports, which occurred in a rather reactive and ad hoc fashion outside the treaty ports prior to 1889, but continued after that date in a steadier and more decentralized manner.

Meanwhile, the domestic infrastructural geography of Japan's rice trade was also being targeted for change as this product was being commodified and mobilized for overseas export. The first step was in getting foreign merchants and their ships to anchor at nontreaty harbors to load Japanese rice in exchange for much-needed foreign currency. This allowed the government to avoid the cost of shipping the rice to the treaty ports, avoid paying middlemen to handle the transactions, and avoid lending funds to Japanese enterprises to export the rice. Many Tokugawa rice hubs were not convenient for overseas shippers, and initially it was those situated along routes between the treaty ports that were successfully used to bolster Japan's efforts to withstand its incorporation into the world economy. Still, equipping ports to handle modern commerce while linking them to wider domestic and international transportation networks was also required for individual sites and the country as a whole to succeed in the new world order.

TŌHOKU SEAPORTS

The complexities and hazards of adjusting early modern systems for modern service are exemplified by efforts to newly mobilize this essential product in the service of the nation. Recalibrating rice's function from tribute tax to cash crop, one to be sold both at home and abroad, shifted the geography of the country's established transportation circuits during the Meiji era. Coastal ports in the Tōhoku region, one of Japan's most significant rice-growing areas, did not adapt as quickly or successfully as did other ports farther south. By contrast, a number of hubs for the management and transport of Tokugawa tax rice, such as Fushiki, Hakata, Shimonoseki, and Yokkaichi, would maintain their prominent position in being named special trading ports. Others with potential became special trading ports later on, as was the case with Hamada and Tsuruga, but many did not gain this status by 1899, including Aomori, Ishinomaki, and Nagoya. The following discussion evaluates some of the ports selected and some of those passed over for early trade and development, along with reasons for success or failure.

A measure of the challenges faced in trying to equip ports and adjust transportation routes to accommodate overseas rice export can be seen in the disappointed expectations of two adjacent ports, Ishinomaki and Nobiru, in eastern Tōhoku. Although Ishinomaki is now known primarily for the devastating earthquake and tsunami disasters that struck this port city on March 11, 2011, it had a centuries-long history as a coastal transportation hub that preceded this crippling moment. During the Tokugawa era, Ishinomaki served as eastern Tōhoku's primary rice port, handling Japanese coastal traffic from Tōhoku to Edo along the *higashi mawari*, or eastern sea circuit. Sendai domain, one of the archipelago's major rice-growing regions, maintained an impressive forty-five granaries at this port. After the Meiji government colonized Hokkaido in 1869, Ishinomaki's prospects rose even higher as it proved a convenient stop on the coastal route between the northern island and the capital of Tokyo.

When Ōkubo Toshimichi created the Home Ministry in 1873, he made establishing a stronger transportation infrastructure an integral piece of his blueprint to promote the country's independent economic development and industrialization.[55] In keeping with this aim, the ministry hired the Dutch engineer Cornelis Johannes van Doorn, who was then serving as a Meiji government adviser, to conduct an extensive survey of Ishinomaki harbor. Van Doorn, however, in concluding that winds, tides, and silting made Ishinomaki ill-suited for large ocean-going vessels, proposed instead constructing Nobiru Port at the entrance to an adjacent estuary and then linking it by canal to Ishinomaki. This solution appeared reasonable to the ambitious yet inexperienced decision makers.

The Nobiru project became part of a broader series of infrastructural investments that the Home Ministry launched in the late 1870s and early 1880s. Ōkubo and his team used public monies for several regional projects, including this one, through the Industrial Development Fund, designed specifically to help Japan modernize without resorting to borrowing foreign funds. Nobiru was thus one of three port construction

55. See Brown, "Ōkubo Toshimichi," 189–93.

projects, known as the big three, or *Meiji san dai chikkō*, subsidized by the central government.[56] Ishinomaki, on the other hand, was chosen to become a primary node in the new Grain Reserve Bureau regulation system being implemented in the late 1870s. As a testament to its significance along the Sanriku coast, it was the only non-treaty-port location listed besides Tokyo, Osaka, Kobe, and Nagasaki.[57]

From the start, however, construction at Nobiru encountered a series of problems that reflected the inadequacies of both the site and the original plan. Despite ongoing attempts to keep the government project viable, a decade and a considerable sum of money later, they conceded defeat, and the plan was abandoned in 1887. Nobiru and Ishinomaki both suffered from this misadventure. As funds were still being thrown at the dying venture, growing railway networks were beginning to impinge on maritime and riverine transport, causing existing shipping at Ishinomaki to decline.[58]

The relatively poor fortunes of Nobiru and Ishinomaki (which would again become a major port in the postwar period) did not, however, obtain for all ports along Sendai Bay. Shiogama, another long-functioning port, was located just south of the other two in Miyagi Prefecture. Although not similarly key to the Tokugawa rice trade, it was also to be linked by canal to Nobiru in van Doorn's plan. After the Nobiru project failed, however, Shiogama still managed to rise as a regional center. The Japan Railway Company selected it as a hub in 1886 because of its favorable location between Aomori and Tokyo. Benefiting from its new position in the railway network, Shiogama would later be designated for harbor improvement in 1903 and within a decade would begin to prosper as a modern commercial port.[59]

The stories of these three ports in Sendai Bay demonstrate how difficult it could be to modernize existing networks. The geographical

56. In addition to Nobiru, these were Misumi in Kumamoto Prefecture and Mikuni in Fukui Prefecture. Nobiru and Mikuni, which was a Tokugawa-era rice collection and distribution hub, were to be rice ports whereas Misumi was primarily a coal port. Of the three ports subsidized by the Home Ministry, only Misumi would later be named a special port of export.

57. Masuda, *Japan's Industrial Development Policy*, 7.

58. Ibid., 23–24.

59. Shiogama was first established during the Nara period and had served as an early naval base (Hiroi, *Nihon chikkōshi*, 313–15).

contours of the well-established national system to get tribute rice to government collection and storage sites would not be able to continue unchanged after state edicts began to commercialize rice and exchange it on the international market. Older pathways and hubs faced variable outcomes. Some, like Ishinomaki and Nobiru, would prove inadequate for modernization, at least with available technologies. Others, as represented by Shiogama (and as we will see with regard to Aomori and Shimonoseki), would gain in status, strengthening their positions as industrialization and new modes of transportation created a "second nature" geography of railroads and modern harbors capably engineered to accommodate larger, deep-draft steamships.[60]

Whether rail would have so completely overtaken shipping along this part of the Pacific coast even if the Nobiru project had succeeded is an interesting question. Might these ports have fared better under a different plan, especially if construction succeeded ahead of the railroad? Could a successfully completed modern harbor at Nobiru, linked to rail connections at Ishinomaki, have gained greater consideration from foreign and domestic shippers, allowing greater steamship traffic in this part of the country? Might they have become special trading ports? It seems unlikely. From the vantage point of the special trading ports, the entire Tōhoku coastline—on both the Pacific and Sea of Japan sides—is a large swath of the country that conspicuously had no sites named as special trading ports at this juncture.

Three reasons for this absence stand out as possibilities with respect to developing direct exports. First, the region may not have been able to keep pace with improved agricultural technologies that would have allowed it to beat out other rice producers. In one unofficial analysis of export rice in the late 1880s, Takeuchi Masato concluded that the regions exporting the highest quantities and qualities of rice were Chūgoku and Kyushu to the southwest.[61] Takeuchi further states that at the May 1888 Tokyo *Genmai* Wholesalers' Competitive Trade Fair,

60. Cronon, *Nature's Metropolis*, 56. See Wigen on employing historical geography as a methodology and on the process of a one-time center becoming a periphery based on shifting national imperatives ("Geographic Imagination" and *Making of a Japanese Periphery*). See also Fox, *History in Geographic Perspective*.

61. Takeuchi, *Dai Nihon bōekiron*, 14. Moreover, Tōhoku did not have coal deposits. Aomori did have sulfur, but this did not tip the balance in its favor for being named a special trading port.

Tōhoku submissions (from the provinces of Mutsu, Iwaki, Rikuzen, Rikuchū, and Uzen) were inferior to those from other parts of the country. Although some Tōhoku regions had better rice varieties and grades than others, and although some showed improvement over previous years, many lost out due to the poor quality of their drying techniques.[62]

A second possibility is that, despite its ongoing importance in national rice production (even if at inferior grades), Tōhoku may, indeed, have been too remote from Japan's center and from other crucial modern resources, like coal, for politicians and industrialists to put the region at the top of a long list of places needing regular rail and steamship routes, especially following the Nobiru debacle.[63] By 1900, the line extending from Sendai to Aomori was the only railroad crossing the vast northern portion of Honshu.[64]

The geography of foreign shipping circuits offers a third explanation. People living on the Sea of Japan coast consistently felt left out of the country's progress during the Meiji era as their part of the country became known as Ura Nihon. Although this region had once been fundamental to Japan's coastal maritime circuits and rice traffic, the modernization of Japan's transportation and a new reliance on foreign steamer traffic had difficulty accommodating it. By the mid-1890s, however, when new opportunities arose, residents would fight to make their ports again relevant to maritime traffic.

The relative neglect of Japan's north does not mean that its leaders and merchants had no options or that they were ignored by Tokyo. The Nobiru project alone proves differently, and other Tōhoku ports that had served as primary nodes in the early modern rice trade still had room to jockey for advantage in Japan's changing transportation geography. For example, in 1877, the Home Ministry approved construction of a new road from Akita, a town along the northern Sea of Japan coast, southward to the port of Tsuchizaki, which had served as a hub on the western *nishi mawari* rice circuit. Two years after road construction began, the Home Ministry bolstered Tsuchizaki's prospects by sanctioning a new

62. Ibid., 3–11.
63. On the importance of coal locations for industrial development, see Pomeranz, *The Great Divergence*, 62–66.
64. See Ericson, *Sound of the Whistle*, 28.

granary there.[65] A decade later, once export restrictions had loosened somewhat with the third wave of special trading ports in 1889, Tsuchizaki's residents also benefited from the recognition that special allowances could improve local circumstances and ameliorate inconsistencies in commercial supply and demand.

Whether or not ports had hinterlands producing any of the five designated special exports, many also diversified and had highly marketable secondary goods. Local boosters in Tsuchizaki, along with those in western Hokkaido's Hamanaka, for example, petitioned the Home Ministry for special allowance to export their product surpluses, including *kombu*, timber (*mokuzai*), and railroad ties (*makuragi*). Reminiscent of Shimonoseki and Yokkaichi, with their rice exports, these two northern sites were granted dispensation to transport their products by rail to nontreaty ports, where they could be loaded onto foreign ships for overseas markets.[66] This measure allowed for a kind of regional safety value, enabling some stability as Japan continued to work its way into the world economy under the treaty port system. Although Tsuchizaki did not become an open port in 1899, it soon became a hub in the national rail system, beating out neighboring Funakawa for this designation. In the first decade of the twentieth century, it ranked as one of the country's second-class major ports (*dai ni shu jūyō kōwan*).[67]

Aomori offers a final example of the difficult issues that Japan's ports faced as commercial and transportation systems adapted in the second half of the long nineteenth century. With naturally calm waters and a convenient location on Mutsu Bay and across the Tsugaru Strait from Hokkaido, the port of Aomori was established for Tokugawa commerce and served the country's vital rice circuits. In the modern age, its strategic geographic position proved to be both a blessing and a curse for commerce.

---

65. DR, gaihen (1871–77): Unsō 8, "Akita-ken ka Akita machi yori . . . ," February 23, 1877; ibid., vol. 3 (1878–79), no. 22: Chihō, "Akita-ken Tsuchizaki minato e komegura shinchiku," May 2, 1879.

66. KR, vol. 13 (1889), no. 28: Zaisei 3, "Kaisha mata wa ikkojin yori haken kanri no hiyō wo benshō suru . . . ," December 14, 1889; ibid., vol. 15 (1891), no. 14: Gaiji, "Konbu mokuzai oyobi ita wo fukaikōjō yori yushutsu suru . . . ," October 15, 1891.

67. Hiroi, *Nihon chikkōshi*, 285–88.

Aomori became a stop on the Honshu rail network in 1891, allowing it to operate more efficiently as a hub for land and sea transport, especially in serving ships crossing the Tsugaru Strait to Hokkaido and Karafuto. This came as Hokkaido was also becoming more fully entwined with Meiji networks. Hakodate sat just across the bay, and Aomori established a fixed route to Muroran in 1893, the year before that port was named for special export status. Because of its growing links, the port's commercial future looked bright.

When Japan's relationship with Russia intensified with the building of the Trans-Siberian Railway, Aomori's status became more difficult to gauge. Commercial opportunity was tempered by its immediate significance as a military port, even when it became clear that the prefecture had significant sulfur reserves. Residents repeatedly championed their port during the decade, but the port's military role was partly responsible for the failure of their bids to gain special trading status in the mid-1890s and again in 1899.

Aomori played an important support role in the Russo-Japanese War, but nearby Ōminato, which was better poised to guard the Tsugaru Strait, was soon named a third rank military port (*yōkōbu*). The two ports complemented each other, and Aomori remained a strategic stop for ships traveling northerly latitudes either to the Russian Maritime Province or to the West Coast of North America. Aomori opened to international trade in 1906 and was quickly named a second-class major port.

Whether due to railroad access, entrepreneurial verve, an inherently strategic location, or perhaps some luck, ports like Aomori, Shiogama, and Tsuchizaki fared better than many other Tōhoku ports, although none functioned as special trading ports prior to 1899.[68] Aomori was the only one of these three in serious contention for that position, but its military function prevented that from happening.[69] Choices made by

68. Being named a special trading port was not necessarily proof of success in either the short or long term, but this was generally considered a desirable designation, confirming the promise of these ports while giving them a chance to launch overseas trade.

69. Moji and Shimonoseki faced a similar conflict between commercial and military functions in attempting to gain greater status in the mid-1890s, which will be discussed more fully in Chapter 6 (KZ [1901], no. 43: Teikoku gikai 15, "Aomori-kō wo kaikō ni tsuika . . . ," April 23, 1901). This document suggests that the Lower House initially approved opening the port to greater commerce in 1899, but

those government officials and private enterprises responsible for developing homeland infrastructures played an important, though not always decisive, role in determining which ports would reach prominence during the Meiji era.

Beyond the domestic politics and material logistics involved in deciding which regions and sites would be included on new routes, the shape of international transportation circuits mattered. The locations of the treaty ports and the amounts of traffic each of them garnered from maritime trade also played a significant role in determining which harbors would prove convenient as ports of call along the best-traveled foreign steamship routes. The Tōhoku region sat outside these major routes, where traffic flowed more regularly through southerly waters between the Chinese coast and Japan's three major treaty ports of Yokohama, Kobe, and Nagasaki.

In the rice trade, the location of Shimonoseki in particular mattered for its ability to export rice. In the 1880s and 1890s, when rice exports began in earnest, the treaty ports shipped rice to foreign countries, starting with relatively small quantities to the four main markets of Australia (55,521 piculs or 3,700 tons), Russia (554 tons), Great Britain (141 tons), and China (18.5 tons), plus another 132 tons to "other" places for a total of just over 4,500 tons in 1880.[70] The total amount of rice exported grew to over 7,000 tons in 1881 and then climbed sixfold to nearly 44,000 tons in 1882. After dramatic rises and falls from 1883 to 1887, rice exports in 1888 reached 4 million piculs (over 250,000 tons) and were destined for at least sixteen different countries. The highest amount (nearly 110,000 tons), or over 40 percent of the total, went to Great Britain. Most of the year's rice exports left from Kobe. After the special ports of export opened, many of the ports handled variable but mostly very small amounts of rice through the 1890s. Shimonoseki is the only site that exported it every year, averaging over 13,500 tons per year for the decade. Moji did not begin exporting rice until 1895 and, after a slow first year, averaged almost 13,000 tons a year.

---

the military may have prevented it, as happened temporarily with Moji in mid-1896.

70. These figures are calculated using the formula that 1 picul equals 133 pounds.

The special trading ports handled approximately 25 percent of rice exports in 1896 and 1897, 20 percent in 1898, and 30 percent in 1899.[71] Kobe handled the great majority of the trade, followed by Shimonoseki and Moji, which traded years in second place. In 1896, 65.5 percent of rice exports went to Australia, France, Germany, Great Britain, and the United States and almost 25 percent to Hong Kong and Russian Asia. The proportion of total exports to Asian countries rose to 28 percent in 1897 and 40 percent (with roughly 85 percent of that to Hong Kong but also to Russian Asia, China, Korea, and a small amount to British India and the Philippines) in 1898. The proportion fell to 30 percent in 1899.[72]

These statistics tell us two main things about rice exports in the 1880s and 1890s. First, rice saw a generally upward export trend that was punctuated by some fairly sharp rises and falls. And even though Kobe maintained the lead in exports by a wide margin, by the late 1890s, together Shimonoseki and Moji carried an average of one-quarter of all rice exports, effectively shifting some of the trade away from the core of the treaty ports westward to the special ports of export. Yokkaichi does not appear in national statistics and did not export any more rice during these years. The second conclusion is that a larger share of exports began going to Asia, especially Hong Kong, starting in 1891. It is not possible to discern from these statistics whether there is a direct correlation between the special exports and the growth in this trade to East Asian markets. Nonetheless, we see an overall dispersal of the rice trade from the core treaty ports to the special trading ports and from destinations in Europe to more in East Asia. Although the central government could not engineer exactly which sites would be able to handle exports, it did increase the overall amounts sent abroad. The coal trade, with different hinterland locations and a specific concentration of export markets, also began to aggregate at the Kanmon ports during this same period.

Creating a New Geography of Overseas Coal Exports

Coal was a limited, albeit growing, commercial product during the Tokugawa era. Although rice was produced nationwide and traveled along well-established paths of collection and distribution, coal circulated mostly

71. Annual totals for these years were 126,000 tons (1896), 86,000 tons (1897), 70,000 tons (1898), and over 145,000 tons in 1899 (*DNGBN*, 1896–99).
72. Ibid.

in northern Kyushu and parts of the Inland Sea. In these areas, coal tended to follow riverine and coastal shipping routes that had originally been created for Tokugawa tax rice, and these proved sufficient even as the domestic coal trade expanded through the early nineteenth century. As this fledgling industry suddenly became drawn into global commercial networks beginning in the mid-1850s, however, the unprecedented demand for coal necessitated expanding transportation systems. In contrast to the start of overseas rice exports, which primarily involved reconfiguring existing transportation networks, providing coal for export required the creation of brand new ones.

When Western steamships arrived in Japan in the mid-1850s, coal was one of the first items that they demanded. Although today the country is generally seen as inherently poor in natural resources, Japan, in fact, had an abundance of the very resource keenly sought during the Age of Steam.[73] Meeting the need for bunker coal with fueling stops on long-distance maritime routes was a crucial component of sustaining overseas commerce and global empires in the nineteenth century. Indeed, many ports that rose to international prominence during the nineteenth century did so as coaling stations for the British empire, including Bombay, Colombo, Rangoon, Shanghai, Hong Kong, and Singapore. Maintaining fuel supplies at locations like these meant carrying coal from home unless and until indigenous coals could be procured in sufficient quantities at competitive prices.

Gaining access to adequate coal supplies was more than an economic endeavor. The rise of steam transportation altered relations among world powers and brought international tensions to East Asia as Great Britain, the United States, and Russia all turned their attention to the region. Steam transportation contributed to a decline in the relative importance of the Atlantic World; it altered port hierarchies in the Indian Ocean as new steamer routes developed and the Suez Canal opened; and it helped bring new attention to the Pacific, especially China but also Japan.[74]

---

73. Sulfur, another special export commodity, was also crucial in nineteenth-century industrialization. As Gerald Kutney states, sulfur "remained a minor industry until industrial demand for sulfuric acid exploded in the early 19th century. Sulfuric acid became the dominant chemical in the entire world, making this era the 'Sulfur Age'" (*Sulfur*, 4).

74. Dubois, "Red Sea Ports," 64–68; Knight and Liss, *Atlantic Port Cities*, 5; McPherson, "Port Cities," 80–92.

These geographical shifts intensified midcentury as steamer tonnage worldwide increased fourfold in the two pivotal decades between 1850 and 1870.[75] By the 1880s, steamers replaced sailing ships worldwide.[76]

Japan found its place in these global processes. Kyushu would quickly prove to be an important supplier of coal—especially for use in steam engines—across transmarine East Asia. What began as an effort to provide fuel for ships calling at Japan's treaty ports turned into a significant business of exporting coal to all of the major Asian hubs by the turn of the century. Moreover, Japan would establish its own coaling stations in Asia, for example, negotiating to do so in Korea when signing the 1876 Treaty of Kanghwa.[77] By the turn of the next century, Japanese coal, as yet with little competition from Taiwan or China, would overtake imported British and Australian coal to dominate the larger markets of Singapore, Shanghai, and Hong Kong and begin moving into markets throughout Asia.[78]

The high external demand for this particular resource helped drive the development of the domestic coal industry even as it struggled to provide a consistent supply to foreign markets. Yet entering the coal market was less fraught than exporting rice overseas. Since coal was not fundamentally tied to the national economy in the same way as rice, making it available for export was chiefly a matter of establishing channels to handle the new trade.

SUPPLYING COAL AT THE TREATY PORTS

The clouds of dark steam billowing from Matthew Perry's "black ships" as they approached Uraga Bay in 1853 offered a visible sign that coal literally fueled the machines of modern empire. Equipped with advance knowledge of Japan's coal deposits and mining operations from contemporaries residing there, notably Dr. Phillip Franz von Siebold at the Dejima trading post in Nagasaki, the Americans intended to secure coal supplies for their developing maritime routes to East Asia.[79] The letter that

75. M. Fletcher, "Suez Canal."
76. Sugiyama, *Japan's Industrialization*, 172.
77. Key-Hiuk Kim, *Last Phase*, 267.
78. Sumiya, *Nihon sekitan sangyō bunseki*, 350.
79. Perry first stopped to purchase coal at the ports of Futami in Ogasawara and Naha in the Ryukyu Islands on his way to Edo. Pursuit of Chinese markets also

Perry handed to Tokugawa envoys from U.S. President Millard Fillmore was addressed to the Japanese emperor. It clearly expressed the
Americans' wish to access Japanese coal, stating in part:

> We understand that there is a great abundance of coal and provisions in
> the empire of Japan. Our steam ships, in crossing the great ocean, burn a
> great deal of coal, and it is not convenient to bring it all the way from Amer-
> ica. We wish that our steam ships and other vessels should be allowed to
> stop in Japan and supply themselves with coal, provisions, and water. They
> will pay for them in money, or anything else your imperial majesty's sub-
> jects may prefer; and we request your imperial majesty to appoint a con-
> venient port, in the southern part of the Empire, where our vessels may
> stop for this purpose. We are very desirous of this.[80]

In measured response to President Fillmore's letter, the shogun's commissioners indicated that although they did have coal to sell, they did not
have experience in either international coal markets or the use of coal
for steamships. As translated by chief interpreter Moriyama Einosuke,
the commissioners stated:

> We recognize necessity . . . and shall entirely comply with the proposals of
> your government concerning coal, etc. . . . commencement can be made
> with coal at Nagasaki, by the first month of the next Japanese year (16 Feb-
> ruary 1855). . . . Having no precedent with respect to coal, we request your
> excellency to furnish us with an estimate, and upon due consideration this
> will be complied with if not in opposition to our laws. What do you mean
> by provisions, and how much coal will be required?[81]

Perry answered simply that they expected American steamers to be
supplied with "reasonable quantities of coal and at fair and equitable
prices."[82]

In the short term, the Japanese gathered coal on an ad hoc basis from
a variety of sites, making its early supply at the treaty ports inconsistent
and, at times, inconvenient and uneconomic. Providing coal at the treaty

---

intensified for the Americans following their own unequal treaty with China in
1844 (Nagasue, *Chikuhō*, 47–48).

80. Pineau, *The Japan Expedition*, 220–21. Perry himself held ambitions for the Pacific, including a desire to establish a profitable transpacific steamship line, which
would require large amounts of coal, one resource California did not have. His
ambitions did not materialize (Brechin, *Imperial San Francisco*, 249).

81. Pineau, *The Japan Expedition*, 222.

82. Ibid., 223.

ports, where no system was in place to ensure adequate supplies, would take time. But within just a few decades, new supply channels grew to meet demand at the treaty ports and the geography of Japan's coal industry and its transportation mechanisms changed considerably.

Although the Chikuhō region of northwestern Kyushu had been the heart of the coal industry during the Tokugawa era, the opening of the treaty ports pushed the *bakufu*, and then the Meiji government, to discover and begin excavating new coalfields on the main island of Honshu and on Hokkaido. These openings also moved the center of Kyushu mining activity, for a time, to that island's southwest as the higher-quality excavable mines near Nagasaki—especially Karatsu, Takashima, and Miike—took precedence over Chikuhō. But as mining technologies improved and overseas exports of Japanese coal increased, however, Chikuhō would quickly rise to dominate foreign exports through the special trading port of Moji.

In addition to changes in the geographies of production and distribution resulting from efforts to supply the country's new ports of call, Japan's own needs for coal were multiplying. Domestic demand continued unabated from several sources, including local fishing villages (where fishermen used coal for onshore bonfires and boat torches and whalers used it to extract whale oil, a powerful insecticide, from carcasses), petty manufacturing industries (where craftsmen used coal in foundries and for heating kilns to make roof tiles or pottery), and urban homes (where merchants and samurai turned to coal for boiling bath water, cooking, and heating living quarters).[83] The highest continuing demand came from the Jūshū saltfields, a key proto-industrial enterprise located along the Inland Sea.[84] Beginning at midcentury, these ongoing needs were joined by new requirements as the *bakufu* and domains endeavored to arm themselves against the Western threat

83. Whalers used coal to extract oil from whale meat, skin, and bones. Domainal officials and rice farmers alike clamored for whale oil once they found it to be a powerful insecticide during the Kyōhō famine (Kalland and Moeran, *Japanese Whaling*, 70, 117; Nagasue, *Chikuhō*, 21). Additionally, coal was generally converted to coke prior to use to both reduce the smell and provide a longer burn (Nishi Nihon Shinbunsha, *Fukuoka-ken hyakka jiten*, 48).

84. The saltfields used coal to boil water for their *irihama* method of salt extraction.

to their sovereignty. In this vein, coal was used in constructing and fueling steamships, casting artillery and munitions, and building coastal batteries.[85]

Japan's coal deposits, which offered a mixed range of quality and access, assisted these endeavors but were not effective for all needs. Ninety percent of Japan's coal is distributed on the islands of Hokkaido (50 percent) and Kyushu (40 percent) and consists of mostly medium- and low-grade bituminous and subbituminous deposits. These grades were quite suitable for steam-driven transportation (steam engine boilers ran more efficiently with higher-quality coals but could certainly use these lower-quality varieties as well) but were largely inadequate for modern heavy industry. As an interim solution, some of the subbituminous coals could be mixed with higher-quality anthracite for use in warships or blast furnaces requiring higher-calorie heat sources, but as Japan developed its own modern industries, supplementary reserves of anthracite would be imported from China and the region of Manchuria. Nonetheless, Japan's domestic coal supply proved more than sufficient to accommodate high foreign demand while meeting most domestic demand throughout the Meiji era.

When the Japanese first endeavored to increase their supplies of coal to meet demand, however, they still had a long way to go. In trying to get coal to the port of Nagasaki in 1854, the bulk of it came from regions near the port, but some was sent from as far away as Chōshū in southwestern Honshu. Even at this early juncture, it was clear that Kyushu was in the best geographic position for exporting coal due to its high quantity and quality, convenience to transportation routes, and year-round access to both mines and ports. Naturally, within Kyushu, there were significant regional differences in coal strata and development. By 1860, coal from Karatsu, in Saga domain, was prized. This castle town and historical hub of foreign commerce (renowned for its Korean-inspired pottery) alone supplied 70 percent of Nagasaki's 60,000 metric tons.[86] One estimate puts nationwide coal production in the 1860s at approximately 400,000 tons, with Karatsu supplying the lion's share of production of more than 120,000 tons.[87] After the Meiji government came to

85. Nagasue, *Chikuhō*, 48.
86. Sumiya, *Nihon sekitan sangyō bunseki*, 21.
87. Aoki et al., *Nihon shi daijiten*.

power, however, it would earmark Karatsu's deposits for the navy, and Takashima and Miike would become the country's top producers for export until Chikuhō rose to challenge them by the end of the century.[88]

Kyushu's coal, however, was a long way from other treaty ports, like Yokohama, where supplying coal proved more challenging. Honshu possessed several minor deposits of lower-quality, mostly lignite, coal, and its largest coalfield, Jōban (spanning eastern Fukushima and Ibaraki prefectures along the Pacific coast), was not discovered until 1855. Excavation at Jōban began in 1858 and soon supplied fuel to the region.[89] In order to respond to the foreign demand for coal, coal sellers (*sekitan-ya*) sprang into action, and at least twenty-eight merchants were conducting sales of coal at the first-named treaty port of Kanagawa when it was officially replaced by Yokohama in 1859.[90] These merchants were subsequently redirected to the latter port, although this switch could not happen overnight. A Russian warship, anxious to load coal at Yokohama during this transition, had to wait while a sufficient labor force was enlisted from Kanagawa.[91]

It took longer still to steadily provide coal at the northernmost port of Hakodate. The decision to designate the fishing port as a foreign stop in 1854 was based on its convenience as a port of call for whaling vessels.[92] Hakodate was required only to supply foreign ships with wood, water, and provisions. The parameters of the agreement did not, however, stop them from asking for coal, which was not yet being mined in Hokkaido.[93] During the *bakumatsu* era (1853–1867), the shogunal administrator (*bugyō*) in Hakodate ordered the prospecting of sites that might yield coal. Over the next decade, excavation began at the promising locations of Kushiro, Shiranuka, and Kayanuma.[94] When the

88. See Tōjō, "Karatsu kaigun tankō," 82–87, on this takeover.

89. Sumiya, *Nihon sekitan sangyō bunseki*, 21.

90. Chikuhō Sekitan Kōgyōshi Nenpyō Hensan Iinkai, *Chikuhō sekitan kōgyōshi nenpyō*, 1, 44.

91. Ibid., 42.

92. Cortazzi, *Victorians in Japan*, 33.

93. Yano, *Sekitan*, 29.

94. Surveying started during the *bakumatsu* era with the help of foreign engineers and these results produced Japan's first geological survey in 1876. Shiranuka's coal was very poor and brought many complaints from foreign shippers. Production there lasted only a short time, ceasing with the discovery of higher quality coal at Kayanuma.

new Meiji government created the Hokkaido Development Agency in 1869, this office continued to conduct surveys to determine the island's resource base, locating several more significant coal seams and assuming management of the best sites, including Kayanuma and the Horonai mine in coal-rich Ishikari.[95]

In addition to supplying the treaty ports, foreign ships and warships occasionally made arrangements with local authorities to purchase coal outside officially designated ports. For example, during the Crimean War, the Takashima mine intensified production and fueled at least ten British, French, and Russian warships anchored on the outskirts of Nagasaki in 1855. Records indicate that in March 1861, a Russian warship procured coal at Shimonoseki, still a domestic coastal port at the time. And as late as October 1864, four warships from different countries stopped at Himejima Island off the northern coast of Kyushu. One of these, a British warship, loaded the relatively large amount of 150 tons of coal.[96]

After the Meiji Restoration, the new government recognized that the production and sale of coal necessitated stronger oversight from a more highly centralized administration, but developing such a system would take place in fits and starts. As the country's new leaders were still becoming aware of the importance of coal—after all, securing precious metals was a more pressing issue when they took power—there was no shortage of parties interested in trying to make the most of the opportunity, from petty excavators to domainal governments still holding monopolies to larger enterprises.

Beyond gaining domestic control, the Meiji government also faced ongoing diplomatic requests that added to the challenge of taking command over this asset. For example, in 1869, Japan's foreign minister, Sawa Nobuyoshi, conceded to British Minister Parkes's demand for duty-free coal. Parkes argued that coal purchased in Japanese ports for use as steamship fuel was not actually an export since it was consumed

95. Ibid., 36. Ishikari is Japan's largest coalfield and is situated just east of Sapporo. It has good bituminous with coking properties (most of Hokkaido's coal deposits tend to be low-grade, with a lot of lignite and inferior non-coking coals). The introduction of new technologies and a mining railroad in the 1880s helped the Horonai mine to develop more rapidly than others in Hokkaido, but overall, Hokkaido lagged behind Kyushu in coal production.

96. Ibid., 34, 46, 52.

in transit.[97] Undoubtedly, he would have known this would create accounting problems and decrease costs for the British. Because usage quantities were difficult to assess, it was easy for shippers to abuse this system by purchasing "transit coal" that would instead be exported without paying the legislated 5 percent tariff.[98] Enforcement was complicated by the fact that the Japanese continued to heavily rely on British commercial shipping for trade throughout the treaty port era. Given the pressing demand for coal, eliminating the tariff did not likely increase sales for the Japanese, but keeping it would surely have helped their bottom line.[99]

Foreign interests also saw other ways to tap into the potential profits to be made from Japan's coal resources. Thomas Glover, the prominent British merchant in Nagasaki who helped modernize the Takashima mine, described the importance of Japan's coal deposits for British use in Asia:

> it is against the interest of England that heavy drafts of coal be yearly made on her [*sic*] already-diminished veins; but it is against the laws of trade to bring "coals to Newcastle," in other words—to make it necessary to furnish our steamers, both navy and merchant, with fuel from distant countries, while Japan can produce it in quantity and quality to supply the whole East, if proper facilities are granted, and encouragement given to capitalists to invest, and engineers to manage the opening up of the mineral districts of this country. In countless ways it would benefit the Japanese as well as the foreigners.[100]

The British did indeed take advantage of Japanese coal as Glover intended, purchasing it in Japan and at their substantial coal markets across Asia. They just as surely gave the Japanese much needed financial, technological, and managerial help as they increased productivity at their mines.

The Meiji oligarchs targeted Karatsu for protection early on. The area had high-quality coal that was fairly easy to excavate. In the *bakumatsu* era, southerly domains like Hizen and Kagoshima were involved in

---

97. Chikuhō Sekitan Kōgyōshi Nenpyō Hensan Iinkai, *Chikuhō sekitan kōgyōshi nenpyō*, 1:66. This would pertain only to coal loaded onto steamers, not sailing vessels, although the latter might travel with and supply steamers.

98. *Japan Weekly Mail*, July 30, 1881.

99. Export coal would not be made duty-free until 1887, just before the special ports of export were established.

100. Quoted in Cortazzi, *Victorians in Japan*, 26.

managing the Karatsu coalfields, largely in the service of establishing a strong military fleet. When the Meiji government took these coalfields over from the newly dismantled domains, even though the Ministry of Industry (Kōbushō) held jurisdiction over the coal industry, the oligarchs placed them under the short-lived Ministry of Military Affairs (Hyōbushō).[101] Designated *yobi tanden* (naval reserve coalfields), Karatsu initially provided a sure supply of fuel for Japan's warships. Within two decades, as Karatsu's limited reserves were rapidly becoming depleted, the Navy Ministry (Kaigunshō) would turn to Chikuhō to meet its fuel needs, appropriating thirty-eight coalfields there in 1886 for its exclusive use.[102]

In Japan's other coal-producing regions, however, a combination of demands from foreign ships and domestic growth in industry and defense caused unprecedented strains on the production, distribution, and consumption sectors of the coal industry by the early 1870s. These new obligations effectively put modern demands on a system developed to meet preindustrial needs, and what was still a fragmented domainal power structure was pushed to its limits. Several pieces of legislation helped ease these stresses. The first was a change in the country's power structure. The Meiji leaders issued edicts designed to reduce the independent power of the domains before abolishing them with the establishment of prefectures in 1872. Other key changes pertained more specifically to coal.

The Dajōkan declared, through the promulgation of a mining directive (*Kōzan kokoroesho*) in 1872, that all mined materials were the property of the emperor. This move formally separated land ownership from mining rights.[103] The document also prohibited foreigners from owning or managing mines, thus protecting these valuable national resources and retaining any profits to be gained from them. On the heels of the directive came the more comprehensive 1873 Japan Mining Law (Nihon Kōhō), which allowed, inter alia, for public ownership and management, gave special rights to the state (*kokka senken shugi*), and established a *shakku* mine concession system, in which those who wished to

101. Tōjō, "Karatsu kaigun tankō," 82. For more on this ministry, see Ōkurashō, *Kōbushō enkaku hōkoku*.

102. The Ministry of Military Affairs, established in 1869, was abolished and divided into Army and Navy ministries in 1872.

103. Samuels, *Business of the Japanese State*, 69.

acquire a concession had to meet certain qualifications and be approved through an application process.[104]

Although the 1873 legislation was issued to cover all mining nation-wide, implementation was less than uniform. As they worked to con-solidate their power and incorporate the unsettled domains, the oligarchs recognized that they needed to protect the country's best assets but could not fully manage or fund the developing coal industry alone. The coun-try's unequal position under the Western powers' commercial treaties did not preclude them from working effectively with foreign merchants who were eager to turn a profit. The relationships between the Japanese and Westerners involved in the coal industry elucidate how it was really in the best interests of individuals, businesses, and government officials on both sides to help Japan's coal mining enterprises succeed. This coop-eration, even if tense at times, is clear in the case of the Takashima mine.

During the *bakumatsu* era, Saga domain joined forces with Thomas Glover, who was then living in Nagasaki, to develop and excavate the Takashima mine. Although the central government briefly acquired the mine from Saga in 1874, Gotō Shōjirō quickly purchased it for the bargain price of roughly half a million dollars.[105] The statesman and entrepreneur, however, could not afford to pay for it without a loan from Britain's Jardine Matheson, then the largest business operating along China's southeast coast.[106] Likely recognizing the mine's high operating costs and the value of this national resource, the oligarchs allowed this purchase even though it defied their new ban on foreign ownership of mines. Gotō even left the management of the mine in the British company's hands. But after a series of misfortunes at the mine, including a fire and flooding, as well as the Satsuma Rebellion and a cholera outbreak, the last two of which took a toll on the mine's work-force, Jardine's wanted out.

Gotō, already in debt, could not pay off the loan and decided to man-age operations and take over sales to China, which had until then been solely the purview of the British company. Even though production began to increase once again, tensions between Gotō and Jardine's escalated

104. Ōkurashō, *Kōbushō enkaku hōkoku,* contains a copy of the Japan Mining Law's 33 articles, 135–48.

105. McMaster, "The Takashima Mine," 226.

106. Ibid., 218.

into an international court case and problems were compounded when unpaid workers who labored under atrocious conditions went on strike. The British company did not recoup all that it had invested in the modernization of the mine when Iwasaki Yatarō, who had strong ties to the central government as the founder of Mitsubishi, came forward to buy the mine in 1881. With this purchase, the connection between the coal and shipping industries began to emerge.[107] Although the mine had an uneven start as a modern enterprise, it benefited from British oversight and funding and would go on to supply Japan and its growing overseas customers before losing ground to Miike and Chikuhō.

The Miike mine followed a somewhat different path than Takashima in the first decades of the Meiji era. Operated by Miike *daimyō* since the early eighteenth century, the mine was acquired by the central government in 1873 and continued under the government's management for several years. It produced high-quality coal but could sell it at lower prices than Takashima by using convicts to labor in the hot, dark, and dangerous mineshafts.[108] Here, too, the Japanese engaged foreigners' help in acquiring and implementing Western technologies to increase production but relied less on such help than was the case at Takashima. Instead, the government soon entrusted the Miike mine to the newly established Mitsui Bussan, which gained a monopoly over sales of Miike coal through personal connections with the statesman Itō Hirobumi. Just over a decade later, in 1888, Mitsui Bussan purchased the mine and continued to handle its coal sales, competing in East Asian markets against Mitsubishi's Takashima coal. In a somewhat similar fashion, the Meiji government would also take over Hokkaido's newly established Horonai mine in 1882. Although this coal mine would eventually be sold in 1889, Tokyo would remain closely involved in production.

The Chikuhō region, in great contrast to the country's other coal-producing regions, was left largely to local control throughout the early Meiji period. The coalfields' operators had difficulty in negotiating the change from the monopoly system (established by the earlier *shikumihō* law) to a more competitive market system, delaying the appearance of Chikuhō coal in East Asian markets. With the end of domainal controls over mining, Chikuhō entered a period of unregulated excavation and

107. Samuels, *Business of the Japanese State*, 70–71.
108. See Hane, *Peasants, Rebels, and Outcastes*, 227–30.

selling.[109] As Kōnoe Kitarō, a writer at the *Moji shinpō* and coal industry insider, later wrote, "for many years there was extreme oppression and then in an instant there was extreme freedom, like a dike suddenly bursting."[110] The Chikuhō coalfields, unlike the large, concentrated mines of Miike and Takashima, were made up of numerous small veins, often referred to as *tanuki bori* (badger holes). After deregulation, the number of these small mines multiplied rapidly. In the first year of Meiji, Chikuzen Province had 160 mines; by 1877, that number had doubled to 315 mines, and after the Satsuma Rebellion, it doubled again, reaching 600 by 1880.[111]

These coalfields would be developed further and become more effectively regulated in the 1880s, as detailed in Chapter 3. Effective production in Chikuhō was crucial to Moji's designation as a special port of export and the appearance of its coal in Asian markets. After it became competitive, Chikuhō coal would quickly dominate, regularly outselling Takashima and Miike coals in East Asia. Well before the special ports of export were designated in 1889, and Chikuhō coal rose to the top, however, the need for more ports to handle Japan's coal was already apparent.

KARATSU

A decade after the Karatsu coalfields had been requisitioned for military use and closed to private capital, the entrepreneur Matsumura Tokimasa established a company to export coal to Shanghai. He knew that much of Karatsu's best coal had already been excavated and the Chikuhō coalfields to the north were gaining Tokyo's attention.[112] Matsumura angled to take advantage of this shift by purchasing the inferior Karatsu coal not being used by the Navy Ministry and exporting it to Shanghai. In his

---

109. Initially the government created Kokura and Fukuoka Prefectures, reflecting the former domainal structure, but in April 1876 they were joined, thus bringing all five Chikuhō counties under Fukuoka Prefecture.

110. Quoted from Kōnoe Kitarō's 1898 *Chikuhō tankō shi* in Imano, "Meiji 20 nen zengo ni okeru Chikuhō sekitan kōgyō," 16. Historians of the Chikuhō coal industry insist that his name is pronounced Kōnoe Kitarō. Kōnoe's biographers have, in fact, tried to get the National Diet Library to change their rendering of his name (as Takanoe Mototarō), but to no avail (personal communication with Tōjō Nobumasa, October 17, 2000). On Kōnoe, see Hidemura and Tanaka's introduction to *Chikuhō tankō shi*.

111. Nagasue, *Chikuhō*, 56–57.

112. Sumiya, *Nihon sekitan sangyō bunseki*, 110–11.

estimation, exporting directly from Karatsu would eliminate the time, money, and risk of shipwreck that came with transshipping it to Nagasaki. After gaining permission to carry out his plan in April 1882, he would have to handle all aspects of the trade. By June, a Nagasaki Customs office was opened in Karatsu, and Matsumura, by agreement, began paying its operating expenses out of his own pocket. Since the Japanese did not own any ships running between Karatsu and Shanghai, he could choose to hire either Mitsubishi ships or foreign ships to carry coal for him. The latter were cheaper, and thus Matsumura contracted individually with a variety of foreign shippers. A Russian ship handled the first run to Shanghai in April 1883, and subsequent trips that first year were handled by both English steamers and sailing ships.[113]

Despite a rough start, partly because coal prices fell just as he launched operations, Matsumura's enterprise survived and continued making shipments until Karatsu's designation as a special port of export. This was no small feat. Other private merchants who had also attempted direct export from both Karatsu and nearby Moji in the 1880s were unable to make it profitable. Matsumura's success surely offered renewed hope, though, that others could succeed as well. In 1889, the year that Karatsu was named a special port of export, it handled the entry and exit of 36 steamships, 84 Western-style sailing ships, and roughly 900 Japanese-style vessels.[114] An 1895 comparison of the value traded at the treaty ports and the special ports of export ranks Karatsu ninth of sixteen sites. With sales valued at 250,000 yen, it fell below other rising coal ports like Moji (1.5 million yen) and Kuchinotsu (over 2.5 million yen) but above Otaru (200,000 yen) and Misumi (22,000 yen).[115] Karatsu proved to be an important forerunner to the special ports of export and held its own for a while before Moji surpassed it.

KUCHINOTSU

The port of Kuchinotsu emerged as a domestic trading hub in the mid-sixteenth century and accommodated foreign ships, both European and Chinese, at that time.[116] But its shipping activity peaked three centuries

---

113. Takeuchi, *Dai Nihon bōekiron*, 166–71.
114. It also exported paper, camphor, wax, oil cake, rice, and salt (ibid.).
115. *Moji shinpō*, October 10, 1895.
116. Kumabe, "Sekitan sangyō hattenki," 69.

later, when it became Japan's main port for Miike coal. After the Meiji
oligarchs appointed Mitsui Bussan to exclusively handle sales of Miike
coal to Shanghai in 1876, Kuchinotsu became central to this effort. Since
Miike could not accommodate large vessels, the trading company immediately set up a branch office at Kuchinotsu, and the government
allowed the port to handle shipping this coal overseas. Although at a remove from the mines, Kuchinotsu offers an excellent harbor on the
southern tip of the Shimabara Peninsula at the mouth of the well-
protected Ariake Sea. The port lies roughly 30 miles by sea from the
Miike mines, but since construction of a suitable anchorage at that site
would not begin until 1902, for more than three decades hundreds of
barges ran daily between Miike and Kuchinotsu, carrying between 100
and 150 tons of coal per load.[117]

The extra leg of the journey from mine to market did not hold back
these exports. Kuchinotsu began exporting coal the year prior to its official opening, sending 200 tons to Shanghai and another 200 tons to
Tientsin (Tianjin). Over the next few years, the volume that it exported to
Shanghai jumped from just over 7,500 tons in 1878 to nearly 35,000 tons
in 1879 and more than 60,000 in 1880. Between 1878 and 1892, Kuchinotsu exported an average of nearly 68,000 tons of coal to Shanghai annually, with 1889 representing the largest single year, at over 100,000
tons. Beyond Shanghai, Kuchinotsu also made regular coal shipments to
Chefoo (now Yantai) (from 1880), Swatow (from 1881), Hong Kong (from
1883), and Singapore (1886) and sent irregular shipments to harbors
ranging from Saigon (Ho Chi Minh City) to Manila and Rangoon and
from Madras (Chennai) to San Francisco. Starting in 1886, Kuchinotsu's
exports to Hong Kong exceeded those to Shanghai and, until 1892, averaged 160,000 tons per year. These numbers represent a decidedly upward
trend during these years for, by 1890, Kuchinotsu was handling an impressive 300,000 tons annually. In 1892, Kuchinotsu's coal exports represented approximately one-third of the national total.[118]

117. Mitsui Bussan Kaisha, *Miike Coal*, 10, 14.

118. Ibid., 15. Exports out of the special trading ports do not make it into the
country's total statistics for these years. In 1890, the national total of coal exports
was reported at just over 11,000 tons and over 12,500 for 1892 (these amounts do
not include coal "exported" for ships' use) (*DNGBN*, 1890, 1892). Looking at later
years that have retroactively included more comprehensive statistics, however, provides a very different picture, showing that in 1892, the national total of exports

These high volumes meant that Kuchinotsu was exporting more than any other nontreaty port in this period, a full decade before being named a special trading port. Its success did not go unnoticed, and it became a model for other ports. The *Nagasaki zeikan enkaku* (*NZE*) traces the origins of the special ports of export to Kuchinotsu. The terms of direct export established at Kuchinotsu in the late 1870s and early 1880s modeled some of the restrictions later used for the special ports of export. For example, trade was limited to ships owned by the Ministry of Industry or specially chartered foreign vessels. A locally installed Nagasaki Customs agency handled tax collection, inspections, and other transactions while also overseeing ships at anchor to load coal. Kuchinotsu functioned as the mine's only specially designated export harbor for a decade before production levels at the mine were high enough that export volumes attracted others wishing to profit. Kuchinotsu's effectiveness in getting Miike coal to market drew competition as boosters at the nearby ports of Hyakkan and Misumi sought permission to begin exporting coal overseas.

MISUMI

In early July 1887, the *Yomiuri shinbun* announced that officials in Kumamoto Prefecture were busy preparing for a ceremony to officially open Misumi on August 15.[119] The event would come a full seven years after the prefecture had applied to the Home Ministry to open a trade port and just two years before Misumi would be designated a special port of export. Expectations for the port were high, but there were many who harbored disappointment that it was Misumi rather than the port of Hyakkan that was opening to trade.

In a scenario reminiscent of Ishinomaki's neglect following Dutch engineer van Doorn's selection of Nobiru in its stead, the port of Hyakkan was similarly passed over for Misumi. When Kumamoto Prefecture applied to have Hyakkan named a trade port, the Home Ministry sent another Dutch engineer, Rouwenhorst Mulder, to investigate the site. Mulder suggested that Misumi's excellent natural harbor would be a preferable location for a modern hub. Misumi, along with Nobiru, was

---

(including lump and dust coal but not ships' use) was more than 900,000 tons (ibid., 1894).

119. *Yomiuri shinbun*, July 7, 1887.

one of the *Meiji san dai chikkō* projects subsidized by the Home Ministry (the third was Mikuni in Fukui-ken). Unlike the case of Nobiru, however, the construction of Misumi proceeded apace, and the port was completed in three years, just in time to be named a special port of export in 1889. It appeared to be off to a good start.

Shortly thereafter, however, word of dissatisfaction with the port began to spread after Tomioka Keimei retired as prefectural governor in 1891. Tomioka had been a staunch advocate of the development of Misumi and, as it turns out, was in league with Mulder in choosing it over Hyakkan a decade earlier. Despite the earlier rejection, "spirited" industrialists in the city of Kumamoto were making plans to go ahead with harbor renovations at the port of Hyakkan as they mounted evidence that it could outperform Misumi. Pulling together a range of statistics, they sought to demonstrate that the high costs of cargo handling and transportation charges made Misumi too inconvenient to attract much business. By comparing these costs to lower ones at Hyakkan, they tried to make the case that Misumi was costing the city significant revenue.[120]

Despite these efforts, Misumi remained the preferred port for development. The Kumamoto Prefectural Assembly budgeted for its renovation and expansion, and it was slated to be linked to the growing Kyushu railroad system by 1895.[121] Unfortunately for all involved, a stunning lack of coordination meant that the Kyushu line never quite made it to Misumi, ending instead at Saisaki over a mile away. Not surprisingly, Misumi never developed as expected, and it certainly did not overtake Kuchinotsu, as had once been hoped.

Evidence of Misumi's poor performance can be found in its early trade statistics. In comparison to the other special ports of export specializing in coal, Misumi ranked last in coal exports every year from 1890 to 1894. In annual statistics, Kuchinotsu (which averaged roughly 385,000 tons of exported coal) just beat out Moji (over 280,000 tons), which was followed by Karatsu (54,000 tons), Otaru (27,500 tons), and then Misumi (which averaged just under 9,000 tons).[122] In 1894, 97 percent of export coal went to Asia—primarily, Hong Kong (nearly

120. Ibid., April 16, 1891.
121. Ibid., December 7, 17, and 19, 1895.
122. *DNGBN*, 1890–94.

444,000 tons), China (about 338,000 tons), and British India (nearly 164,000 tons), followed by relatively small amounts to the Philippines, Korea, and French India. The other 3 percent was divided mostly among the United States, Russia, France, Hawai'i, and Australia.

Nonetheless, both Misumi and Kuchinotsu went on to become open ports in 1899. By then, Moji was exporting twice as much coal as Kuchinotsu, and Misumi was still far behind. Ranks would shift yet again with the opening of the mechanized port of Miike (situated 2–4 miles from the mines) to handle coal exports in 1908. This changed the fortunes of Kuchinotsu, "the old export harbour . . . some 40 miles away," for the worse.[123] Still later, the renovation of Saisaki sealed Misumi's decline as a coal port.

The development of these three major ports in Kyushu—Karatsu, Kuchinotsu, and Misumi—occurred in tandem with significant changes in the Japanese coal industry. The central government took important steps to bring coal under its purview to protect the fuel sources that it needed, especially coal for the navy at Karatsu. The central government also did two things for coal that it did not do with regard to the early rice trade: it allowed foreign investors and advisers to help develop the coal industry, as at Miike and Takashima, and it allowed private enterprises to handle coal sales overseas. The Mitsui firm had unique permission to export coal from Kuchinotsu; Jardine Matheson and Gotō Shojirō exported Takashima coal from Nagasaki; and Matsumura Tokimasa was authorized to export coal from Karatsu. Although the government began its development of Misumi's harbor in the early 1880s, it would not export coal from that site until after it was named a special trading port in 1889.

Conclusion

Although rice and coal were handled quite differently by the central government during the early Meiji period, both played an important role in aiding Japan's entry into the world economy. By the time the country had recovered from the worst of the economic shocks, it had a fully monetized economy, the beginnings of a modern transportation system, and a growing export trade in several key commodities. The year 1889 proved pivotal for both rice and coal legislation. Since national revenues were

123. Mitsui Mining Department, *Mining Enterprise*, 9–10.

no longer based on rice (the last allowances for tax payments in rice having ended in 1888), the government decreased its level of direct intervention in rice markets. In keeping with Matsukata's deflationary policy of selling off government enterprises, the Miike mine was sold to Mitsui in 1888. That same year, the Ministry of Finance eliminated export tariffs on coal. These major changes made it possible for the government to promote greater export in these commodities, ushering in the "second era" of export promotion.

The next phase of gradual opening, the naming of the special trading ports, took place only after it was safe for the central government to allow an increase in export trade—and less risky for Japanese merchants to begin direct export. These openings were based, in part, on earlier experiences with exporting rice and coal. Not only had both of these commodities already been tested in export markets, but some ports and transportation networks—after a series of trials and errors—were ready to accommodate them. Yokkaichi, Shimonoseki, and Fushiki would be among those designated to handle rice and Karatsu, Kuchinotsu, and Misumi to export coal.

Despite the central government's efforts to create a port infrastructure to enhance trade, many of their efforts failed due to technological, planning, and financing problems, especially in the case of Nobiru. Moreover, Japan's dependence on foreign ships to handle these cargoes meant the major shipping routes bypassed some regions. Even where ports were positioned optimally and had the necessary facilities, some, like Yokkaichi, still did not succeed in these early years. Nonetheless, in the 1880s and 1890s in both the rice and coal trade, we see an important shift in the locations from which the country traded its commodities, one decreasing undue reliance on what were still the main treaty ports of Yokohama, Kobe, and Nagasaki and moving toward other sites, the most successful of which were to the southwest. Moji, Shimonoseki, and the other Kyushu coal ports were all gaining in strength. At the same time, we see an increase in the exports heading to destinations in Asia, even if the consumers were primarily from the Western countries. Unlike with the rice trade, a direct correlation between the special ports of export and the increase in coal sold to East Asian markets is simple to make.

The end of the decade proved pivotal in another way. In February 1889, the Meiji government promulgated a constitution with the promise of establishing a national assembly the next year. By this time, local voices were also calling strongly for new development and commercial opportunities. Although local efforts are apparent in this discussion of the early Meiji era, this chapter has primarily paid attention to the central government's heavy intervention in the direct overseas export of some of Japan's key commodities and the oligarchs' often unsuccessful attempts to orchestrate the development of certain ports in support of broader economic policy initiatives. Chapter 3, by contrast, focuses on national-to-local dynamics during the 1880s, to demonstrate the high degree to which localities were involved in trying to create modern ports and draw trade to them. We turn now to the Chikuhō coal region and the dramatic rise of the port of Moji.

PART II

Ports in the Nation

THREE

The Making of Moji

Land and sea routes came together at Moji at a time when railroads were newly consolidating the nation and foreign steamships were offering ready-made links to global commercial networks. Moji's origins as a modern seaport express these two distinct yet interrelated processes of integration. Just as the laying of extensive railroad tracks in the mid-1880s began to significantly alter the shape and speed of Japan's domestic transportation networks, Japan's recently demarcated prefectures were also beginning a new phase of national political and economic centralization, one that enabled greater popular participation. And just as steamships were accelerating Japan's international ties, Moji and its citizens were increasingly entering into relationships that crossed local and national boundaries. In short, Moji's greater consolidation into the fledgling nation-state occurred simultaneously with the start of its integration into an East Asian commercial system. The port operated within these interlocking dynamics.

From the beginning, a multitude of local interests were vital to the establishment and operation of this port. In the mid-1880s, Moji drew unprecedented attention from local coal concerns, county leaders, and prefectural authorities as well as from national railroad interests, government ministries, and investors in Tokyo and Osaka. Together these various groups—local and national—intensified the site's participation in wider networks and industrialization projects. As the efforts that went into the making of Moji demonstrate, this port's development was by no means a top-down process. Instead, local agents operated within new institutional, economic, and geographical frameworks while using official and unofficial channels to enlist broader support in achieving their ambitions and quite literally putting this port on the national map.

This chapter explores the ways in which local entrepreneurs, politicians, and boosters challenged and encouraged national authorities and capital holders to help them create this port and connect it to national and international transportation circuits and coal markets. First, it sketches the conditions of the late 1870s and 1880s to explain the timing of Moji's rise. Changes in the national climate enabled local actors to attract national resources to their projects. In the process, these local actors helped influence the shape of Japan's industrial and infrastructural geography at a crucial moment in their creation. Their contributions and ability to create and connect Moji are clear at each stage of its making. Second, this chapter shows how mine owners in the Chikuhō coal region developed their businesses and worked to make them productive. They created the conditions that allowed Chikuhō to begin rivaling the larger Takashima and Miike mines to the south and gain the attention of national conglomerates. The creation of the port of Moji was based on the "re-regionalization" of Chikuhō and the development of large-scale production in this coal hinterland. Third, this chapter examines the establishment of the *Moji shinpō* newspaper and reveals the founder's worldview from Moji. By delineating a very clear geography of the port, the Chikuhō region, and their wider networks, this worldview is reflected in the paper, generating a sense of the port from within at the very moment it was poised to become a key transportation and information hub. Finally, the chapter looks at the port's domestic and East Asian coal markets to demonstrate Moji's strong connections to transmarine East Asia. Importantly, this process of network creation took place concurrently at the local, national, and international levels. The informal empires in East Asia, with their great appetite for coal, were vital to Moji's "remarkable" rise.[1]

---

1. The word remarkable (*ichijirushii*) is a trope often repeated in contemporary assessments and later histories of both the port of Moji and the Chikuhō coalfields. For example, *MKS*, 3:102–3; Nagasue, *Chikuhō*, 10; Nakano, *Kaikyō Taikan*, 63.

Moji's Remarkable Rise

In 1854, when the United States imposed the first unequal treaty on Japan, Moji (then known as Mojigaseki) supported a small fishing village of fewer than 500 people.[2] Most villagers made their living either toiling in the coastal salt fields or plying local waters in search of fish. The village lay on the outskirts of early modern regional power centers, most notably the castle towns of Kokura and Chōfu.[3] The nearby villages of Dairi and Tanoura (both later incorporated into the town of Moji) were regular spots for crossing the strong currents of the Kanmon Strait to the shipping hub of Shimonoseki.[4] But Moji, despite its position directly on vital east-west coastal shipping routes leading to the commercial centers of Osaka, Kobe, and Edo, did not become a major port for domestic trade in the early modern period.

Even thirty years after the first unequal treaties were signed, this local scene was little changed. Moji's industries were limited to one sake brewer, a single soy sauce maker, and six salt manufacturers.[5] Nonetheless, the regions surrounding it had been undergoing rapid change. Sea traffic on the Kanmon Strait grew in volume as treaty ports opened Japan to foreign trade and shipping routes expanded. Regional land and river routes reached capacity as dramatic increases in Chikuhō coal production overwhelmed them. Newly delimited prefectures coordinated plans to stretch railroad lines across Kyushu. As projects to modernize transportation systems around the country gained steam—especially in constructing ports that could serve as nexuses to join railroads and shipping routes for both commercial and military use—Moji and Chikuhō together entered the fray.

2. This population is just for the village of Moji, but when it was joined with Kuzubara, Tanoura, and Komorie in 1889, its total population rose to roughly 3,300 people (*MKS*, 7).

3. Chōfu was an ancient but thriving castle town in the eastern part of Chōshū domain on the Kanmon Strait. It served as an important base of operations for the Meiji Restoration. Hagi, located on the western edge of Chōshū, was the domain's main castle town.

4. Tanoura was Shimonoseki's counterpart on Edo *kitamaesen* cargo ship routes traveling the Kanmon Strait (*KKS*, 19–20).

5. *KKSGS*, 22.

The timing of Moji's rise in the late 1880s was not accidental; it came at a watershed moment for the country when many longer-term local and national initiatives were bringing new results. Moji's early development reflects the great interplay between national centralization and decentralization as Japan's center and peripheries continued to negotiate distributions of political power and economic responsibility following the twin upheavals of opening the country and the Meiji Restoration.[6] Some of the larger political struggles borne of the post-Restoration consolidation were quieting down, and new economic opportunities were multiplying as the economy stabilized and the government released more control to localities and the private sector.

On the domestic political scene, 1878 had witnessed the end of the "era of centralized power."[7] This shift was symbolized dramatically by the assassination of Ōkubo Toshimichi, a key architect of Japan's modern infrastructure. Although his legacy of development would continue, he was the last of the Meiji Restoration's original triumvirate.[8] The changing tenor of government was also heralded by the Three New Laws (*Sanshinpō*). Promulgated just weeks after Ōkubo's death, these laws, which the oligarchs Kido and Ōkubo had helped write, created a new foundation for local government, allowing for the greater politicization of local citizens, especially through newly established prefectural assemblies.[9] By the mid-1880s, these bodies were increasingly effective in advocating for the specific wants and needs of the areas that they served.[10] In the case of Fukuoka, assemblymen soon became vocal mediators between their districts and the prefectural authorities and many would use their political experience at the prefectural level to gain seats in the national Diet.

Economically, the Matsukata deflation was proving successful in generating new levels of private investment through lower interest rates, stable prices, and speculative stock returns.[11] An important component of the resulting "First Enterprise Boom" was the financing of local development projects.[12] Spending cuts at the national level in the early 1880s

6. See McClain, "Local Politics and National Integration."

7. Pittau, "Inoue Kowashi," 259.

8. The other two, Kido Kōin and Saigō Takamori, had both died the previous year (ibid.).

9. Kim, *Age of Visions and Arguments,* 206.

10. McClain, "Local Politics and National Integration," 66.

11. Ericson, *Sound of the Whistle,* 115.

12. Nakamura, *Chihō kara.*

meant that prefectural governments had already begun taking over the funding and management of more public works and services.[13] By mid-decade, local elites in Fukuoka and other prefectures were channeling their capital into infrastructural improvements, such as the building of ports and railroads.

National political and economic policies simultaneously trended toward allowing greater opportunity and growth for local communities. As domestic investment in commerce and industry expanded, interest in tapping global markets swelled. Tokyo's late-1870s push for direct exports took a new turn during the enterprise boom, when more private entities pursued selling in overseas markets. Not only did Japanese merchants have more capital to invest in such ventures but a global decline in the price of silver further encouraged exports.[14] In northern Kyushu, mine owners and merchants saw new potential for the private export of Chikuhō coal to promising East Asian markets. Moji quickly became central to their early plans and trial runs.

Fostering conditions that would allow for the overseas export of Chikuhō coal proved to be in the interests of both local and national powerholders. As seen with the Ministry of Finance's promotion of export rice in the late 1870s and early 1880s, the oligarchs clearly recognized that increasing exports was a fundamental method for raising revenues to fund the country's costly development. By the 1880s, as the oligarchs began to promote private ownership and oversight of industrial enterprise, and once railroads began creating new possibilities for matching ports to key hinterlands, an expansion of export bases became increasingly justified. The special ports of export, with their pivotal allowance for chartering foreign ships, represent a new phase in Japan's openness to trade.

The special ports of export reflect not only Tokyo's willingness to increase the number of domestic sites able to handle exports but also a change in the official stance toward greater liberalization of trade. The government now allowed foreign ships to enter specified nontreaty ports to load cargo, without the express per-voyage stipulations that had applied in earlier, discrete cases of direct export. Such special authorization came of practical necessity. Beyond the continuing desire to restrict foreign access to Japanese territory under the unequal treaties was the

13. Vlastos, "Opposition Movements."
14. Ericson, *Sound of the Whistle*, 115.

simple fact that the country did not have the steamship tonnage needed to carry more cargo.

The special ports, and Moji in particular, demonstrate that much of Japan's export trade depended on the Western presence in East Asia. The Western powers used modern steamships to maintain their economic networks and activities in the region, making them at once the main consumers of Japanese coal and the owners of the predominant means of transport for near seas and transoceanic hauls. The arrangement was mutually beneficial—the Western powers would have greater regional access to coal, which supported their economic and military undertakings, while offering a cost-effective return cargo in their runs between Japan and the continent. The Japanese, in turn, would have ready markets and the willing assistance of Western, primarily British, fleets to carry their goods.

Still, rapid growth was by no means a foregone conclusion for Japan and certainly not for this particular harbor. In fact, the odds were against Moji's success. An 1881 investigation by the Tokyo Chamber of Commerce reported that of 176 Japanese ports, only 64 were capable of handling steamships. Of the latter, only ten became special trading ports.[15] Moreover, this port faced repeated obstacles as early attempts to export coal ended in failure, and initial bids to link it by rail were rejected. Initial plans to construct a port at Moji that was suitable for overseas trade proceeded slowly. Putting this port on the map required dogged local efforts, which were underwritten by central politicians and capitalists. Yet identifying exactly who advocated for this port reveals the late nineteenth-century formation of a new geography of capital interests with roots extending across Kyushu.

Centered on the port, with strong ties to the Chikuhō region, Moji was created in both material and discursive terms. Moji's proponents began composing a narrative that outlined its emerging character and generated a vision for its future position in national and international systems of transportation and exchange. The process of defining Moji can be found in bids to establish the port and the railroad but is most apparent in the establishment of the *Moji shinpō*, which served as the voice of the port. As early as the newspaper's incorporation in 1892, it shaped perceived and real geographies, tracing the flow of coal from Kyushu's

15. Kokaze, *Teikoku shūgika*, 203.

mining regions, to Moji, and on to coal markets in Japan and throughout East Asia. While reflecting existing pathways, the paper's editors regularly printed segments offering strategies for bettering the port and advancing its trade along new routes. The paper was instrumental in establishing Moji and providing a consistent narrative celebrating what it saw as the singularity of the port's striking development.

When Japan's special ports of export opened to foreign commerce in 1889, most had long histories as key nodes in Tokugawa transportation networks. Some, like Shimonoseki, readily added special exports to their commercial repertoires while others, including Yokkaichi and Fushiki, had more trouble generating new business. Among the ports with meager activity prior to being named for special export were those, like Otaru, that acquired the suddenly expansive qualities of boomtowns.[16] Moji, in particular, appeared as if from nowhere. Its days as an active trade center during the premodern era had left barely a trace. But within only a decade of its establishment as a special port of export, this once-sleepy port sat at the vanguard of Japan's commerce, industrialization, and military pursuits across transmarine East Asia. By the early twentieth century, Moji would rank among Japan's top ports, and the Chikuhō coal that it shipped would dominate East Asian markets.

There was no shortage of illustrative phrases invoked to describe the significance of Moji at the turn of the twentieth century. Moji was a "first-class harbor" that served as the "empire's front door."[17] It was "the embodiment of coal" and held a key location commanding "the throat of western Japan."[18] It was a "prodigy" that performed extremely well and held unique promise.[19] Describing Moji as an extraordinary place was easy, even if such portrayals were at times overblown, since it did become a major port practically overnight. And although local and national efforts both proved vital in opening this port, these phrases reveal that its development owed much to a high demand for coal, its place in broader trade circuits, and its key location at the western edge of the country,

16. Otaru also became the central point of entry for Japanese immigrants moving into Hokkaido.

17. Tanaka, *Teikoku no Kanmon*, 1.

18. Takeda, *Chikugo hana mushiro Moji sekitan chōsa*, 3; Tsuda, "*Moji shinpō* kabunushi meibo," and prospectus, "*Moji shinpō* hakkō no shushi oyobi hōhō."

19. *MKS*, 1.

standing between Japan's commercial and political centers and the continent.

Linking Coal, Rail, and Port

RATIONALIZING THE CHIKUHŌ COALFIELDS

A conjunction of events taking place between 1885 and 1889 shows how Moji's latent potential, rooted in its geographic position, and its added potential, generated by those seeking to profit from its location, led to the designation of Moji as a special port of export. The place was right and the time was right for three interrelated processes to converge on this once-ignored promontory. The first was the rationalization of the Chikuhō coalfields, a move initially championed by the Fukuoka prefectural government but soon joined by local mining interests with the establishment of the Chikuhō Coal Mining Industry Association (Chikuhō Sekitan Kōgyō Kumiai, or CSKK). The second was the founding of the Kyushu Railway Company and the Chikuhō Industrial Railway Company (Chikuhō Kōgyō Tetsudō, or Chikutetsu), and the third was the establishment of the Moji Port Construction Company (hereafter Moji Chikkō). The interdependent relationship among these three entities—coal, rail, and port—is summed up in this vivid statement made by coal industry insider Kōnoe Kitarō in 1897: "The railroad is Moji's father and Moji Chikkō its mother. And if we look at Moji as a living being, then Chikuhō coal is the blood that makes the limbs and body move. . . . In short, coal is Moji's life. Moji was born of coal. And the rapid progress and prosperity it has attained today is due entirely to coal."[20] Kōnoe wrote during the florescence of the Age of Steam, upon which Moji's success wholly depended. Before Moji could become a modern harbor with railroad and international steamship connections, however, its coal hinterland, the Chikuhō region, had to undergo a process of "re-regionalization."

Chikuhō found a new cohesion in the coal industry during the 1880s, when the people of this region joined together to gain economic advantage in a climate in which success required combining risk-taking entrepreneurship with large-scale production. The domestic political restructuring of the 1870s afforded its inhabitants the ability to move

20. Ibid., 53.

beyond earlier provincial and domainal factionalism in coordinating their efforts. Favorable domestic conditions notwithstanding, however, the primary impetus for change emanated from the developing East Asian economy centered on the treaty ports. That is, although Chikuhō necessarily had to operate within a national framework, the process of its re-regionalization drew heavily on international demands for coal, especially as pinned to the treaty ports.

The idea of re-regionalization indicates a breakdown and recasting of a geographical formation that is made and unmade in response to changing circumstances, especially as seen within the framework of modern nation-states, but applicable to processes of globalization as well.[21] In the case of Chikuhō, re-regionalization took place as Japan was drawn into the modern world order. The economic and political transformations that came as the new Meiji government centralized its power did not simply absorb or dismantle earlier regional formations. Instead, as Chikuhō demonstrates, regions, as both material and imagined places, are "constitutive of and never merely additive to the centers of power."[22] As a place struggling to keep pace with the vicissitudes of Japan's fortunes during the treaty port era, Chikuhō became a kind of economic bloc for the purpose of gaining advantage within national and East Asian markets. Viewing Chikuhō in this way—as a region consolidated for economic expediency within a shifting economic and political landscape—in part rejects the "hulking presence" of the nation by exposing local efforts and allowing for the "self-formation" of this specific place.[23] Its reconfiguration, though, is not limited to its relationship with the nation for it also exposes the crucial dynamic at work between the broader East Asian economy, a supernational region, and this subnational zone.

Re-regionalization is captured by the very name Chikuhō, which was coined in the 1880s with the establishment of Chikutetsu. The Chikuhō region was an amalgam of Chikuzen (筑前) and Buzen (豊前) Provinces,

---

21. Applegate, "A Europe of Regions," 1163; Rafael, "Regionalism," 1218.

22. Rafael, "Regionalism," 1208. On regionalism and the construction of regions, see Arrighi, Hamashita, and Selden, who apply the concept of "re-regionalization" to East Asia as a world region ("Introduction," 9), and Wigen, "Culture, Power, and Place," 1196.

23. Applegate, "A Europe of Regions," 1159; Barlow, "Asian Women in Reregionalization," 287. By *self-formation,* Barlow means that the political economy of a place is mutually constitutive with its discursive formulation.

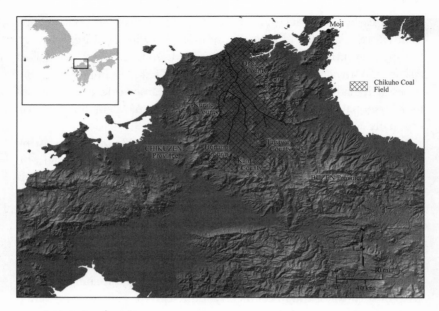

MAP 6 Chikuhō Coal Region.

under the domains of Fukuoka and Kokura, respectively (see Map 6).[24] The name Chikuhō (筑豊), formed by combining the first characters of each province's name, refers to the geographic area encompassing portions of all five of the region's main coal-producing counties: Onga, Kurate, Kama, Honami, and Tagawa.

Although it was not specifically named until the 1880s, the area's cohesion predated this period. Despite domainal factionalism that divided the two provinces during the Tokugawa era, the navigable Onga River and its many tributaries flow through both of them, demarcating an organic watershed. Mountains surround the drainage basin to the east, west, and south. Inhabitants of the Onga basin developed their own sense of culture based on life in this spot and their experiences

24. In early Meiji, before the spread of the name Chikuhō, the region was somewhat awkwardly referred to as Chikuzen Buzen ni shū tanden or "the coalfields of Chikuzen and Buzen provinces" (Kadokawa Nihon Chimei Daijiten Hensan Iinkai, *Kadokawa Nihon chimei daijiten*, 868). Provinces, established in the eighth century, continued to hold considerable significance for local identities through at least the nineteenth century (Wigen, *A Malleable Map*, 9–14).

with the river, especially regarding river transport and flood control. The area also contains both fertile plains that provided large quantities of high-quality rice to the domains of the early modern era and abundant scattered coalfields that would come to define it in the modern era.[25]

The re-regionalization of Chikuhō and its establishment as a coal production center that spanned over 300 square miles, an area roughly the size of New York City, took place in three main phases during the Tokugawa and Meiji periods.[26] The first phase was precipitated by the Kyōhō famine of the 1730s, which hit northern Kyushu hard, depriving Chikuzen Province of as much as one-third of its population.[27] Poverty-stricken farmers, desperate to earn subsistence wages, turned to excavating coal as day-laborers. Resorting to mining for survival during these difficult times carried a stigma, and the mining of Chikuzen's coal was known unfavorably as a "famine industry," inaugurating a long legacy of discrimination against miners.[28] The famine coincided with widespread deforestation, a problem throughout Japan, which increased demand for coal as already-scarce wood became unaffordable.[29] Farmers worked to improve their own situation while excavating coal to meet the demands of this newly commercializing industry.

Coal sales outside Fukuoka and Kokura domains, the primary areas of excavation, intensified with the growing demand of the salt manufacturing industry along the Inland Sea. In order to ensure sufficient supplies at home, domainal authorities took over management of coal sales, along with a good percentage of its profits, through the *shikumihō* monopoly system of 1788. Integral to this system were coal exchanges located at the

25. The basin itself covers an area of about 400 square miles varying from 8 to 16 miles east to west and ranging across 31 miles north to south (Katsuki, *On-gagawa*, 2–15, 68).

26. W. D. Smith, "Gender and Ethnicity," 204.

27. The estimate of one-third of the population, or 100,000 deaths, is often used, but Kalland and Pederson calculate it closer to 70,000 people, or 22% of the population. Either way, it was a very ruinous event, since as Kalland and Pederson point out, the province did not recover its prefamine population for more than 100 years ("Famine and Population in Fukuoka Domain," 34).

28. Nagasue, *Chikuhō*, 20–23. Sasaki argues that discrimination against all types of miners, not just those extracting coal, was at least partly due to the *bakufu*'s purposeful separation of mining from agriculture, one a money-making enterprise, the other self-sufficient (*Modes of Traditional Mining Techniques,* 11–12).

29. Totman, *The Green Archipelago,* 80.

day's important shipping junctions of Ashiya and Wakamatsu, which connected the Onga River and its coal-rich basin with coastal waterways leading to the Inland Sea. By the end of the Tokugawa period, this area had become the country's foremost coal producer.

Despite the region's head start in coal mining, Chikuhō would lose its position in the second phase of regional restructuring to mines located closer to Nagasaki in western Kyushu. Nagasaki's handling of increased steamer traffic in the 1850s heralded the start of Chikuhō's temporary decline. This regional breakdown persisted for most of the first two decades following the Meiji Restoration, when the Chikuhō coalfields, in contrast to the government-owned mines, were left largely to local control. Two early pieces of mining legislation allowed for this decentralization. The 1871 edict establishing prefectures effectively stripped *daimyō* of their domainal monopolies over mining and led to the divestment of late Tokugawa systems of exchange (*takiishi kaisho*). Two years later, the comprehensive Japan Mining Law established procedures for privately owned mines, while new prefectural laws granted permission to sell coal outside Fukuoka's borders.[30]

These laws led to significant changes in mine ownership and coal sales across northern Kyushu. Without the old controls, and in the absence of effective new ones, mining in Chikuhō turned chaotic, leading to a period of get-rich-quick speculation and reckless excavation.[31] The coalfields were operating on a very small scale and saw rapid turnover during what proved to be a generally turbulent post-Restoration decade in Fukuoka Prefecture.[32] The industry's fortunes changed so rapidly that the situation was "measured by day and night." Despite the great financial uncertainty, many people, including farmers of the lower and middle ranks, risked their livelihoods attempting to find their fortune in this precarious

30. The Japan Mining Law was preceded by an 1869 "release of mines" to the private sector and the 1872 Rules on Mining (Kōzan kokoroesho), which, among other things, prohibited foreigners from owning or managing mines (Nagasue, *Chikuhō*, 54–56). By 1876, a short-lived Kokura Prefecture was merged into Fukuoka Prefecture, placing most of the Chikuhō region then under the latter. Only the eastern portion of Buzen Province fell under another jurisdiction, that of neighboring Ōita Prefecture.

31. See ibid., 54–55.

32. Latent social unrest came to the fore with political and economic instability after the Meiji Restoration in the form of riots and farmer insurrections. The political situation did not begin to stabilize until after the 1877 Satsuma Rebellion (ibid., 55–58).

business. Those involved in small-scale mining enterprises, many of which failed, came to be known pejoratively as "speculators" (*yamashi*).[33]

Apparently the resultant chaos was too much for some, for in 1874, a group of miners went to the prefectural office and requested a return to the old system.[34] Prefectural officials, recognizing the problems of un-regulated mining operations, established offices at Ashiya and Wakamatsu, the former centers of the *shikumihō* monopoly system, in an effort to reestablish some control over the industry. The new system was not a monopoly; the prefecture supervised, rather than dictated, the handling of excavation and sales, collecting nominal taxes and establishing branches in each county.[35] Their ability to manage the situation, however, remained tenuous, and the industry as a whole began to stagnate.

In the longer term, Fukuoka Prefecture, along with concerned investors and industrialists, ended mining abuses and reckless selling by creating the legislative, organizational, and physical conditions that would enable Chikuhō to begin large-scale production. These efforts mark the start of the third phase, building the region anew. Recognizing that the country's other primary coal-mining areas—the Takashima and Miike mines in western Kyushu and the Horonai mine in Hokkaido—were per-forming well under government ownership, Fukuoka's policymakers re-quested central assistance.[36] In 1878, the Ministry of Industry dispatched surveyors to investigate the area's coal seams but made no commitment to further involvement. The surveyors concluded that improving the industry would necessitate two fundamental steps: draining water and eliminating the profusion of petty, unregulated mines.

Chikuhō's rocky coal outcrops had been nearly exhausted by this time, and although drilling samples indicated significant underground deposits, high water levels prevented the excavation of these deeper, po-tentially lucrative seams. Local mine owners, notably Katayama Itsuta, Kaijima Tasuke, and Sugiyama Tokusaburō, worked to introduce steam pumps to their mines with help from foreign engineers.[37] Although windfall profits from higher nationwide coal prices during the costly

---

33. Ibid., 57.
34. Imano, "Meiji 20 nen zengo," 16.
35. *KKSS SK*, 2:7.
36. Nagasue, *Chikuhō*, 63–67.
37. Kaijima Tasuke, unlike many other Chikuhō mine owners, was born to a poor farmer and worked in the coal mines from an early age. He was able to take advantage of high coal prices during the Satsuma Rebellion to purchase mining

Satsuma Rebellion enabled these attempts, a lack of ongoing financing, technological know-how, and training slowed progress. By 1881, only Sugiyama had managed to begin removing water from his mines successfully. Subsequent attempts to spread this new technology more broadly across the region were further hampered when domestic demand fell as a result of the Matsukata deflation. Nonetheless, the pumps, together with the introduction of dynamite blasting, a technique effective in cutting vertical mine shafts, helped to increase production volumes dramatically over the course of the next decade.[38]

The second barrier to large-scale development was the size of mining lots. Even after the Meiji government amended the Japan Mining Law in 1882 to prohibit stakes (*shakku*) of less than 10,000 *tsubo*, or roughly 8 acres, compliance in Chikuhō was minimal. Local owners who would have otherwise lost their mines found ways to evade the financial qualification process. In 1883, less than 3 percent of Chikuhō concessions conformed to the new regulations; over 60 percent still managed pockets of less than 1,000 *tsubo*.[39] Chikuhō mining would not become more efficient until a coordinated effort was made to directly regulate all aspects of the highly dispersed industry.

The opportunity for stronger regulation arose after the Ministry of Agriculture and Commerce laid out new rules for trade associations in January 1884. The next year, Fukuoka prefectural authorities moved quickly to unite mine operators into a self-regulating body by issuing their own "Rules for Coal Miners' Associations."[40] Chikuhō's five counties initially had their own coal mining associations but united to pursue common interests. The resulting organization was the CSKK, which consisted of roughly fifty committee members from the five Chikuhō counties, including several of the region's most powerful mine owners.[41] Ishino Kanpei, a prefectural official and mine manager, was elected as

---

concessions and successfully build the base for what would later become the Kaijima conglomerate (*KKSGS*, 15).

38. Excavation amounts jumped from 75,000 tons in 1877 to quadruple that amount across the next decade (*KKSS SK*, 1:52–55; Sumiya, *Nihon sekitan sangyō bunseki*, 212–16; Tōjō, "Chikuhō sekitan kōgyō," esp. 2–8).

39. Nagasue, *Chikuhō*, 67–69. 1,000 *tsubo* roughly equals 35,500 sq. ft.

40. Ogino, "Meiji chūki," 1; Nagasue, *Chikuhō*, 67–69.

41. The group was first called the Alliance of Chikuhō's Five County Coal Associations, but with reorganization in 1893, it was renamed the Chikuhō Coal Industry Association. On membership, see *KKSGS*, 253.

the association's first president and is credited with "restoring dignity to the industry."[42] Under his leadership, the organization worked with alacrity to improve production, transportation, and sales.

A principal step toward these improvements was the consolidation of mining stakes into much larger lots. Increasing the scale of operations helped ensure better management and created some uniformity. The prefecture also made the application and approval process more rigid and punishments for noncompliance harsher. Pressure to carry out redistricting and enforcement came in 1886, when the Navy Ministry began seizing coalfields (*tanden fūsa*) for naval use, laying claim to mines in thirty-eight towns in and around Chikuhō. More than a decade of heavy excavation had left the *yobi tanden* reserves in Karatsu depleted when the surveys by Fukuoka Prefecture and the Home Ministry made plain that Chikuhō held rich caches of underground coal. Fukuoka Prefecture immediately created twenty-four mining lots, the smallest of which was 190,000 *tsubo*—at least doubling a significant portion of the mines.[43] The new districts took the names that would identify Chikuhō coals in Moji and East Asian markets for the next several decades, including Namazuta, Tagawa, Akaike, Komatsu, Ōtsuji, and Hōkoku.

Gathering the necessary capital to take over these suddenly immense districts (*kōku*) proved challenging. Many local mine owners lost their holdings, and even the largest ones had to scramble to consolidate their claims, some joining together to co-own lots. For example, Hiraoka Kōtarō, a mine owner as well as a founder and president of the ultranationalist Genyōsha, purchased the Akaike mine with Yasukawa Keiichirō and bought the Hōkoku mine with Yamamoto Kisaburō.[44] With deep roots in the industry, Yasukawa and his brother, Matsumoto Hisomu, who had each been adopted into other families, opened Yasukawa Shōten in 1877 in Ashiya at the site of the old exchange. It was an ancestor of theirs who had established the first coal exchange in Ashiya earlier in the nineteenth century. Some of the original CSKK members, including

42. Ogino, "Meiji chūki," 25. The quotation is from *MKS*, 62.
43. *KKSS SK*, 1:53. The CSKK also launched a movement, joined by Mitsubishi and Mitsui, petitioning the Navy and Home ministries to release the mines. By 1891 they succeeded in having most of them returned and made available for private development.
44. *KKSGS*, 21.

Sugiyama, Hoashi Yoshikata, Matsumoto, and Konomi Takasuke, also managed to survive the redistricting, at least initially.

Soon, however, the coal market entered a three-year slump following the 1890 financial panic, which Hugh T. Patrick says has been called "Japan's first capitalistic crisis." A rice crop failure the year before coincided with changes in the global silver market, causing the country to move from a trade surplus to its largest trade deficit yet.[45] The slump presented mine managers with still more difficulties in garnering sufficient funds to mechanize and run their newly expanded mines. Adding insult to injury, severe flooding in the Chikuhō area in 1891 pushed some owners over the edge. Konomi had been dubbed Chikuhō's "Coal Mine King" before heavy floods deluged his mines, forcing him into bankruptcy.[46] Others, including Yasukawa and Kaijima, had to borrow money in order to stay afloat.

Asō Takichi, finding it difficult to finance his enlarged operations, had already sold part of his Namazuta mine to Mitsubishi in 1889. The purchase was handled through the mediation of Yasukawa and Hiraoka, who thus helped pave the way for the future *zaibatsu*'s push into Chikuhō.[47] Having lost out to rival Mitsui when the government sold the Miike mine in 1888, Mitsubishi was already turning its attention northward when the financial panic accelerated its advance. Within five years, the company had moved its mining headquarters from Nagasaki to Wakamatsu, and its penetration of Chikuhō intensified, especially following the Sino-Japanese War of 1894–95.[48] Asō, Kaijima, and Yasukawa all weathered the slump and used profits from mines that they sold during the crisis to reinvest in Chikuhō and diversify their holdings. These owners would subsequently rise to the top as the region's "big three" families and expand their businesses to become local conglomerates, or *chihō zaibatsu*, by the end of the Meiji period.[49]

45. Patrick, "External Equilibrium," 203.
46. *KKSGS*, 21.
47. Ibid., 13.
48. The company first moved to Nōgata in 1892 before relocating to Wakamatsu the next year *KKSS SK*, 1:59–60.
49. In the early twentieth century, Asō would expand into banking, electric power, railroads, and cement. Yasukawa became involved in enterprises such as cotton spinning and the manufacture of steel and pig iron. Kaijima initially remained

Fukuoka Prefecture encompassed most of the Chikuhō region, and its officials and elected assemblymen alike encouraged the rationalization of the coal industry within its borders. Although the prefectural and national governments provided legislative conditions that enabled restructuring, the tenacity of Chikuhō business owners who cleaned up the industry made it viable prior to the era when big conglomerates and external capital swooped in to overwhelm many of them.

Chikuhō had undergone significant transformations as Japan changed from a relatively closed early modern polity into a modern nation-state. The restructuring of this region for the purpose of managing excavation and promoting the sale of coal came to be embodied in local organizations like the CSKK, Chikutetsu, and the Five County Riverboat Association. The riverboat association formed in 1885 and quickly joined forces with the CSKK to improve coal transport. The term Chikuhō was more than a convenient geographical title, and its use signified the deliberate organizational grouping of individual concerns for mutual benefit. Through the intense geographical reconfigurations of the 1880s, the regional formation of Chikuhō endured and today connotes the heyday of fuel coal, brutal labor conditions, and continued economic hardship in a post-mining age.

In the early twenty-first century, Japan's coal mining is associated with harsh and dangerous working conditions, especially at such notorious sites as Mitsubishi's Gunkanjima (Battleship Island), recently opened to tourists, and through large-scale tragedies like the 1963 Miike coal mine explosions. Reaching further back in time, however, reveals an unyielding history of oppression. When the government took ownership of the Miike coal mine in the 1870s, it used prison labor and then granted Mitsubishi permission to continue doing so after it purchased the mine in 1888.[50] The Takashima mine in turn reduced wages and used corporal punishment to enforce obedience and meet mining quotas in order to compete. At the end of the century, the first Koreans were brought to Japan to work in its coal mines. To remedy labor shortages during the boom economy that came after the First Sino-Japanese War, Chikuhō's

---

heavily in coal mining and sales but by the 1920s diversified into timber, lime manufacturing, and dry distillation. On the *chihō zaibatsu* (with a particular focus on the Yasukawa-Matsumoto family) see Nakamura, *Chihō kara,* 193–242.

50. Hane and Perez, *Modern Japan,* 293–94.

coal mines recruited 230 Korean laborers to work for them, but the attempt resulted in difficult relationships among those involved and the recruitment ended after only six months.[51] But it was during the 1930s that Japan established a systematic regime of forced labor that was composed primarily of colonial Koreans but included Chinese laborers and prisoners of war as well. At Chikuhō, coerced foreign labor began replacing Japanese miners with the 1937 outbreak of the Second Sino-Japanese War (1937–45) when demand increased and Japanese left the mines to fight or support the war effort. By the closing months of World War II, roughly 125,000 Koreans made up more than 31 percent of Chikuhō mine labor, and, at some mines, they comprised as much as 70 percent of the workforce. These numbers do not reflect the total number of laborers who worked in the mines over several years or tally the thousands who died in Japan's mines during the war.[52]

Long after Japan's last coal mines closed, as postwar energy needs began to be filled by oil, Chikuhō is still marked by numerous *bota yama* (slag heaps), and the region remains economically disaffected.[53] Despite the hardships of mine work, for many of the men, women, and children who labored in Chikuhō, this was the only life they knew, and it generated strong community ties.[54] Today the Chikuhō region continues to represent the shared socioeconomic and cultural history of the mining life, but more so with regard to the Japanese rather than the foreign miners who labored under Japan's imperial regime. The region has recently become known on the world stage in association with Yamamoto Sakubei, whose writings and paintings were accepted by the UNESCO Memory of the World register in 2011. As the mines began closing permanently in the 1950s, Yamamoto, himself a miner from childhood, began to document the living and working conditions of the Chikuhō mines since the Meiji era. His corpus of roughly 700 paintings was recognized

51. See Tōjō's articles, "Nisshin sengo no Chikuhō" and "Meiji-ki Nihon."
52. Nagasue, *Chikuhō*, 185.
53. On the cultural history of the region, see Katsuki, *Ongagawa*, and on its postwar history see Allen, *Undermining the Japanese Miracle*, and Hein, *Fueling Growth*. For photographic depictions of the miners and their children, see photojournalist Domon Ken's *Chikuhō no kodomotachi*.
54. W. D. Smith, "Gender and Ethnicity," and Allen, *Undermining the Japanese Miracle*.

locally as an important record of the region's heritage before it gained attention on a global scale.[55]

SELECTING MOJI

Just as the re-regionalization of Chikuhō hinged on the interests and co-operative activities of local business owners, the establishment of both the Kyushu Railway Company and Moji Chikkō depended on the dreams and hard work of local agents. Even more clearly than in the case of Chikuhō's rationalization through the CSKK, building port facilities and railroads reveals how the pursuits of various groups and individuals came together in creating linkages across Kyushu while garnering national-level political and monetary support. A number of the same local figures who had assisted Chikuhō's development were also active investors in and promoters of Kyushu's railroads and the port of Moji, making the connection among these three constituent parts inescapable.

After the prefecture's authorities and mine owners began consolidating operations across Chikuhō, new possibilities for overseas export of the region's coal emerged. Their concern for development did not stop at Kyushu's northern shores but extended outward to markets throughout Japan and on the Asian continent. And after it became connected by rail to the hinterland, Moji would become the indispensable link between Chikuhō coal and the lucrative markets of East Asia.

Yoshida Chitaru was a businessman residing in Fukuoka when he decided to try exporting coal overseas. Although not the first person to export Japan's coal from outside the treaty ports, he was the first to try doing so from Moji. Yoshida was active in the Chikuhō coal industry and had previously established the Coal Export Company in Waka-matsu to ship coal to Inland Sea salt manufacturers. Eager to expand his business, he petitioned the central government in 1885 for permission to ship coal to Shanghai. Yoshida had already been using Moji's shores for coal storage and transport for his domestic shipments and named this port specifically in his plans. Upon approval, as the trader Matsu-mura Tokimasa had done two years earlier in Karatsu, he agreed to pay the fees to have Nagasaki Customs oversee his exports. Yoshida's

---

55. City of Tagawa's Yamamoto Sakubei website, http://www.y-sakubei.com /english/ (accessed June 20, 2013).

endeavor marks the first time that a customs agency was established at Moji, nearly four years before its designation as a special port of export would lead to the installation of a more permanent office.[56]

In addition to gaining official sanction, Yoshida pursued his plan in consultation with the CSKK, which established an Overseas Export Office in early 1886, and other local concerns. Some had national ties, such as the Kokura branch of the Eighty-Seventh Bank and the Waka-matsu office of the Ōsaka Shōsen Kaisha (OSK).[57] The mine owner and CSKK member Hoashi Yoshikata contracted with the Nippon Yūsen Kaisha (NYK) on Yoshida's behalf to transport coal from Moji aboard the company's steamship *Etchū Maru*.[58] The next January, Yoshida exported nearly 1,500 tons of Chikuhō coal to Shanghai, but did not sell as much as he expected; prices at the time were much too low for him to trade competitively, and the expense of doing business was simply too high for this small enterprise.[59] After only a year and a half, he applied to have his permit withdrawn, and Moji's first customs office closed its doors.[60]

Yoshida's choice of Moji is interesting given that other nearby ports, notably Wakamatsu and Kokura, were better equipped to handle a venture of this sort. At the time, Wakamatsu ranked as the primary coal collection and distribution center for the Onga River basin, a capacity that it had slowly appropriated from the long-dominant hub at Ashiya.[61] Waka-matsu's importance can be seen not only in the fact that Yoshida based his own export company at the port but also in the CSKK's relocation

56. *KKSGS*, 24–25.

57. Ibid.

58. This iron screw steamer had been built in London in 1881 with a gross tonnage of 954GT (Kizu, *Nippon Yūsen senpaku*, 57).

59. 2.2 million catties (*Fukuoka nichi nichi shinbun*, January 13, 1886, reprinted in *KKSGS*, 254). Also in 1887, CSKK president Ishino along with other organization members went to Tokyo to petition against the high costs of transporting coal, arguing they hampered possibilities for export (Ogino, "Meiji chūki," 4).

60. Chikuhō Sekitan Kōgyōshi Nenpyō Hensan Iinkai, *Chikuhō sekitan kōgyōshi nenpyō*, 1:135.

61. The 1762 completion of the Horikawa Canal linked Wakamatsu to the Onga River, thus providing a shortcut to the Inland Sea. As coal shipments to the Jūshū saltfields grew, coal shipping started to concentrate at Wakamatsu, initiating the decline of Ashiya's dominance at the Onga's natural estuary farther west.

of its headquarters there and in its selection as railhead for Chikutetsu, which opened in 1891.[62]

Kokura, by contrast, was home to many of the area's most important capital networks. Despite its decline after taking a pro-*bakufu* stance in the *bakumatsu* era and ending up on the losing side of the Meiji Restoration, Kokura still mattered. At the time of Yoshida's venture, many prominent inhabitants were engaged in renovating the former castle town's harbor in the hopes of re-establishing its earlier prominence and turning Kokura into a modern commercial city. The town had found redemption and some prosperity as a military base during the 1877 Satsuma Rebellion, prompting its elites to strategize about a comeback. Kokura's leading citizens—including Tsuda Koreyasu, who would become both a chief advocate for the port of Moji and the founder of the *Moji shinpō*, and the famous early domestic coal broker Nakahara Kazō—had ambitious plans for port renovations that had been in the works since 1878. In fulfillment of early funding plans, the town opened a brothel in 1883.[63] This fairly common strategy for earning harbor revenues, however, was not enough when the project ran into problems with dredging, docking, and bridge building, all of which raised cost estimates quite significantly and delayed the endeavor. Although a scaled-back version of the planned renovations were eventually completed, these setbacks were enough to shift focus away from Kokura.[64]

Kokura's larger problems notwithstanding, it still would have been a reasonable choice for Yoshida, as would Wakamatsu or the neighboring towns of Dairi or Tanoura. Indeed, any of the ports along the northern Kyushu coastline held their convenient placement on the Kanmon Strait and their relative proximity to Chikuhō in common. Moji, however, possessed two distinct advantages. First, it had a naturally favorable harbor. Not only was it surrounded on three sides by mountains,

62. *FKS CKT*, 27. Wakamatsu and Moji developed in a somewhat symbiotic relationship with each other in exporting coal from the late 1880s. Their success and proximity to each other along the Kanmon coast contributed to the later decision to place the Yahata Steelworks nearby in 1894, thus establishing this zone as one of Japan's key industrial belts.

63. *KKS*, 24–27.

64. A full-scale modernization of the port, however, would wait until the early twentieth century (Hiroi, *Nihon chikkōshi*, 370–73).

providing both protection and defense, but its inlet offered a calm refuge from the strong and fast currents that are a hallmark of the Kanmon Strait.[65] Despite the great variability in depth along the strait, Moji's offing, the waters just beyond the main anchorage, bestowed uniformly deep waters able to accommodate steamships. Further, its open and flat saltfields furnished ample room to store the coal that would be loaded onto these steamships. The second decisive advantage was its nearness to Shimonoseki. Safe and timely passage between Honshu and Kyushu was a growing concern, and Shimonoseki was slated to be a rail hub directly linked to Tokyo. Locally, schemes for cooperation across the Kanmon Strait started to congeal in the idea of a Dai Kanmon-kō, or single large port that would encompass both Moji and Shimonoseki.[66]

One such plan was hatched by Sano Tsunehiko, an influential native of Kiku County (and founder of Shinrikyō, one of the thirteen Shintō sects). He recruited Toyonaga Chōkichi, a former retainer from the Tokugawa-era castle town of Chōfu, who had become a wealthy and powerful merchant. At roughly the same time that Yoshida was attempting to operate his coal export business out of Moji, these two men were taking initial steps toward surveying the harbor and reclaiming land for port construction. Understanding that developing each shore of the Kanmon Strait would benefit both sides, Toyonaga agreed to help develop Moji for trade, backing the undertaking financially while Sano managed the day-to-day affairs.[67]

As important as reclaiming land, building embankments, and erecting warehouses were to the project, Sano's greatest energies went into gaining the consent of the people living in the adjacent towns of Kusubara and Moji. To gain the support of the many who strongly opposed the plan, including saltfield operators and the notoriously oppositional fishermen along the coastline, he promised monetary compensation for

65. The natural features of the Kanmon Strait make it hazardous to navigate. It is fast-moving (reaching up to 10 knots), narrow at its entrances (between half and three-quarters of a mile wide), and of variable depth (the deepest part of the channel is 33 to 43 feet deep, but along its shores it is 16 feet or less). The strait, and its entrances in particular, are also littered with sand bars, rocky reefs, and sunken vessels (Kanmon Kōro Kōji Jimusho, *Kanmon kōro*, 4; *KKS*, 479).

66. Although the two ports are often identified together as Kanmon, they never officially merged.

67. Yonezu, *Meiji no Kitakyūshū*, 139.

displacement and land allotments, and choice jobs as coastal boat operators and laborers on the new docks. With their acquiescence, Sano then
applied to the newly appointed Fukuoka governor, Yasuba Yasukazu, to
reclaim nearly 6 square miles of land from the coastal zone in these
towns so that he could move forward with this undertaking.[68]

Yasuba quickly rejected Sano's application, but not because it lacked
merit. Rather, it was because the governor himself was considering a similar project, one tied directly to the establishment of a Kyushu trunkline
railroad. It appears that many such "men of discernment," including
Yasuba, and likely Sano and Toyonaga as well, had advance word that the
central government was planning to open special ports, as rumors to this
effect had been spreading throughout the country.[69] Whether or not such
knowledge directly informed local plans, the promotion of both the port
and the railroad in advance of these designations was undoubtedly crucial to Moji's selection as railhead. Governor Yasuba would also be pivotal
to their success.

LAYING THE RAILROADS

Governor Yasuba, a firm railroad advocate and early stockholder in Japan's first private railway, had come to Fukuoka with a strong belief in
developing a regional industrialization policy. This son of a Kumamoto
samurai was a career politician and bureaucrat with deep ties to the new
government. He had fought to bring down the shogunate in the Boshin
War and helped force the surrender of Edo Castle, traveled abroad with
the diplomatic and information-gathering Iwakura Mission, been a member of the Chamber of Elders (Genrōin), and governed Fukushima and
Aichi Prefectures before being assigned to Fukuoka in early 1886.[70] This
appointment came after Yasuba helped put an end to the nationwide Freedom and People's Rights Movement by suppressing western Kyushu's
Reform Party (Kaishintō), headquartered in his hometown of Kumamoto, and its drive for parliamentary democracy. Used to getting things

68. *KKS*, 28–29.
69. Yonezu, *Meiji no Kitakyūshū,* 139.
70. See Yasuba, *Yasuba Yasukazu den,* and *KKS*, 29. He later became a member of
the House of Peers (*Kizokuin*), where he advocated a firm foreign policy. From 1897,
as magistrate of Hokkaido, he supported policies for development through such
means as deforestation and colonization (Rekidai Chiji Hensankai, *Nihon no rekidai
chiji,* 28–29).

done and with considerable political clout both nationally and across Kyushu, Yasuba thought that building the railroad was too important to be left solely in local hands.[71]

The governor was also a pragmatist, however. He understood the need for local cooperation in carrying out his plans, especially given that they were to be built on foundations laid by local residents prior to his arrival. This was true not just of the port but also of the railroad. The movement to create a railroad to service Kyushu and its coal industry had been in the works since at least 1879. Prefectural assemblyman Uemura Jisaburō (who would become known as Kyushu's "railroad zealot") and Fukue Kakutarō (a member of the Diet who would fight for Moji's greater opening in the mid-1890s), together with businessman Okada Koroku and Governor Kishira Shunsuke (Yasuba's predecessor), first advocated building a line between Moji and Kumamoto. Although Uemura had enlisted the firm backing of Kokura merchants, especially Nakahara Kazō, local support was not enough since the central government was still reluctant to allow railroad building by the private sector. The plans were shelved.[72] With the government's turn toward allowing privately owned railroads and the enterprise boom of the mid-1880s, however, Yasuba quickly took the opportunity to spearhead Fukuoka's railroad drive.[73]

During his first year as governor, he met with power holders in Fukuoka and worked to coordinate efforts across prefectures to establish a Kyushu railroad. From the start, Yasuba was determined to make Moji its railhead. The governor went to the Fukuoka Prefectural Assembly in November 1886 to request funding approval for the construction of an extension from Dairi to Moji. Original plans called for ending passenger and cargo service in Dairi, just southwest of Moji along the coast, but Yasuba argued that Moji's natural geographical advantages—namely, its protected inlet and proximity to Shimonoseki—would better facilitate transportation and bring greater profits. His impassioned pitch, however, failed to sway the assembly to pay for a spur that they viewed as a needless ancillary cost, and they roundly voted it down.[74]

71. *KKS*, 29.
72. *FKS CKT*, 25–26; Kodama and Kawazoe, *Fukuoka-ken no rekishi*, 278.
73. Ericson, *Sound of the Whistle*, 108–16.
74. *MKS*, 11.

Undeterred, Yasuba met with the governors of Kumamoto and Saga, the two other prefectures through which the line would pass. Together, they formulated a proposal to run a private railroad from Moji to Kumamoto via Kurume and Misumi. Six delegates accompanied the three governors on a trip to Tokyo to present their proposal. The central government, with the sanction of the Navy Ministry, approved the establishment of the Kyushu Railway Company on two conditions. First, they were to link their project to the pending Nagasaki-Sasebo line, which the Nagasaki Chamber of Commerce and the Private Industry Association (Shiritsu Kangyōkai) had recently proposed.[75] Second, they were to name Takahashi Shinkichi, then Commercial Bureau Chief of the Ministry of Agriculture and Commerce, company president to oversee construction and operations.[76]

Having agreed to the conditions, the promoters immediately began to raise capital for the Kyushu Railway Company, which was established in August 1888 with 7.5 million yen. Over 70 percent of the original stock issued was held by residents of Kyushu's four sponsoring prefectures of Fukuoka, Kumamoto, Saga, and Nagasaki. Local shareholders included many from Chikuhō, including the big three mine owners (Asō, Kaijima, and Yasukawa), Konomi Takasuke, and members of the Fukuoka Prefectural Assembly. CSKK president Ishino personally held close to 100 shares, but most of the remaining investors, such as prominent businessman Ōkura Kihachirō and the great industrialist and financier Shibusawa Eiichi, were based in Tokyo.[77]

As the approval and funding for this north-south Kyushu line proceeded, a parallel movement to establish a mining railroad for Chikuhō coal was also under way. Even though the Kyushu Railway Company would certainly benefit the coal industry to some degree, it was intended primarily to carry passengers and general cargo.[78] Only a designated mining railroad could ease the congestion on the Onga River, which was becoming severe as coal production volumes increased with new districting and the mechanization of the coalfields. Within just three years of the CSKK's establishment, river traffic had risen by 50 percent, from

75. Ibid., 30.
76. *FKS CKT,* 25–27; *KKSS SK,* 1:61 .
77. *FKS TH,* 1267–72.
78. The Kyushu line did also carry some Miike coal to Moji for export.

just under 3,000 to over 4,600 boats, and fare hikes became frequent. Moreover, irrigation needs mandated that mining shipments be periodically suspended, making coal supplies inconsistent at best. The bottleneck of vessels carrying coal on the Onga River, in turn, had a negative effect on the transport of agricultural products, especially rice. Building a railroad and improving coastal harbors to alleviate these conditions for the good of industry and agriculture alike took on new urgency.

Chikutetsu was established to carry the region's coal, and although it was not the country's first mining railroad, it was the first private one. The Horonai Railway (Hokkaido) and the Kamaishi Ironworks Railway (Iwate Prefecture) were both established in 1880 as government-operated enterprises, built to link directly to their nationally owned mines.[79] The Horonai Railway, the routing of which was essential for the development of the port of Otaru (named a special port of export in 1889), was used as a model for the development of the Chikutetsu line.[80] Yet, as with other aspects of the coal industry in Chikuhō, the central government did not orchestrate the laying of its rails. Tagawa County's elected prefectural representative, Hayashi Yoshitarō, proved integral to establishing the new line. Overseeing the fundamental stages of its creation, Hayashi held a founders' meeting to establish the company in June 1888 with capital of 750,000 yen. He located the main office in the central Chikuhō city of Nōgata and commenced construction the next year. Many of the region's usual suspects, including Asō, Hiraoka, Saitō Michihiko (director of the Eighty-Seventh National Bank branch in Kokura), Shimizu Yoshimasa, and Yasukawa, helped fund the project.[81]

Despite substantial local investment in the project and a solid start, financial troubles from the 1890 panic, its subsequent coal mining slump, and the 1891 Chikuhō floods quickly mounted, causing Kyushu's new lines to waver. Many shareholders were forced to sell, precipitously decreasing the percentage of stock held locally and allowing capital from Osaka and Tokyo to move in. Mitsubishi, in particular, took advantage of the situation, buying up railroad stock and purchasing mining

79. For more on Kamaishi Ironworks and its railroad, see Wittner, *Technology and Culture*, esp. ch. 4.

80. *FKS CKT*, 24–25.

81. *KKSGS*, 29, 35.

concessions in one stroke. Mitsubishi soon owned majority holdings in both Chikutetsu and the Kyushu Railway Company and moved its mining offices from Nagasaki to Wakamatsu, planting itself firmly in the midst of Chikuhō's coal industry.[82]

BUILDING THE PORT

Meanwhile, Moji's harbor development was proceeding apace. Following rejection of his plan by the prefectural assembly, Governor Yasuba ordered a survey in late 1888 to assess requirements for port renovation. The governor enlisted three Buzen county heads (Kumagai Naoyoshi, Tsuda Koreyasu, and Shimizu Yoshimasa) to oversee on-site inspections and survey the area between Dairi and Moji. The Home Ministry, for its part, sent in some of its more seasoned engineers for consultation: the Dutch engineer Rouwenhourst Mulder, who assisted in Misumi's town-planning and harbor development; the Home Ministry engineering chief Ishiguro Isoji, who also worked on the ports of Kure, Sasebo, Miike, and Wakamatsu; and Prefectural Engineering Chief Koyama Kaizō.[83]

Locally, even though Sano and Toyonaga were not defeated by Yasuba's earlier rejection, they continued to encounter problems in their own efforts to develop the port. Unexpectedly, key figures supporting the larger Dai Kanmon-kō project on the Shimonoseki side suddenly applied to expand their port independently of Moji. Perhaps they believed that their chances were better if they went solo. After all, Shimonoseki's strategic importance as a commercial center was already widely recognized, as signaled by the Western powers' repeated attempts to turn it into a treaty port and the 1883 designation allowing it to embark on the Korea trade.[84] Nonetheless, this move left Moji supporters quite short of funds. Kiku County head Tsuda Koreyasu called on fellow Fukuoka native Suematsu Kenchō, who would soon become Itō Hirobumi's son-in-law, for assistance. Suematsu famously recruited Shibusawa Eiichi to invest in the Moji project. By this time, Moji's private sponsors—headed by Sano and still supported by Toyonaga—and its official backers, most

---

82. *FKS TH*, 1267–72; *KKSS SK*, 1:66–68.
83. *MKS*, 12–14.
84. *KKS*, 28–29.

notably Governor Yasuba, had recognized the need to join forces in building the port.

Unlike the heavy base of Chikuhō mine owners who supported the CSKK and the railroads, Moji Chikkō drew most of its funding from elites in Kyushu's northern cities and counties. Shimizu Yoshimasa then retired as head of Miyako County to become the company's president and serve as co-director with Toyonaga.[85] Other notable people who signed the port construction application included several of Kiku County's economic and political leaders, such as Fukue Kakutarō (who had been serving as a prefectural assemblyman since the first election in 1878), Saitō Michihiko, Tsuda Koreyasu, and Uemura Jisaburō.[86]

These individuals comprise a partial list of Moji's most important founders and backers, and many were connected to nearby port construction projects at Kokura, Wakamatsu, and Tanoura. The participation of these local heavy hitters was vital to moving this project forward. Their funds alone, however, were insufficient, requiring Moji Chikkō to find investors among some of Meiji Japan's great capitalists. In addition to Shibusawa and Ōkura, Yasuda Zenjirō and Asano Sōichi also contributed funds to the project.[87] With great anticipation, a groundbreaking ceremony initiated Moji's port construction in July 1889, the very same month that the port received designation as a special port of export.[88]

Moji Chikkō was only ever intended to be a temporary enterprise and was incorporated for just ten years "for the purpose of building Moji harbor and constructing a wharf for business." Its original three-phase plan encompassed reclaiming a land area that totaled more than

85. Shimizu also became involved in the Moji Coal Exchange, the Kokura Chikkō Port Construction Company, and the Kyushu Railway Company.

86. *KKSGS*, 17, 256.

87. *KKS*, 29.

88. The Moji Chikkō Company oversaw the three planned phases of construction, lasting from 1889 to 1899. Most of the labor, however, was contracted out to the newly created Nippon Engineering Company. Owners Shibusawa and Ōkura (both investors in Moji), along with Fujita Tensaburō, established Nippon Engineering, Japan's first engineering company, in 1887 to construct naval stations at Japan's five military ports as tensions with China escalated in the mid-1880s. This company also handled numerous construction jobs, including work on the Kyushu railroad (*KKSGS*, 51, 258).

120,000 *tsubo* (about 100 acres) laying roads, digging ditches, and building a wharf. During the second phase, the *Moji shinpō* described the laborious work of port construction: "Currently more than twenty daily laborers and more than twenty stonemasons are engaged just in building stone walls. Sixty-seven ships transport earth and sand, and everyday more than 60 *tsubo* (about 2200 square feet) is reclaimed." It further expected "a great increase in the number of people and extent of construction" over the course of the next month.[89] Owing to steady progress, the company would complete all three phases before its scheduled dissolution in 1899.

During the late 1880s and 1890s, Moji was not the only port under construction. This was a period when local and national attention turned to the development of Japan's transportation infrastructure, with interest in both the laying of tracks and the creation or renovation of connecting ports. As is clear in the hard work required to rationalize the coalfields and establish the port of Moji, it was very difficult for local groups alone to support the heavy costs of financing such large-scale and capital-intensive projects. Even though both initiatives in northern Kyushu grew from local efforts, completing them required support at the national level. After the basic infrastructural elements of the port and its connecting rail lines were more or less in place to handle Chikuhō's coal, two other components had to come together: a reliable source of information about both the coal industry and the port and success in the East Asian coal markets.

Narrating Moji in Multiscalar Perspective

During the extended process of seeking and maintaining support for the development of the port and its hinterland, boosters had to be clear about defining their plans and visions. In so doing, they began to clearly articulate their visions for Moji and rhetorically position it in domestic and international trade and transportation networks. The key surviving record of Moji is the *Moji shinpō* newspaper, which offers a reflection of life at the port, a chronicle of daily activities and extraordinary events, and a map of the real and imagined geographies that situated this port in the world.

89. Moji Chikkō Gaisha, "Moji chikkō gaisha teikan"; *Moji shinpō*, July 20, 1893.

Tsuda Koreyasu, one of the port's early backers, founded the *Moji shinpō* in early 1892. The newspaper's coverage centered on Moji but intentionally moved beyond it to encompass its regional setting, its maritime connections, and East Asian markets. In designing this daily to provide up-to-date coverage of Moji and the coal industry that was its lifeblood, Tsuda boldly defied convention to produce the kind of reportage that he believed would best serve the port, and the paper, in a new age.

In deliberate counterpoint to the politically affiliated, opinionated newspapers that spread during the Freedom and People's Rights Movement and still prevailed in the early 1890s, Tsuda launched what promised to be a nonpartisan and factually accurate daily focused on business matters and the economy and designed unabashedly to facilitate commerce and profit-making.[90] The paper would eschew "irresponsible" reports and political harangues and, instead, "adhere to strict neutrality." Tsuda's belief in responsible journalism was evident in his view that a newspaper's duty was both to function as "society's eyes and ears" and to serve as a "beacon of civilization."[91] Tsuda's commitment to objective and comprehensive reporting was aimed at creating an informed readership. His vision preceded the more general adoption of these principles by the country's newspaper industry, which, as a direct result of the First Sino-Japanese War, came to espouse the idea that "news lay at the core of journalism."[92] In this regard, Tsuda and his paper were ahead of the curve.

The *Moji shinpō*'s inherently geographical approach to the news and its coverage further demonstrated a commitment to putting business ahead of convention. Again intentionally turning away from contemporary norms, the paper gathered information on commerce and industry from all over Kyushu, in the process repudiating territorial divisions that lingered from the Tokugawa era. In the paper's prospectus, Tsuda expressed his dismay over the tendency for other Kyushu papers to reinforce feudal conventions by limiting their coverage to the prefecture in which they operated, "never crossing the border, just like during the

90. For some of its fifty-year run, however, it was sympathetic to, if not directly involved with, the Seikyūkai political party.

91. Tsuda, "*Moji shinpō* kabunushi meibo," and prospectus, "*Moji shinpō* hakkō no shushi oyobi hōhō."

92. Huffman, *Creating a Public,* 220.

former age of the *bakufu* when *daimyō* protected their own territory, not daring to infringe on another domain."[93] At a time when prefectural officials still struggled with consolidating their authority, Tsuda was urging the adoption of broader horizons.

His solution for overcoming ingrained conservatism was to station correspondents in towns and cities throughout Kyushu where business conditions, market prices, and events would bear most directly on his intended readers: the people of Kiku County and those involved in the coal industry and related enterprises. In concentric fashion, correspondents were initially located at the eight proximate commercial centers of Shimonoseki, Kokura, Wakamatsu, Nōgata, Hakata, Kurume, Saga, and Kumamoto, so that coverage of markets and coal production, both crucial to Moji, could extend across Chikuhō's five counties and beyond. Information from these locations would be transported daily by rail or sea and published in the paper the following morning so as to be immediately useful in business transactions.

Beyond these proximal regions, the prospectus also stated that the paper would dispatch correspondents to Japan's largest urban markets: Tokyo, Osaka, and Kobe. Noticeably, he left out Nagasaki, where Chikuhō coal would have difficulty making headway, given that the much nearer Takashima and Miike mines were dominant there. Turning to foreign markets, he first listed Shanghai and Pusan, two key East Asian markets and sites of Japanese settlement that were directly linked to Shimonoseki by regular shipping service. After the *Moji shinpō* obtained sufficient monetary resources, the ambitious prospectus continued; it would send correspondents to what it identified as the next tier of significant ports, namely, Hong Kong, Tientsin, Chefoo, and Vladivostok. Coverage during the first two years of the paper indicates that regular news did, in fact, come from the first set of locations named, but circumstances soon changed and Moji's connections would reach farther than Tsuda had anticipated. The outbreak of the First Sino-Japanese War largely determined where news broke in the short term and expanded the geography of Japan's coal markets, and the paper's ambit, in the long term. Adapting coverage in an effort to report consequential news was consistent with

93. Tsuda, "*Moji shinpō* hakkō no shushi oyobi hōhō." Each of Kyushu's prefectures had daily publications by the end of the 1870s (*KKSSKB*, 725).

Tsuda's vested and entwined interests in the survival of his paper and the growth and prosperity of Moji.

Tsuda's rationale for choosing Moji's as the paper's home rested on its favorable location. He explained his decision as follows:

> To begin with, as one of the special export ports, Moji's name will resound overseas, especially as a result of its coal markets. But it is also the railhead for the Kyushu line, it commands the throat of western Japan, and it is separated from China by only a narrow strait. The comings and goings of domestic and foreign ships increase in frequency day by day, and it is most convenient for traffic between this shore and the shores of foreign countries. All of these [advantages] are closely related to the port's economy, politics, education, hygiene, and all things. These are the grounds on which I have decided to publish a paper from Moji.[94]

Similar arguments about the port's advantages had been made in the efforts to win Moji's selection as the Kyushu railroad's starting terminal and as a special port of export, endeavors in which Tsuda had also played an instrumental role.

Tsuda established the *Moji shinpō* following a long career in local politics and a fourteen-year tenure as the head of Kiku County (1878–1892). During this time, he ardently promoted the development of the towns and ports of both Kokura and Moji, gaining friends and making enemies along the way. But the record of his life, as indicated by a memorial published in the *Moji shinpō* shortly after his sudden death in December 1894, emphasized his commitment to public service as something he held dear, like "quality sake."[95] Among the more than 1,000 people who attended his funeral procession were employees, officials, and executives of many of the region's most prominent establishments, including the Kyushu Railway Company, Moji Chikkō, Kokura Hospital, Kokura Courthouse, and Kiku County's Educational Association, as well as several banks, town halls, schools, and private businesses.[96]

Creating the *Moji shinpō* was consonant with Tsuda's deep involvement in local development. To begin with, securing the requisite start-up capital and subscriptions required tapping into his extensive community networks. Sixty-eight people invested in the newspaper prior to its publication, the great majority (roughly 72 percent) of whom came from Kokura and Moji. Many of them were local notables already involved in

94. Tsuda, "*Moji shinpō* hakkō no shushi oyobi hōhō."
95. *Moji shinpō*, December 20 1894.
96. Ibid., December 21, 1894.

urban infrastructure projects, such as providing electric street lighting and expanding transportation networks, as well as essential services like banking, commerce, manufacturing, shipbuilding, and even politics.[97] Their involvement in civic growth was often wide-ranging. Some of them, for example, had been integral to establishing Moji Chikkō, while others would become principal actors in the mid-1890s movement to gain import privileges for Moji.[98]

Investors in the paper who were directly engaged in coal mining included Morinaga Katsusuke, Kanzaki Tokuzō, Hayashi Jirōta, and Ichioka Seizō. Yasukawa Keiichirō, now a mine owner, coal agent, and industrialist, was the most illustrious name among them. Still, other Chikuhō mine owners, such as Asō Takichi and Kaijima Tasuke, are noticeably absent from the list.[99] Although the *Moji shinpō* did come to serve, in part, as an organ for the coal industry, it was launched as a local paper, and at first its sales centered on Moji and Kokura.

In addition to soliciting investors, Tsuda had to enlist the help of editors and hire employees to handle production. His first recruit was Sumida Hirokichi, who resigned as village head of Mojigaseki-mura to help establish the paper and manage its business affairs.[100] Tsuda himself oversaw the paper's operations, consulting nationally with executives in the newspaper industry. He hired the experienced Nishikawa Tsūtetsu, who had worked as general editor at both the *Ōsaka nippō* and the *Kansai nippō* and recruited Yoshimoto Akitei to serve as fiction writer and literary editor. He also coaxed Mōri Yasutarō—a native of Fukuoka Prefecture who had been an editorial reporter at the *Kyoto nippō* and then director of the *Shizuoka daimu* newspaper—into becoming editor-in-chief. Following Tsuda's death, it was Mōri who took over as company president and kept the *Moji shinpō* running until it ceased publication in 1938, after a forty-six-year run.[101]

97. These local personages included Morinaga Katsusuke, Kanzaki Tokuzō, Ieiri Yasu, Ishida Heikichi, and Shimizu Yoshimasa.
98. The latter group included Ishida, Kanzaki, and Tsugawa Ikuzō.
99. Others who did not hold shares included Hasegawa Yoshinosuke and Fukushima Ryōsuke, Tokyo-based capitalists who had invested in Moji Chikkō.
100. Mojigaseki-mura is the early Meiji name for what in 1894 became Moji-machi and then in 1899 Moji-shi.
101. *KKSS KB*, 728–33. Mōri did not maintain the same stance held by Tsuda regarding political affiliation and the paper came to be associated with the Seiyūkai, the party under which Mōri himself, during his tenure as head of the *Moji shinpō*, served four terms (1902–1924) in the Lower House of the Diet. The paper's demise

In keeping with the optimistic tone and ambitious scope of Tsuda's prospectus, the company originally resided in what at the time would have been one of Moji's more impressive buildings. A Western-style two-story mansion with a stately entrance flanked by pine trees, it was large enough to be used later as a small hospital.[102] Despite the image of success engendered by its rhetorical and material architecture, the *Moji shinpō* had a rocky start. During the first year, daily circulation reached just 1,000, but Tsuda maintained faith in both the port's promise and the importance of the paper's mission, keeping it afloat with substantial contributions from his personal accounts. With the advent of the Sino-Japanese War of 1894–95, the paper's fortunes began to change through its impressive and ground-breaking reportage. Sales jumped to over 6,000 papers per diem, nearing distribution figures of the prominent *Fukuoka nichi nichi shinbun*.[103] After the war, subscriptions fell off and would not again match 1895 sales until the outbreak of the Russo-Japanese War nearly a decade later.

Just as Tsuda had originally done in sending reporters to sites representing a clear economic geography of the port and its transactions, the paper similarly dispatched correspondents to key battle sites on the continent during these wars so as to receive the latest news as quickly as possible. Whether reporting on casualties in distant battles or documenting fluctuations in the world of commerce, the *Moji shinpō* consistently presented an overt geography in its presentation of the news, one that resonated with the wider encounters and integrations occurring across Japan and East Asia from the vantage of Moji. This was, in part, a function of presenting key stories with bylines—not only providing the author's name but marking them as received by the paper's offices at a specific date from a specific location. More broadly, though, Tsuda's decision to send correspondents to specific locations and have them report back to Moji in a timely manner reflects the new landscape

---

followed a series of events that overwhelmed it: the advance of the *Ōsaka mainichi* and *Asahi shinbun* newspapers into northern Kyushu in 1921, the 1923 Tokyo earthquake, which hampered reports on Tokyo's industries, and finally, in 1935 the *Ōsaka mainichi* and the *Asahi shinbun* simultaneously started printing evening editions in Moji. The *Moji shinpō*'s final publication date is unclear, but no papers published after June 30, 1937, remain in existence.

102. Imamura, *Shashinshū*, 68.
103. *KKSS KB*, 726–29.

(and seascape) of the industrial age, one being conspicuously shaped by advanced technologies like railroads, telegraphs, and steamships.

Nonetheless, the *Moji shinpō*'s regular features—statistics on coal production, sales, and pricing; ship and railroad schedules; and word of the latest economic, political, and social happenings—were accompanied by a consistently narrated appraisal of Moji and an abiding sense of its position as a nexus for a larger network. Kōnoe Kitarō had memorably stated that Moji was born of coal, but it equally came about as a transportation center; its links to other places were integral to its very makeup. Coal passed through as its lifeblood, but, as Tsuda understood, Moji could be animated only by its extensive connections, requiring steady flows to its hinterland and, just as vitally, to those ports where its coal was in demand.

Domestic and East Asian Coal Markets

From the time that foreign ships began coming to Japan, they needed coal and comprised a main source of demand for this resource. Although Moji would help fulfill domestic industrial and fuel needs, it was primarily the foreign ships stopping for fuel and loading coal for continental markets that would enable the port to thrive. As the foreign coal trade developed, the great majority of it was in Japanese hands. In 1896, before the end of the treaty port system, Japanese merchants handled just over 90 percent of Japan's total coal exports.[104] At the same time, just under 90 percent of coal exports, the bulk of which went to China and Hong Kong, were carried by Western-style vessels.[105] Thus, by the 1890s, sales of foreign bunker coal and overseas exports provided Japanese merchants—in an increased number of ports throughout the country—with a growing foothold in regional commercial networks. In other words, Moji and other special trading ports exporting coal developed in conjunction with the great consumption of this vital fuel source by the Western imperial powers in East Asia.

Prior to the development of significant overseas markets in the 1890s, the largest *bakumatsu* and Meiji-era consumers of Japanese coal, in order, were the domestic salt manufacturing industry, foreign ships fueling at

104. *DNGBN*, 1896.
105. Sugiyama, *Japan's Industrialization*, 202–3.

Japanese treaty ports, and overseas coal depots, which mainly supplied bunker coal for foreign ships. During the Meiji Restoration, salt manufacturing's demand was more than triple that of foreign ships.[106] In 1886, just prior to the opening of special ports of export, demand for foreign bunker coal only slightly exceeded that for domestic salt manufacturing, each commanding close to 30 percent of the total. By comparison, coal for domestic ships and overseas exports each accounted for 15 percent of total demand. After Moji opened in 1889, the large quantities of export coal that it handled comprised the largest proportion of total demand for Japan's coal.[107]

Overall, these trends indicate a rapid series of shifts in Japanese consumption and distribution patterns. These changes were borne partly of the economic and political shifts in the 1880s and 1890s that enabled a boom in private industry and an accompanying increase in levels of trade. Demand for Japanese coal by domestic and foreign consumers climbed sharply at the end of the century, the amount sold nearly doubling every five years between 1880 (nearly 10 million tons) and 1900 (over 94 million tons).[108] By 1900, coal demand for domestic factories began to overshadow that for all other uses. Domestic industry would then continue to lead overall demand, making the country a net importer, rather than net exporter, of coal by the 1920s. Nonetheless, East Asia's major coal markets had become the primary destination for Moji's coal, and its share in these markets rose sharply during the 1890s.

The three most important East Asian entrepôts at the end of the nineteenth century were Shanghai, Hong Kong, and Singapore. All were British military and commercial strongholds that sustained international steamship traffic from around the globe. Each port attracted prominent steamship companies and coal sellers to their shores. Early on, they imported coal from distant mines in Britain, Australia, and America, but took advantage of growing productivity at more proximal mines in Taiwan and, especially, in Japan. Coals from Takashima, Karatsu, and Miike began to dominate these markets in the three decades before Chikuhō coal made its appearance in the 1890s. Japanese coal supplied great quantities to these markets, enhancing the country's overall revenues.

106. Yasuba, "Gaikō kaiun," 43–44.
107. Ibid., 51.
108. Ibid.

But these mining regions also competed against one another, reflecting and reinforcing regional shifts at home as Chikuhō and Moji in northern Kyushu made gains over Japan's large mines and ports to the south to capture the largest share in these overseas markets.

SHANGHAI

Takashima coal was the first from Japan to gain a share of Shanghai's market in the 1850s and 1860s, and after coal from Karatsu and Miike also became available, these resources from southern Kyushu sold well. Japanese coal comprised 13 percent of the Shanghai market by 1870, approximately 50 percent by 1875, and nearly 80 percent by 1890, outcompeting British, Australian, and American imports.[109] Japan's bituminous grades were generally of sufficient quality to fuel commercial ships, but their real advantage was lower transportation costs.[110] Warships required higher-calorie anthracites; coal from distant Cardiff was preferred despite the added transit cost. The importation of superior anthracite from Welsh docks notwithstanding, the lower price and decent quality of Japan's coal cinched its market share in the region.

In Shanghai, Chikuhō coal was used for a variety of purposes: as fuel for factories (such as cotton spinning, shipmaking, and arms manufacturing), railroads, and smaller jobs like distilling, home heating, and heating water at public bathhouses. But the bulk was consumed by steamships. Major shipping companies with offices in Shanghai at the turn of the twentieth century included the British firms of Jardine Matheson, Butterfield and Swire, and the Peninsular and Oriental Steam Navigation Company (P&O), as well as East Asian concerns such as OSK and the China Merchants Steam Navigation Company. These companies purchased or contracted coal supplies from agents who had also established businesses in Shanghai. Among the most important were Japan's top-selling Mitsui, Mitsubishi, and the Taniguchi Katō Company, which operated alongside several other foreign as well as Chinese agents.[111]

Although Mitsui Bussan entered the Shanghai market selling mostly Miike coal in the early 1880s, the development of the Chikuhō

109. Sugiyama, *Japan's Industrialization*, 173.

110. Nagasaki, Kuchinotsu, and Moji were each approximately 500 nautical miles from Shanghai (ibid., 178).

111. Yamashita, "Nihon shihonshugi seiritsuki," 84–88.

coal industry in the mid-1880s enabled the company to dominate the Shanghai market after 1893.[112] Of all the coal imported into Shanghai between 1897 and 1901, Japanese coal gained steadily against the others to supply 65 percent (of roughly half a million tons imported) in 1897 and almost 78 percent (of nearly 850,000 tons) in 1901. Of these totals, Moji's portion of Japanese coal at Shanghai also grew from just 30 percent in 1897 to nearly 70 percent in 1901. The next highest amounts from Japan were Miike and Takashima coals, which were shipped out of Nagasaki and Kuchinotsu, followed distantly by coal from Karatsu and Hokkaido. Moji's share of all coal imported into Shanghai grew from 20 percent in 1897 to over 50 percent by 1901, thus dramatically establishing its ascendancy.[113]

Even as proximity to Shanghai helps account for the success of Japanese coal, it also raises the question of why Chinese coal did not hold greater prominence in this market. Initially, Chinese coal was limited to that being mined in Taiwan, which comprised only about 10 percent of Shanghai's total coal imports before the 1890s. The Kaiping coal mines (in Hebei Province) were not developed until the late 1870s and would only become more competitive in Shanghai with increased productivity and distribution beginning in the 1890s.[114]

The advance of Kaiping, which relied heavily on foreign borrowing and took place in parallel with growing Western interest in China's deposits, did concern the Japanese. Aware that Japan's newfound dominance in Shanghai could easily be threatened, the CSKK considered having an inspector investigate Chinese mining first-hand as early as 1898, but did not do so at that time. In 1902, however, the Ministry of Agriculture and Commerce dispatched engineers to investigate, prompting the CSKK to petition the ministry to send a Chikuhō industry expert. In the end, the CSKK did receive a report from a mining engineer, Wada Tsunashirō, who inspected mines in North China, about coal production there.[115]

112. Sugiyama, *Japan's Industrialization*, 175. Mitsui Bussan was Japan's largest coal seller, handling more than 50 percent of the country's exports by 1905 (Yamashita, "Nihon shihonshugi seiritsuki," 83–85).

113. Sugiyama, *Japan's Industrialization*, 175.

114. Ibid., 181–82.

115. *FKS CSKK*, 37.

Despite legitimate concerns about competitors, however, Chinese coals still held less than 20 percent of this market at the turn of the century.[116]

HONG KONG AND SINGAPORE

Although coal sales to Hong Kong began later than those to Shanghai, Japan quickly took over the lion's share of that market from Great Britain and Australia, supplying more than 75 percent of the total by the mid-1880s. Hong Kong was a free-trade port that functioned primarily as a transshipment center with major trading partners in India, Australia, the United States, Germany, and Great Britain. The British handled most cargo for the port, which also served as a chief military base for the same. Due to the nature of the port's role in transit trade and its high volume of steamer traffic (it ranked roughly third in the world and first in East Asia by the time of the Russo-Japanese War of 1904–5), Hong Kong supported a lively coal market aimed at fueling steamships.[117]

Takashima and Miike coal held the lead in Hong Kong for the first two decades of sales, but, as at Shanghai, Chikuhō's development allowed its coal to climb rapidly to the top of Hong Kong's imports. In 1896, when Japanese coal supplied three-quarters of the Hong Kong market, Miike and Chikuhō each accounted for half of that amount. By 1901, however, when Hong Kong imported nearly one million tons of coal, Japan held close to 85 percent of the market, and Chikuhō outpaced Miike by more than three to one, a ratio that held steady until the outbreak of World War I.[118]

Singapore likewise functioned as an important East Asian transportation hub and saw a significant amount of steamer traffic. Although the coal it imported was used mostly to fuel the many ships anchored there, it did not deal in the same volumes as either Shanghai or Hong Kong. Japanese coal was first imported into Singapore in 1883 and at first held a relatively small share of less than 18 percent. By 1893 it controlled roughly 36 percent of the market, not garnering more than 50 percent

116. Yamashita, "Nihon shihonshugi seiritsuki," 86.

117. Sugiyama, *Japan's Industrialization*, esp. 182–87; Yamashita, "Nihon teikokushugi seiritsuki," 6–13.

118. Coals from Tonkin (northern Vietnam) and India also began to climb in Hong Kong's market at the turn of the century (Yamashita, "Nihon teikokushugi seiritsuki," 15).

until after 1896. By 1897, Chikuhō coal from Moji supplied more than 50 percent of that sent to Singapore by Japan. Whereas Japanese coal had initially competed against British and Australian coal, more and more during the 1890s, they faced competition from mines in India and Malaysia. Most of these sales were handled by British rather than Japanese companies, especially Mansfield and Paterson Simons, which had been a major trading company in Singapore since the 1820s. Nonetheless, Mitsui Bussan still managed to gain ground against these older, more established companies while also besting Mitsubishi.[119] Looking at these key markets in East Asia demonstrates the overall rise of Chikuhō coal compared to other varieties, both Japanese and foreign, in the last decade of the nineteenth century. These statistics show the high demand that helped enable Moji's "remarkable rise."

Conclusion

The local population played a leading role in effecting the re-regionalization of Chikuhō and establishing the port of Moji in the late nineteenth century. Although the two places became quite interdependent, each one's development is attributable to the efforts of local groups whose cores were to be found in the CSKK membership and elites in Kiku County. These groups joined prominent figures from across Fukuoka Prefecture and Kyushu, bringing in national heavyweights to establish the railroads that provided the essential links between the two sites and enabling Moji to rise quickly as a major coaling port.

New associations and organizations bridged earlier divides as local, prefectural, and national powerholders found shared benefit in a series of key projects that began with the rationalization of the coalfields in the mid-1880s. Tokyo's loosening of central control afforded local actors new opportunities to take charge of their own prospects. The activities of the Fukuoka prefectural government, embodied by Governor Yasuba and the prefectural assembly, were crucial in bringing new prosperity to this region—in efforts to create a coal association, enforce new districting, and link the Kyushu railroad to Moji. But neither national nor prefectural authorities remade Chikuhō, funded the building of Moji, or

119. Yamashita, "Higashi Ajia sekitan shijō."

orchestrated the new interdependence between the two. All of these projects grew from deep local roots.

The timing of these developments, though, is significant at the national level. The mid-1880s, in Fukuoka Prefecture as in other locations, was a decisive moment. It was a time when local entrepreneurship could flourish and influence where and how capital-intensive and large-scale enterprises developed. It was a moment between an era of centralized industrialization and the growth of the *zaibatsu* conglomerates. Moreover, these local efforts paved the way for business conglomerates to begin moving in easily when financing became more difficult in the early 1890s. Although many did not survive this influx, local enterprises were not completely overshadowed.

Importantly, we also find that overseas coal exports from Moji to key East Asian markets developed ahead of both the Sino-Japanese War of 1894–95 and the end of the unequal treaties in 1899. The dramatic advances in Japanese industrialization following the Sino-Japanese War are less dramatic when seen in light of the significant groundwork that preceded and contributed to this moment. Moreover, the local populations of Moji and its environs already held a significant stake in the wider East Asian economy.

This chapter has shown how key elements came together to establish a major port. First, coal, rail, and port facilities—specifically, the re-regionalization of the Chikuhō coal hinterland, the building of the Kyushu and Chikutetsu lines, and the construction of the port—formed the material base of Moji's networks. Second, the *Moji shinpō* provided a source of reliable news about coal supplies and markets while also discursively narrating this place and its geography of information networks. Third, the East Asian markets for its coal established the demand necessary for Moji's early success. Yet another element still merits discussion. Although the port's hinterland supplied Moji with coal, its life force, its "blood," this special trading port had an equally strong maritime orientation. Since it was the water through which ships traveled and where they dropped anchor, Moji's harbor and its offing also delineated a principal space of foreign exchange. We turn now to Moji's waterfront and shipping networks, situating these with respect to the country's maritime commercial and military capacities.

FOUR

The Paradox of Informal Imperialism

In the late nineteenth century, Japan did not have control over the waters and shipping lanes surrounding its archipelago. This was true with regard to both commerce and naval defense. Japan's maritime vulnerabilities had been made abundantly clear when Commodore Perry opened Japan with gunboat diplomacy in the mid-1850s. They were clear with the signing of the unequal treaties and the recognition that much of Japan's new commerce would be handled by foreign vessels. They were clear with the 1866 Tariff Convention allowance that the treaty powers could carry Japan's coasting trade, disrupting what had been a practiced and efficient national system of transportation.[1] Maritime weaknesses were exposed several more times during the next half-century, both at Japan's outermost edges and along its vital inland waterway, before the country became the "unchallenged maritime power in the West Pacific," with victory over Russia in 1905.[2]

Before Japan established its maritime authority in East Asia, however, the country was dependent on foreign shipping for overseas trade, and meager naval forces compounded its tenuous position. Since the growth of commercial enterprises outpaced the country's shipping capacity, Japan's ships handled a mere 10 percent of its overseas trade before 1895.[3] Establishing adequate fleets, support industries, and administrative structures took time to develop. As Japan worked to gain

1. Perez, *Japan Comes of Age*, 57.
2. Evans and Peattie, *Kaigun*, 133.
3. Chida and Davies, *Japanese Shipping*, 17.

maritime independence by ending the unequal treaties, creating a commercial shipping industry, and establishing a strong navy, the special ports of export proved an expedient step along the way.

The government granted the 1889 special ports of export—unlike all other types of special trading ports—unique dispensation for chartered foreign vessels to carry their freight. The reason was straightforward: Japan's commercial fleet did not have the necessary tonnage to carry these cargoes. Even though by the mid-1880s Japan was in a better financial position to enhance its transportation grid, the country continued to struggle with raising the number of its steamships and profitably expanding their routes. And without adequate shipping capacities, hard-earned ports and railroads would be of limited use. The Meiji government permitted foreign vessels to call at select harbors to help compensate for this predicament of development, calculating that the benefits of this allowance outweighed any potential risks.

The decision had immediate results. As soon as Moji received designation as a special port of export, small businesses moved in, coal sellers wasted no time loading exports, and the harbor immediately began receiving visits from foreign and domestic ships of various makes and sizes. That commerce grew rapidly suggests an eagerness on all sides for the services that Moji was slated to provide. It also points to the existence of shipping traffic and consumer markets that Moji could readily support. Local statistics claim that in 1896 over 10,000 domestic steamships, 100,000 Japanese-style sailing ships, and 1,200 foreign steamships entered and cleared the port. Close to 150,000 steamship passengers, 750,000 train passengers, and 700,000 patrons made round trips across the strait to Shimonoseki. Additionally, nearly 100,000 travelers lodged in town and the resident population approached 30,000, a dramatic increase from roughly 500 the decade before. In terms of cargo, Moji exported more than one million tons of coal that year alone.[4]

Although national statistics list a smaller number of foreign ships handled at Moji that year, the figure is still impressive. The *Dai Nihon gaikoku bōeki nenpyō (DNGBN)* for 1896 states that 358 merchant steamships entered Moji from foreign countries, 41 of which were Japanese. The majority were British (147), followed by ships from Germany (89), Norway (62), Austria (10), and one each from China, Denmark, Russia,

---

4. *MKS*, 3.

and Spain. These statistics indicate Moji's activity represents 16 percent of the national total, placing the port behind only Nagasaki (28 percent) and Kobe (18 percent) and ahead of Shimonoseki (13 percent) and Yokohama (10 percent).[5] These figures are not an aberration, for across the highs and lows from 1891 to 1900, Moji regularly handled from roughly 10 to 20 percent of the national total.

Moji's place in the national port hierarchy and its volume of international steamer traffic are surprising, given that it was not a treaty port. The circumstances at Moji show that even though Japan had to proceed cautiously until it could revise the unequal treaties and gain equality in the comity of nations, it could, in the meantime, benefit from the presence of the Western imperial powers in the region.[6] As such, Moji's position reveals a paradox of informal imperialism.

On the one hand, East Asia was a dangerous place.[7] Under the dynamics of informal empire, in which outside powers sought access to national resources and markets, and home governments sought to limit such access, ports served as gateways between jealously guarded interiors and international oceanic networks. Japan had successfully negotiated to limit the Western presence to the treaty ports even though its own naval capabilities were meager and it lacked a modern commercial fleet. The Ansei Treaties plainly defined the limits of Western privilege in the treaty ports, which comprised the territorial core of informal empire in Japan. Yet jurisdiction outside these zones—in Japan's coastal waters and in nontreaty harbors—was ill-defined and, at times, proved controversial. As the modern system of nation-states and Western international law took hold in this region, the establishment of clearly demarcated territorial and maritime jurisdictions remained incomplete.[8] The treaties did not protect Japan against further encroachment, leaving the country still exposed in a competitive international environment.

---

5. *DNGBN*, 1896.

6. The treaty port system provided some clear protections and even privileges for the Japanese. Sugiyama, for example, argues that the treaty port system worked to obstruct the activities of Western merchants, and where "by several ironic twists of fate," the system worked in favor of Japanese merchants who were either importing or exporting" (*Japan's Industrialization*, 74). See also Duus, "Japan's Informal Empire," xi–xxix.

7. See, for example, Beasley, *Japanese Imperialism*, 71; Jansen, "Japanese Imperialism," 62–70; Larsen, *Tradition, Treaties, and Trade*, 45; Peattie, "Introduction," 8–9.

8. See Benton, *A Search for Sovereignty*, 30–39.

On the other hand, the Western presence revitalized transmarine East Asia as a site of passage and commercial and cultural interaction. Multiple entities, from countries to individuals, gained new opportunities to create power and wealth. Within this space, circumstances were not absolute. Advantage could be gained from disadvantage. Even as Japan worked to come back from political and financial turmoil and establish itself as a modern power, it was able to take advantage of the foreign presence, tapping into networks that enabled it to engage in commercial and military endeavors that it was not otherwise prepared to undertake. The complexity of Japan's position and the paradox of informal imperialism becomes manifest when we look at larger questions of shipping and maritime sovereignty. The special trading ports in particular demonstrate how Japan could be a dependent and vulnerable semicolony at the same time that it benefited from mutual accommodation, a degree of autonomy, and growing strength to launch its own imperialist pursuits.

Commercial and Military Symbiosis

Shipping was essential for this island nation to modernize both commercially and militarily. These two drives developed in conjunction with each other at the time of Japan's forced opening, and they remained closely linked for the rest of the century. A decided lack of large, modern ships had made Japan vulnerable to exactly the kind of gunboat diplomacy that forced its opening in the mid-nineteenth century. The country's domestic shipping industry, which had been severely curtailed under the shogunate in the 1630s, started to revive during the *bakumatsu* era, when the Tokugawa government and domains alike began to purchase foreign ships.[9] Both national and local leaders were anxious to provide an effective naval defense against the encroachment of foreign ships, but they were too late to prevent informal empire from reaching the country's shores. The unequal treaties and establishment of commerce at the treaty ports then created a second worry in the form of trade deficits, which were exacerbated by an immediate dependence on foreign shipping and the loss of coastal routes to foreign shippers.

9. By the time of the Meiji Restoration, the shogunate owned 44 ships and various domains owned 94 ships, for a total capacity of 17,000 tons (Chida and Davies, *Japanese Shipping*, 3–5).

After the Meiji Restoration, the new oligarchs acted immediately to protect domestic shipping. Deliberate government efforts to decrease the country's dependence on foreign powers, apparent in their desire to refrain from taking out foreign loans, also guided the early establishment of a modern shipping industry. Although maritime defense and trade autonomy both remained serious concerns, limited funds compelled them to choose among pressing needs. Rapid development of a large modern naval fleet was prohibitively expensive. By the mid-1870s, government leaders gave precedence to the army over the navy in national security and budgetary calculations. Since a "static defense" (shusei kokubō) of shore batteries along the country's coastline proved the best available option in the short term, national defense came under the purview of the army. In turn, the navy was relegated to providing support with warships that could patrol coastal waters.[10]

Beyond making the navy secondary to the army, the oligarchs also effectively gave higher priority to strengthening commercial shipping than to building a dedicated naval fleet. Since military transport and supply could be handled adequately by commercial ships, the two developed hand in hand. As the acquisition of commercial vessels could be financed partly by private entities, strengthening state ties to Mitsubishi proved a feasible solution for meeting both commercial and military needs. Even so, the difficulties in launching a domestic shipping industry were legion: modern ships were expensive to buy, build, and operate; competition among shipping interests in East Asia was severe; and freight rates were high, particularly if cargo holds were not filled to capacity.[11]

Deficiencies in support industries also had to be addressed along the way. Japan lacked steel mills to stock shipyards with basic materials for construction and repair. Modern steamships lacked locally trained pilots and crews, making them reliant on foreign captains. Businesses had to learn the management of routes and cargoes while setting reasonable rates that could return profits on runs that were always costly. Basic coastal installations were also required. Local administrators at ports around the country worked with the Home and Navy ministries to determine where to place lighthouses, buoys, and coastal batteries. In short, establishing a

10. Evans and Peattie, *Kaigun*, 8.
11. See Wray, *Mitsubishi and the N.Y.K.*, on competition among national and international shipping entities.

strong maritime presence would prove to be one of the country's more challenging commitments to modernization and sovereignty. Yet, over the course of the next three and a half decades, the country would, in fits and starts, begin to build commercial and naval fleets worthy of a modern world power.

In the early years of the Meiji era, foreign ships carried large amounts of domestic goods between the treaty ports. Many Japanese citizens traveled domestic circuits aboard non-Japanese vessels, and growing numbers of foreign ships were chartered under Japanese names to trade at closed ports. But in the fight against Western dominance, the Japanese government banned chartered foreign ships from entering all but the open ports in 1869. Government leaders tried to curb foreign passenger service by requiring Japanese to purchase a special pass to board foreign steamships. Additionally, they issued legislation in 1869 and 1870 encouraging the private building and ownership of Western steam and sailing ships as well as the remodeling of existing Japanese-style vessels to sturdier Western construction.[12]

Further, Tokyo worked to return coastal shipping to Japanese hands through subsidies, lending out government ships, and consigning tributary rice shipments to domestic carriers.[13] The national government began to support Mitsubishi's shipping business in order to remove foreign concerns from coastal routes.[14] Diplomatically, members of the Iwakura Mission attempted to renegotiate the allowance for Western vessels in Japan's coastal shipping, to no avail.[15] When Ōkubo Toshimichi established the Home Ministry in 1874 and detailed his industrial promotion policy, he advocated an independent national transportation system, arguing that it was not only foundational for the country's industrial growth but essential for maintaining political independence.[16]

Regaining full sovereignty vis-à-vis the foreign powers remained a consistent goal as the new government simultaneously handled unrest at home and pursued military action in East Asia. The Meiji government's

12. Yamamoto, *Technological Innovation*, 5–6.

13. Ibid. Japan Mail Steamship Co. carried some of the tribute rice (Masuda, "Policy," 10–11; "Coastal and River Transport," 34).

14. Masuda, "Coastal and River Transport," 34.

15. Coastal shipping would remain a concession even in the final revised treaties (Perez, *Japan Comes of Age*, 172).

16. Wray, *Mitsubishi and the N.Y.K.*, 92–93.

early military endeavors aimed to ensure domestic stability and define Japan's national territory, but it also had the corollary effect of increasing the country's shipping tonnage. When Japan planned its 1874 expedition to Taiwan to avenge the murder of shipwrecked Ryukyuans and thus lay claim to the Ryukyu island chain, the Western powers refused to allow the Meiji government to charter their ships for the mission. Tokyo instead purchased thirteen steamships from abroad to carry Japanese troops. After the successful conclusion of the venture, the new vessels were turned over to Mitsubishi, ostensibly as compensation for its service in handling the transport. The Home Ministry further offered the company annual subsidies of 250,000 yen for a period of fifteen years and also hired it to transport government mail.[17] In employing and rewarding Mitsubishi, the government established a direct link between the country's early commercial and military endeavors.

This pattern of developing commercial and military power through a symbiotic relationship only grew stronger over time. The 1876 Treaty of Kanghwa, which opened three Korean treaty ports to trade with Japan, enabled Mitsubishi to create a monopoly over routes to Korea. The national government provided the company with eleven ships along with monetary compensation for its help with the incident that led to the treaty.[18] Over the course of the next five years, Mitsubishi opened regular lines to Korea. Most ran once a month and originated in either Nagasaki or Kobe. From there, the ships often went to the special trading port of Shimonoseki as well as the Gotō Islands and Tsushima before continuing to the Korean treaty ports of Pusan, Wonsan, and Inchon.[19] When the Dajōkan ordered the Home Ministry in February 1881 to open a line from Kobe to Russian Vladivostok via the Korean treaty ports, Mitsubishi reluctantly ran it with the goal of helping to maintain the security of the Korean Peninsula rather than generate profitable trade.[20]

Again in 1877, as the Satsuma Rebellion tested the new government and its military preparedness, the Meiji leaders assisted Mitsubishi in the purchase of ten steamships to provide military transport. After the

17. Masuda, "Coastal and River Transport," 34–35.
18. Wray, *Mitsubishi and the N.Y.K.*, 88.
19. Kokaze, *Teikoku shūgika*, 230–32.
20. Wray, *Mitsubishi and the N.Y.K.*, 158.

rebellion was put down, these ships bolstered Mitsubishi's commercial lines, and the company continued to prosper.[21] Over the next several years, the additional vessels enabled Mitsubishi to plow its profits into subsidiary activities, especially coal mining, instead of adding tonnage to its now sizable fleet.[22]

In the early 1880s, Mitsubishi controlled the only exclusive overseas shipping network that the country held: Japan's Korea monopoly. Mitsubishi increasingly transported Korean cargo among the three treaty ports, taking over its coastal shipping as Western powers had done in Japan.[23] Its control of the Korea trade, however, officially ended in the spring of 1882, when, encouraged by China, the Western powers signed unequal commercial treaties with Korea as well. That October, China and Korea also signed a watershed agreement in the 1882 Regulations for Maritime and Overland Trade. Since these other countries were slow to add Korea to their shipping routes, Japan maintained its dominance in this trade for a time. By the end of the decade, however, China opened maritime routes to Korea, further intensifying the competition between the two countries over trade rights and political influence on the peninsula.[24]

In the midst of handling these overseas concerns, however, domestic tensions began to alter Mitsubishi's privileged position. As was true of the development of the Chikuhō coal industry, railroads, and the port of Moji, the mid-1880s proved pivotal for the country's shipping enterprises. Mitsubishi's expanding interests, especially in mining, caused the navy to begin eyeing the company's intentions with suspicion. While

21. Masuda, "Coastal and River Transport," 35.

22. Beyond improving Mitsubishi's fortunes, the Satsuma Rebellion also vitalized small shipowners who transported cargo from a government supply base in Osaka. These competing carriers soon joined together to form OSK, creating what would be the country's second-largest shipping company (Wray, *Mitsubishi and the N.Y.K.*, 108, 187).

23. Kokaze, *Teikoku shūgika*, 230–32. Wray argues that Mitsubishi held little interest in opening or maintaining lines to Korea (*Mitsubishi and the N.Y.K.*, 158–59).

24. Kokaze Hidemasa refers to this shipping competition between China and Japan as a "war by proxy" (*Teikoku shūgika*, 229). Paine states that the Sino-Korean 1882 commercial treaty granted "China exclusive economic privileges that would enable it to dominate Korean trade" and together with Li Hongzhang's other policies, Korea would, within a year, become "a Chinese protectorate in all but name" (Paine, *Sino-Japanese War*, 55–56).

recognizing that it had to rely on the company for national defense, the navy nonetheless wanted to keep Mitsubishi from gaining undue prominence in military affairs. The emergence of competition in shipping helped to resolve the issue. A new alliance of shippers, the Kyōdō Un'yu Kaisha, which included Mitsui, aimed to compete against Mitsubishi. This viable alternative to a single-company monopoly soon began receiving subsidies from the government in a bid to encourage competition in the industry. Unexpectedly, however, the rivalry proved devastating to the finances of both enterprises as each slashed prices to outsell the other. They ended up joining efforts to form the NYK in September 1885.[25] This merger, combined with the establishment of the OSK just the year before, not only helped the industry revive but allowed Japan to begin to recover its coastal routes and slowly launch new ones overseas.

The navy did not sit on the sidelines during these dramatic vicissitudes in shipping. During this critical decade, commercial and naval shipping took increasingly independent paths. Although commercial shipping tended to support naval endeavors through the early Meiji years, by the mid-1880s, the navy could better support commerce, especially by providing coastal defense, containing smuggling, and working to establish control over Japan's coastal waters.

Militarily, Tokyo worked to improve the country's offensive and defensive capabilities at this juncture, including the enhancement of its naval fleet and military bases. The Army, Navy, and Finance ministries independently created new districts for military and commercial endeavors. Moreover, just as tensions with China were increasing, domestic security concerns were subsiding (particularly after the national conscript army defeated the Satsuma Rebellion), leading the oligarchs to reconsider military priorities and enabling the proponents of a powerful navy at last to gain a bigger share of attention and financing.

The situation in Korea provided some of the impetus for these changes. Within months of the Korean commercial treaties that heralded the end of Japan's trade monopoly there, the Dajōkan approved a naval expansion bill calling for the construction of forty-eight warships over

25. On the companies' competition and merger, see Wray, *Mitsubishi and the N.Y.K.*, esp. ch. 5.

an eight-year period.[26] By the time Japan and China signed the Treaty of Tientsin (Tianjin) in 1885, both sides were actively pursuing military strengthening programs, at least partly in anticipation of a future battle over Korea.[27] On the peninsula, the Imperial Japanese Army had begun systematically surveying and mapping Korea after the 1882 Imo Incident paved the way for Japanese military officers to gain access to the Korean interior.[28] This mapping took place ahead of equivalent army surveying of the home islands.[29] Within Japan, new policies advocated expanding the navy for national security reasons, and public bonds issued beginning in 1886 helped to pay for the costly buildup.[30]

China took similar actions as it faced new diplomatic realities that went beyond the rivalry with Japan. In the wake of the country's defeat at the hands of France and the loss of its tributary state of Annam (Vietnam), the Qing government pushed to overcome regional factions and centralize its four independent fleets.[31] Despite the failure of this brief attempt, Li Hongzhang strived to modernize his Beiyang fleet. Stationed principally at the naval base of Port Arthur (now Lüshun), this became China's largest fleet and would alone fight Japan during the Sino-Japanese War of 1894–95. As part of this effort, Li purchased two German ironclad battleships and pointedly had them pay a visit to Japan. When these impressive hulks called at Yokohama and Nagasaki in 1891, as intended, they created a stir among Japanese officials and citizens alike.[32]

26. Schencking, *Making Waves*, 34. Schencking attributes the victory solely to a new level of Satsuma support for expansion, but the developments in Korea would undoubtedly have encouraged government approval as well.

27. This treaty ensured the two powers equality in military response in the event of either's armed intervention in Korea.

28. The settlement of the incident (in which rioters attacked the Japanese legation in Seoul) resulted in revisions to the Treaty of Kanghwa as well as the Treaty of Chemulpo. The military maps these surveys created would be distributed to military personnel at the outbreak of the Sino-Japanese War in 1894. See Kobayashi, Watanabe, and Yamachika, "Shoki gaihō sokuryō."

29. See Hara, *Meijiki kokudo bōeishi*, 275.

30. Schencking, *Making Waves*, 33–37.

31. Rawlinson, *China's Struggle*, 110, 129.

32. Evans and Peattie, *Kaigun*, 19; Rawlinson, *China's Struggle*, 165; and Schencking, *Making Waves*, 55.

Taking a divergent path, Japan focused on purchasing torpedo boats and establishing a different kind of fleet; one with a concentration of smaller, faster vessels. This difference in ship types would end up favoring Japan when the two countries went to war a decade later. Even though Japan still had to order its best capital ships from overseas, it worked to establish its own modern shipbuilding facilities at home. Additionally, the Japanese were busy establishing their own arsenals at Tsukiji and Yokosuka for the production of armaments as well as smaller iron warships.[33]

In addition to building up their fleets, both countries also turned their attention to naval training in the 1880s. Although the British had a strong hand in training the navies of both China and Japan, the Japanese were said to foster more discipline among their officers and sailors.[34] The Japanese navy also spent time honing its tactical formations and combat strategies. The port of Shimizu, which would be named a special port of export at the end of the decade, was being used as an anchorage for a portion of Japan's naval fleet. When the navy began an extended study of naval tactics, it selected Shimizu as a testing site. In the summer of 1887, the port hosted a naval conference, and its inhabitants watched as sailors practiced maneuvers in the harbor. Owing to this moment, Shimizu has been considered the "cradle of Japanese naval tactics."[35] Shimizu, like many of the special trading ports, including Muroran, Moji, and Shimonoseki, held some naval responsibilities in addition to its main role as a commercial hub.

Beyond attending to their naval fleets, armaments, and tactical strategies, the Japanese also gave new weight to coastal surveillance and defense. Reorganizing central oversight of both naval and customs districts enabled ports to take on new functions. With regard to military considerations, Tokyo created five naval districts, dividing the country into sections that would each be handled by *chinjufu* (naval bases). In December 1884, the country's eastern naval base moved from Yokohama back to its prior position at Yokosuka. In May 1886, after investigating a number of sites, the navy selected Kure and Sasebo as the bases for two of the districts. These would open July 1, 1889, just two weeks

33. Evans and Peattie, *Kaigun*, 14.
34. Rawlinson, *China's Struggle*, 166.
35. Evans and Peattie, *Kaigun*, 36.

before the special ports of export were announced. Establishing these bases was an important precondition to opening the special ports of export, which would necessarily have to accommodate foreign vessels to transport their cargo.

The other two naval bases slated to open—Maizuru (in Kyoto Prefecture along the Sea of Japan) and Muroran (in southeastern Hokkaido near the Tsugaru Strait)—were selected in 1889 and 1890, respectively. These choices were based on strategic concerns about Russia's growing presence in East Asia. In particular, if Russia completed the Trans-Siberian Railway and placed warships at Vladivostok, it would pose a direct threat to the Sea of Japan. These ports were positioned to counter a possible attack from that direction. Financing continued to be an obstacle, however, and the opening of these naval bases was delayed. Officials determined that neither Maizuru nor Muroran would be of great value in a battle against China, which Tokyo considered a more pressing concern. Moreover, some officials questioned whether maintaining five bases was necessary since these stationary defenses would pull funds away from strengthening the naval fleet. Thus, the opening of Maizuru would be pushed back to 1901 while Muroran's opening would end up being cancelled in 1903.[36]

Although Muroran would not become a naval base, it had been functioning as a coal storage site for the navy since 1883 and would be named a special port of export in 1894.[37] Muroran was established not just to promote the export of local products but also to curb smuggling in the region. Its designation, then, was meant to both encourage legitimate trade and police this remote maritime zone. Although perhaps Muroran was at one extreme, all special trading ports had to assume a policing role.

The unusual situation of Muroran notwithstanding, special trading ports were, by nature, sites where foreign vessels had to be carefully monitored, especially since visitors were not necessarily limited to merchant vessels. This was particularly true at Kanmon, where Moji and Shimonoseki sat at a vital national chokepoint. Since the 1850s, foreign ships passed their shores when traveling through the Kanmon Strait to

36. Hara, *Meijiki kokudo bōeishi*, 227–33; KR, vol. 13 (1889), no. 12: Heisei 3, "Kaigun kanyōchi wa chinjufu jōrei daisanjō ni yori . . . ," July 15, 1889.

37. Ibid., vol. 7 (1883), no. 17: Heisei 3, "Kaigunshō Sapporo-ken ka Iburi-no-kuni Muroran-gun Muroran-kō ni oite . . . ," March 7, 1883.

the Inland Sea as they moved among the treaty ports of China and Japan. Hailing from countries like Great Britain, Germany, Russia, and France, warships were a constant presence in transmarine East Asia, there to protect their merchants and diplomats and ensure their countries' commercial and strategic interests.

Far fewer in number than commercial vessels but more impressive in size and appearance, modern warships could be regularly seen passing by or stopping at Moji. Foreign warships usually sailed on through but did occasionally stop at the port, sometimes in service of their country's visiting dignitaries.[38] For example, in 1893, the Austrian warship *Elizabeth* anchored in Moji's offing while the Austrian prince met with military leaders and visited military installations across the strait in Shimonoseki. Domestic warships also called at Moji, their numbers increasing after the opening of naval bases at Kure and Sasebo. In 1893 alone, twenty-nine imperial warships entered the port of Moji for a variety of purposes, including inspection tours, monthly practice maneuvers, and a celebration for the installation and inspection of Moji's newest battery.

Naval redistricting and the opening of the special ports of export also took place at the same time as important changes in the Imperial Army's strategy. The national garrison system, originally a domestic police force, was reconfigured in 1888 to dispatch army divisions overseas. These new divisions, with their ability to make use of the growing national shipping and railroad networks, mark a decisive shift in Japan's ability to launch offensive military operations.[39] It seems likely, moreover, that enhancing the capabilities of additional domestic ports capable of serving the country in an offensive battle was a consideration in the selection and opening of special ports of export the following year.

From yet another direction, Tokyo worked to improve its oversight of the country's growing commercial activities. On the heels of opening special ports of export, the Ministry of Finance established new customs districts in 1890. Japan's six customs houses were responsible not only for the specific port that accommodated them but also for managing branches at nearby special trading ports. The overseeing customs house

---

38. *Moji shinpō*, January 1, 1894. See also *Moji shinpō*, July 20, 25, and August 8, 10, 1893.

39. Lone states that Japanese historians generally agree that 1888 marks the date when "military strategy shifted irrevocably from defence to offence" (*Japan's First Modern War*, 21).

was responsible for collecting duties, inspecting cargo, and suppressing smuggling. Customs districts were similar, but not identical, to the newly limned naval districts. Nagasaki Customs, for example, covered the entire shoreline of Kyushu, in addition to the coasts of the Ryukyus, Tsushima, and Iki. By contrast, the naval districting split Kyushu between Sasebo and Kure, which covered its western and eastern coastlines, respectively.[40] Prior to the re-districting of 1890, the jurisdiction of Nagasaki Customs stopped at the ports. Japan's coasts were in effect "open" (*kaihō*) without specific zoning or settled jurisdictions. Therefore, when foreign ships sought refuge, called at ports, drifted ashore, or foundered on the shoals, it was simply the "nearest" customs house that dispatched an official to manage the cargo (presumably while other entities handled passengers and crews, disabled vessels, and other related matters).[41]

The government clearly relied on these offices. In February 1892, the minister of finance issued a directive to all prefectures stating that if foreign ships were to enter unopened ports or were found smuggling or poaching in Japan's coastal waters, local authorities were to consult with the appropriate customs house. Upon being informed of the location of the ship under suspicion, the customs house was to then notify an imperial warship to approach the vessel. In such a situation, the final word over whether a ship was to be confiscated rested with the minister of the navy.[42] In addition to providing instructions to those who would confront these transgressions, this legislation also established a clear hierarchy of authority, one that placed the Navy Ministry ahead of the Ministry of Finance, which held responsibility for the country's customs administration.[43]

---

40. KR, vol. 13 (1889), no. 12: Heisei 3 "Kaigun kanyōchi wa chinjufu jōrei daisanjō ni yori . . . ," July 15, 1889.

41. In 1875, Nagasaki Customs established a branch at Shimonoseki (nearly a decade ahead of its designation as a special trading port) to help handle such situations (*NZE*, 219).

42. Ibid., 220.

43. For a brief period (from September 1894 to March 1896) local police officers were also allowed to manage trouble on ships when special permission to enter unopened ports had been granted. In such cases, it was the Home Ministry that would direct local authorities about how to handle the situation (ibid.).

Even though commercial and military shipping operations began moving in separate directions in the 1880s, their interests remained closely linked. The need for mutual support was especially apparent at the special trading ports. In addition to monitoring all foreign ships stopping at the ports, these local sites also functioned to help police the country's waterways, especially at Japan's farthest reaches, where coastlines remained poorly controlled. Muroran and Naha, along with Tsushima's ports of Sasuna and Shishimi, were all designated special trading ports, in part, to discourage illegal dealings in these outlying areas.

Japan's commercial and military operations were closely intertwined throughout the treaty port era. In the first decades after the Meiji Restoration, Japan's efforts to increase its modern tonnage were driven by three overriding goals: to recover shipping rights, to support military endeavors, and to expand commercial shipping routes via nationally subsidized companies. By the 1880s, as both commercial and naval fleets were expanding and modernizing, Tokyo was able to devote new attention to maritime administration, working to regulate its growing overseas commerce—and ongoing dependence on Western ships—while gaining fuller control over the country's coastline and enhancing military capabilities. Overall, maritime activities had greater levels of national oversight by 1890, and the special trading ports proved an important tool in this process as national commercial and military strategies increasingly took this substructure of local gateways into account.

Dependence on Foreign Shipping at Moji

Coal exporters in particular relied heavily on chartered foreign ships to transport their coal overseas. This had been true since at least the early 1880s, when Tokyo became concerned over the "disturbing trend" of increasing numbers of foreign charters used by Mitsui and Mitsubishi, which had to transport coal out of their major mines in Kyushu and Hokkaido. Japan was paying outside concerns the considerable sum of 600,000 yen annually for trips to Shanghai and Hong Kong.[44] Increases in the overseas export of coal as the industry developed only exacerbated the problem. Channeling this money to foreign enterprises undercut Japan's ability to build a fleet capable of handling this trade on domestically owned vessels, which in turn compounded high freight rates. Despite

44. Wray, *Mitsubishi and the N.Y.K.*, 147, 156–57.

the disadvantages of conducting business in such a manner, however, there was no easy solution to correcting the imbalance.

These concerns notwithstanding, as the Japanese worked to build their own maritime presence, they took greater advantage of the situation through the special trading ports. These ports were dependent on the regional networks of port cities and shipping routes systematized by the British informal empire in Asia. Although these ports were governed by different rules than the treaty ports, shipping, trade, information, and administrative networks structurally linked the two. As a result, special trading ports did business with and through treaty ports across Asia, taking advantage of the regular shipping routes and various tramp liners that ran between them.

By introducing the special ports of export, the Meiji government recognized the need to allow chartered foreign ships to carry Japan's trade. At the same time, it understood that doing so at these new sites would introduce potential avenues of unwelcome ingress into Japanese trade. The special ports of export, therefore, bore two important restrictions. First, only exports could be accommodated at these sites; they were not allowed to handle any trade in imports. A second, related limitation forbade coastal trade and assessed fines of between 500 and 1,000 yen for violations.[45] The government designed these clauses to prevent foreigners from encroaching on Japanese commerce while under charter to carry special exports. Since this batch of special trading ports were specifically intended to promote Japan's export trade, government authorities were anxious to maintain narrow transactions and keep them in the hands of Japanese merchants.[46]

Daily arrival and departure notices published in the *Moji shinpō* reveal Japan's heavy reliance on foreign shipping and the high level of foreign demand for Chikuhō coal. Japan's regular *shasen* lines, most notably NYK and OSK, do account for many, but not all, of the steamships dropping anchor at Moji.[47] Both companies maintained operations at the Kanmon ports. NYK had a branch office in Shimonoseki and a smaller office in Moji. As an affiliate of Mitsubishi, which owned a growing share

45. *NZE*, 58.
46. Unfortunately, this had the side effect of creating a barrier against exports. In the case of Yokkaichi, the inability to import meant they did not conduct much trade at all for the first five years as a special port of export.
47. See Wray, *Mitsubishi and the N.Y.K.*, on NYK's extensive relationship with the Meiji government.

of Chikuhō coal mines, it also held coal storage sites on Moji's shores. OSK, by contrast, located its branch office in Moji. Aside from ships headed to Korea, which departed from Shimonoseki, the majority of the company's departures left from Moji.[48]

At this time, NYK was now Japan's foremost international carrier whereas OSK predominantly handled coastal cargo and passengers. Their routes through Moji reveal some of the ongoing limitations of Japan's shipping capacity even after the new developments of the mid-1880s helped ameliorate the situation. Japan's dependence is revealed by the numbers of foreign ships stopping at the country's ports and the routes dominated by Western vessels. But it is also clear in the fact that many Japanese-owned vessels were built and piloted by Westerners.

Nonetheless, Japan's shipping companies were increasing their fleets and routes in the 1890s and their regular stops at the special trading ports surely aimed at boosting the profitability of their runs. The *Moji shinpō*'s printed schedules for the month of January 1894 reveal that ninety-six OSK trips departed from Moji on twenty-five ships and NYK made thirty-eight trips on fifteen ships.[49] OSK only handled one over-seas route to Pusan (3 trips) and ten domestic routes (93 trips), some with daily service, whereas NYK ran six overseas routes (9 trips) and eleven domestic routes (29 trips).[50] By 1897, NYK had twelve scheduled routes through Moji, only two of which were domestic, running from Yokohama to Misumi and from Kobe to Otaru. Of the international routes, three traveled to China, and the others had final destinations in Europe, America, Australia, India, Taiwan, and the Philippines. Although most ran once a month, the Kobe-Kelung route, for example, went four times as often.[51]

48. By the turn of the century, OSK had built its own wharves, located only 250 yards from Mojikō Station, complete with a waiting room attended by "redcaps" to assist passengers with luggage and other needs as they made travel connections between ship and rail (Harada, *Ōsaka shōsen*, 63–65).

49. This month was selected for the completeness of its records and because it falls on the eve of the Sino-Japanese War. It is fairly representative of monthly statistics for all of 1893 and up to the start of the war in August 1894.

50. *Moji shinpō*, January 1894. Ships for OSK's route to Pusan left from Shimonoseki, not Moji.

51. *MKS*, 153–56.

In terms of each company's ships, all fifteen of the NYK ships were built in England or Scotland, mostly in mid-1880s, and ranged between approximately 700 and 3,500 gross tons.[52] Japan did not produce such large steamships until the early twentieth century. Westerners captained the nine largest of the fifteen ships, while the smaller vessels tended to have Japanese captains.[53] By contrast, the OSK ships were equipped primarily for coastal routes and were domestically built. They had smaller capacities, ranging from less than 200 to just over 700 gross tons. All twenty-five had Japanese captains.[54] NYK and OSK's Moji service for this month on these forty ships indicates, perhaps not surprisingly, that although Japanese companies' domestic routes were primarily in Japanese hands, their foreign routes continued to rely on Western assistance.

The degree to which Moji's early fortunes depended on the Western presence becomes clearer when looking at the full range of steamers stopping there. In 1893, the first year for which detailed local records are available, nearly 350 steamships entered Moji to carry export coal, averaging close to 30 per month.[55] The great majority of these ships—roughly 70 percent—were British. Half of the remainder were German, with a sprinkling from Norway, Austria, Holland, Russia, and China. Many, but certainly not all, of the foreign ships calling at Moji were relatively large, recently built (approximately 40% since 1890), and designed as ocean-going vessels. Japan possessed few such vessels at this time.[56] One

---

52. Kizu, *Nippon Yūsen senpaku*, 26–113.

53. The purchase of foreign steamships for commercial purposes preceded appropriate training for captains and crew (including engineers and navigators) and so initially skilled foreigners were hired to operate them. By 1887 all deck officers (including captains) of coastal vessels were Japanese and, in 1892, the first Japanese captain commanded an ocean-going ship (Chida and Davies, *Japanese Shipping*, 19–20).

54. Lloyd's Register of British and Foreign Shipping, *Lloyd's Register*.

55. *Moji shinpō*, January 1, 1894. This figure represents a significant increase over the 215 foreign steamships logged the year before, and is more than double the number recorded in 1891 when, just two years after opening, 116 foreign steamships dropped anchor at Moji (ibid., January 12, 1893). These numbers correspond closely to those found in *DNGBN* for the same years.

56. In fact, a number of the ships that called at Moji, such as the *Priam*, *Orestes*, *Myrmidon*, and *Glengyle* (all British), would later be purchased by Japanese firms or individuals.

of the largest ships to anchor at Moji was the British *Samoa,* at nearly 7,000 gross tons. It loaded an undetermined amount of coal during its ten-day stop en route to Hong Kong.[57]

All but a few ships that tried to load coal at Moji were able to do so. The few that left without it were generally hampered by either a shortage of coal or bureaucratic misunderstanding. The British ship *Kurrara,* for example, arrived during a temporary coal shortage and had to leave without receiving its intended supply. In another case, the Austrian ship *Melpomene* did not follow proper procedure in securing Ministry of Finance approval to take on coal and so had to continue on to Kobe without loading any.[58]

Of these ships, most were headed to the three major coal markets in East Asia. Hong Kong was the most common destination, followed by Shanghai and then Singapore, but some headed for other Chinese ports. Those that left Moji for European or American ports were primarily loading fuel coal for the long journey. Ports of origin other than Kobe include the treaty ports of Nagasaki, Yokohama, and Hakodate as well as Shanghai and Hong Kong. Some vessels solely made round trips from Shanghai or Hong Kong to Moji, and because shippers faced difficulties gathering an economically sufficient volume of freight at Japan's treaty ports, they actively sought return cargo at the special trading ports. Knowing that their export-only limitation was costing them business, Mojiites would later fight for the right to import foreign goods in the mid-1890s Open Ports Movement.

The high level of steamer activity at Moji required the support of a busy multitude of smaller vessels. In its harbor, Japanese-style ships (*wasen*) and wooden sailboats operated alongside ironclad steamers and traveled in the shadow of hulking warships. Ships at anchor amplified the congestion created by the through-movement of assorted foreign and domestic vessels. In addition to pilot boats plying the Kanmon Strait were ferries, lighters (*nibune*), row boats (*goheitabune*), steam launches (*kojōkisen*), and other small craft. These modest boats, many of which were owned and operated by small businesses, added up to thousands of vessels in

57. *KKS,* 474. This analysis is based on *Moji shinpō* statistics during 1893 (except for the months April to June, for which there are no copies of the paper). These nine months cover the activity of 233 foreign ships, or nearly three-quarters of the year's total.

58. *Moji shinpō,* August 19 and 29, 1893.

the waters immediately surrounding Moji. An 1897 estimate puts 500 or 600 of them just making round trips between Moji, Shimonoseki, and Wakamatsu; a full third of these were coal-carrying lighters running between Moji and Wakamatsu.[59] Many boats also traveled the short distance between Moji and ships in the offing to provide fresh water supplies, convey stevedores to load coal shipside, and conduct offshore trade.

All these figures provide important snapshots of Moji's harbor during its early years. Allowing foreign ships to serve the special trading ports was essential to their success. The majority of Moji's coal was carried to other East Asian ports by these vessels until the balance shifted to domestic ships in 1906.[60] Foreign ships were thus a regular feature of Moji's harbor and represent a fundamental part of the port city's character. The effectiveness of Moji's operations, however, did not depend solely on the shippers. When domestic and foreign vessels arrived at port, they required the support of local laborers, enterprises, and associations.

Coal Sales and Stevedores

The effective functioning of Japan's ports and port facilities had a direct bearing on the costs and profitability of the businesses that depended on steam transportation. Elite businessmen and manual laborers alike were essential to ensuring the smooth operation of these gateways. Because Moji developed rapidly to accommodate significant amounts of traffic, it also witnessed an influx of workers to help coal flow in and out of the port. As such, Moji comprised a new zone of national integration and modernization and provided much-needed employment for Japan's underclass, who now moved to the frontlines of Japan's East Asian trade. At the same time, the rapidity of the port's development, its population of mixed classes and backgrounds, as well as its multiple and sometimes

---

59. *MKS*, 150–51. Since Wakamatsu's harbor proved inadequate for handling large ocean-going vessels, this port concentrated on the domestic coal trade. Large amounts of coal from Chikuhō continued to be transported first to Wakamatsu by river. Smaller boats then hauled up to two-thirds of it eastward along the Kanmon Strait to Moji in order to supply foreign trade there. Despite continuing reliance on river transport, the shift from river to rail hurt Onga riverboat pilots as they lost work and had to turn to mining in order to survive (Sumiya, *Nihon sekitan sangyō bunseki*, 352–53; *Moji shinpō*, July 21, 1893).

60. Moji Shiyakusho, *Shize chōsa shiryō*; idem, *Moji-shi tōkei nenpō*.

vague jurisdictions, meant that Moji, like other special ports of export, also, as we will see, became a liminal site of contact and transgression.

Most of the town's businesses operated either directly for the coal and transportation industries or in support of them, including warehouses, inns and restaurants, ship repair facilities, customs, police, banking, communications (newspapers and telegraphs), and prostitution. Further, the port's own transportation systems provided vessels to attend ships at anchor, ferry passengers across the Kanmon Strait, and assist with loading coal. The smooth operation of all these services, especially those directly related to the selling and loading of coal, were vital to the success of the port as well as to the coal industry as a whole.

Exporting coal overseas from Moji in the 1890s was an involved process, one that required the aid of both Japanese coal sellers and shipping agents. A common scenario for advance direct export orders began when a foreign client, often a major foreign-owned East Asian shipping line such as Ocean Steamship or China Navigation, placed an order with a coal store in Moji, designating the amount of coal needed and a shipment date. After the client or buyer placed an order, the store would complete a number of steps to fill it: sending a sample to the client, determining the market price, inquiring about shipping fares, and hiring a steamship from a shipping wholesaler.[61] One of the parties would also apply to the Ministry of Finance for a license to charter a foreign ship and notify the Moji branch of Nagasaki Customs of the anticipated quantity of coal and final destination of the shipment. After the ship was in port and loading had started, the ship's captain approved the final tonnage to be taken on board and authorized the invoice. Prior to the ship's leaving port, the client, or client's agent, would pay a provisional price, up to 95 percent of the captain's invoice. Final payment was settled after the coal was unloaded at its port of destination and the quantity confirmed.[62]

Moji's coal sellers operated out of storefronts, many of them Western-style buildings, lined up alongside trading companies and banks near the

61. The *Moji shinpō*'s foreign shipping notices for 1893 generally indicate volumes and types of coal loaded for export, which were delivered to Moji from twenty-five named Chikuhō mines, and on occasion, from the Miike coal mine as well.

62. *MKS*, 111–12.

harbor.[63] Larger coal sellers had come to Moji starting around 1891, or within two years of Moji's designation as a special export port. Their numbers and handling capacities rose quickly, with the Sino-Japanese War boom contributing greatly to their growth. For example, in 1895, Moji had ten established coal stores, but by 1898, there were forty-one.[64] Moreover, in 1895 the Moji Coal Sellers Association (Moji sekitan shō kumiai) was organized. In addition to certifying its thirty-two members and having them clearly display nameplates in their store windows to demonstrate membership, this organization conducted examinations of a seller's coal upon request of the buyer.[65] The association struggled to eliminate ongoing problems by regulating quality. Articles 9 and 10 of the association's rules, for example, forbade falsifying coal types when buying or selling and also prohibited any transactions under phony names. Although providing poor-quality coal might turn a fast profit, ensuring consistently high quality was necessary for Japanese coal to earn and maintain good standing in overseas markets.[66]

After coal was purchased, it had to be shipped. Mitsubishi and Mitsui both functioned as shipping agents for export coal, often handling arrangements from offices in Kobe, Osaka, Tokyo, or Nagasaki. More locally, the Shimonoseki-based Uriu Hajime was one of the most prevalent names among shipping agents for Moji coal. On the surface, his company, Uriu Shōkai, appears to be a Japanese operation, but in reality, it served as a front for the Nagasaki-based British company Holme Ringer. As a foreign entity, Holme Ringer was not legally permitted to establish a branch outside the treaty ports, but through Uriu it found another way to open business in Kanmon.[67] Uriu Shōkai arranged charters via foreign shippers active in the region, often using Ocean Steamship, China Mutual, and China Navigation ships. These companies most

63. Moji Shiyakusho, *Minato to ayunda*, 5.

64. *MKS*, 100, 111, and 278.

65. Ibid., 97–100. The organization's members include many of the port's well-known businesses, including the Matsumoto-Yasukawa, Nakajima, and Asano stores, as well as the Mitsui, Mitsubishi, and Sumitomo agencies, and also some labor groups like the Iroha- and Isobe-gumi (the latter of which also had a store).

66. Ibid., 91–97. Ogino states that such measures did not stop the offense partly because they only fined the perpetrators ("Meiji chūki," 24).

67. Williams, *Story of Holme Ringer*, 47–49. Holme, Ringer & Co. still operates at the Port of Kitakyushu.

commonly made runs from Kobe to Hong Kong, but Uriu also arranged for many trips originating in Shanghai. The presence of a Japanese-fronted British company operating at Kanmon in the early 1890s, one doing business with companies owned by Western entities, reminds us that these international networks were still dominated by the Western powers.

Nonetheless, Japanese companies at Moji knew that providing well-regulated port facilities and services was crucial to doing business in a timely and cost-effective manner. The length of time that each ship spent in port reflected efficiency in customs processing, business transactions, and cargo handling. Most ships stopping at Moji in 1893 loaded at least 300 tons of coal, if not much more. Larger ships frequently took on between 1,000 and 2,000 tons of coal, and even smaller ships often loaded several hundred tons. Since twenty-five stevedores using the traditional method of manual hauling could typically load between 25 and 35 tons an hour, a crew of this size would finish loading a small cargo of 300 tons in approximately ten hours.[68] This was intensive labor requiring a sizable work force. A trade report written by British consul Chalmers, based at Shimonoseki, states that "in January, 1904, the Pacific mail steamship 'Siberia' made a trial call to test the coaling facilities of the port, with the result that 2,006 tons were put on board in 10 hours." Chalmers determined this to be an impressive result, although he indicates neither how many stevedores were used in this trial nor how typical such rapid loading may have been. Doing the math against the earlier estimate suggests that loading 200 tons per hour would have required between 150 and 200 stevedores. Tracking the stays of nearly half the foreign ships calling at Moji that year reveals that the great majority stayed in port only two nights or less.[69] Most ships, therefore, were able to receive their coal and quickly get on their way.

The stevedores who loaded Chikuhō coal onto the steamships were as important to the success of the port as the coal sellers and shipping agents.[70] In keeping with the diverse roots of Moji's boomtown

68. *KKS*, 451–52; Hayashi, *Kaikyō no onnatachi*, 46; PRO FO 262/918, 44.

69. Of the remainder, two stayed a lengthy eleven nights and the rest from three to nine nights (the reasons for the longer stays are not provided). The *Moji shinpō* only provides complete entry and exit information for roughly half the ships and these statistics are apparently not available elsewhere.

70. In 1893, close to half of Moji's resident population of nearly 10,000 consisted of stevedores (*MKS*, 119–20).

population, a majority of the port's laborers had migrated there from elsewhere, many coming from the Kansai region to the northeast along the Inland Sea. Although at this time many of Japan's coal mines used impoverished farmers and prison labor to extract this vital resource from the ground, those who labored on Moji's docks were also people on the margins of Japanese society who were often in desperate need of employment. Most of the stevedores were male, but as many as one in ten were girls and women, ranging in age from twelve to fifty.[71] They were divided into two kinds of toilers: the *okinakashi*, who worked more demanding jobs in the offing on lighters and steamships, and the *rikunakashi*, who worked on shore.[72] Women and children, regardless of which type of work they did, earned only 50 to 60 percent of a man's daily wage.[73]

Stevedores worked under one of eight contracting labor groups, or *gumi*, active in Moji by 1892 (by 1919 there were 22 of these organizations). These groups and the labor they provided were integral to the port's functioning. Some groups were headed by Moji's more prominent founding fathers. The Isobe-gumi's Isobe Matsuzō and the Jinen-gumi's Jinen Kinzō, for example, used their position as labor bosses to launch other enterprises. A native of Kobe, Jinen originally contracted with NYK to handle its cargo in 1891 and brought fifty stevedores with him. After successfully establishing his business, Kinzō's son Harujirō took over and turned it into one of two *chihō zaibatsu*.[74] Both the Jinen and Isobe families gained political and financial influence as labor contractors, landowners, shippers, and shipbuilders. Similarly, the head of the Muratagumi, who also came from Kobe, formed his own labor group when he first contracted to handle coal for Yasukawa Shōten. In order to

---

71. Hayashi, *Kaikyō no onnatachi*, 60.

72. MKS, 115.

73. Takeda, *Chikugo*, 25.

74. The other was headed by Ishida Heikichi, a Fukuoka native who was one of Moji's more prominent residents. He got his start operating roundtrip ferry services between Moji and Shimonoseki in 1889 and then helped coordinate the efforts of competing ferry owners to provide steam launch services between Moji and Shimonoseki at the rapid pace of one boat every ten minutes. Ishida's venture continued to best its rivals and in 1896, he established the Kanmon Steamship Company, which operated twenty-three ships within a year (*KKS*, 489; *MKS*, 151–52; *Moji shinpō*, August 26, 1893).

avoid competition and fighting among the eight groups, they joined together in 1896 to create the Moji Coal Stevedore Association.[75]

Loading coal was a highly labor-intensive process. After coal arrived at Moji either by rail or boat, the stevedores manually unloaded it and stacked it in mounds in designated coal storage piles, arranged according to coal seller, along the shore.[76] The coal would already have been processed at the mines prior to transport but might be blended at Moji to meet the energy requirements of the particular ships fueling there. A portion of the *rikunakashi* would work from the storage piles, filling bamboo baskets with coal. Others then carried the laden baskets, balanced on poles across their shoulders and up an elevated pier before emptying them into a waiting lighter.[77] After being loaded with 50 to 60 tons of coal, the lighter would head to the offing, about half a mile away, where it would draw alongside a waiting steamship.

Meanwhile, in preparation for loading the steamship, the *okinakashi* would hang a series of shelves by rope off both sides of the ship for balance and efficiency, creating an image likened to a Hinamatsuri doll display.[78] The number of shelves used depended on the height of the ship, ranging from three to twelve boards.[79] Stevedores would then line up on the hanging shelves to vertically haul baskets heavy with coal up from the lighter. A second group of *okinakashi*, often women, would remain in the lighter filling the baskets using special hoes (*irekuwa*) while yet another, smaller group of stevedores on the steamship's deck laterally moved the deposited coal to the ship's bunker hold. At the final stage in this sequence, a worker down in the hold leveled the coal as it accumulated, with the unfortunate side effect of becoming covered from head to toe in black dust. The *okinakashi*'s method was known as *tengutori*, which was later vividly referred to as a "human conveyor belt."[80] This loading

75. See Dōyashiki, *Kitakyūshū no jinbutsu*, 2, 20; Hayashi, *Kaikyō no onnatachi*, 23, 37; and *MKS*, 115.

76. *KKS*, 451–52. Moji's newspaper also reported almost daily on amounts of coal stored at the port (these figures did not, however, include Mitsubishi's supply).

77. Hayashi, *Kaikyō no onnatachi*, 64. An 1896 contract wage scale distinguished among thirteen different jobs performed by stevedores. Total wages were then calculated in terms of the weight of the coal a worker handled (*MKS*, 115).

78. *KKS*, 451.

79. Ibid., 452.

80. *Tengutori* is believed to be a corruption of the word *taguru* meaning "to haul or reel in." The term "human conveyor belt" was a loanword from English.

method started in Nagasaki, but it was perfected and made famous in Moji, eventually assuming the status of a Moji *meibutsu* (local specialty).[81] The sight of these experienced stevedores, working collectively, often while chanting, was considered a "grand spectacle" for Japanese and foreign visitors alike.[82] Despite the difficult life of its dockworkers, one gets a sense that citizens of the port city took pride in their honed efficiency at loading coal, which was, after all, their most important undertaking.

Foreign Contact and Transgression on the Waterfront

The port's heavy reliance on foreign steamships that routinely anchored at port for hours or days at a time as stevedores loaded them with coal meant that foreign captains and crews spent days or weeks in Moji's harbor. Although forbidden to come ashore without the requisite papers, and despite the government's intention to minimize the foreign presence, these outsiders nonetheless had professional and personal contact with Moji residents in a variety of ways.[83]

Although interactions occasionally took place in town or on the docks, more often than not they occurred on the water. Moji's deep-water anchorages offered an important site of regular communication between ordinary Japanese citizens and foreign visitors outside the treaty ports. Japanese stevedores, prostitutes, innkeepers, tugboat and ferry pilots, and salespeople were in regular contact with the personnel of the ships that provided their livelihood.

A prime opportunity for cross-cultural encounter came during the coal-loading process, when stevedores naturally came into contact with the crews of the steamships. Occasionally, these meetings were acrimonious, and stevedores fought with foreign crews over the job at hand. The day-to-day policing and regulation of such encounters fell to local law enforcement. In one incident, for example, two stevedores from the Isobe-gumi disagreed with a crewman of the British steamship *Menmuir* over the amount of coal being loaded. Mutually exchanged gestures escalated into a "serious quarrel" (*ōtachimawari*) that subsided only after Moji's police intervened.[84]

81. Hayashi, *Kaikyō no onnatachi*, 60–61.
82. Nakano, *Kaikyō taikan*, 67.
83. *NZE*, 58.
84. *Moji shinpō*, August 29, 1893.

Generally speaking, however, stevedores did not get into fights while loading the ships. Indeed, they were more likely to fight with one another or engage in drunken conduct when off-duty. But other segments of the local population also encountered trouble with foreign sailors and captains. For example, while selling goods to personnel on steamships from his small vessel in Moji's offing, a Shimonoseki salesman, Mr. Koga, had trouble with Captain Adams of the British steamship *Samoa*. The captain purchased three goats, drinking water, fish, beef, and vegetables from Mr. Koga for approximately 150 yen. According to Koga, Adams paid 1 percent less than the total he owed and then refused to pay the rest. When Koga protested, Adams literally shoved him out the door. As the angry salesman disembarked from the steamer, other officers aboard the *Samoa* reportedly told him that the captain had done the same thing repeatedly in Yokohama and Kobe. Koga lodged a complaint with the Moji police. Deciding that it was a civil rather than an international matter, the police called on the captain of the British *Ismailia*, also in port, to mediate. The captain was unable to settle the matter, and Adams steered the *Samoa* toward Hong Kong without having paid Mr. Koga any more money.[85]

In another case, Captain Johannsen of the German ship *Protos* went ashore at Moji and attempted to stay at the Ishida Ryokan (an inn owned by Ishida Heikichi) even though he did not have a permit to travel in Japan. Since a Western pilot from Kobe who accompanied him did possess the appropriate paperwork, Johannsen likely thought that he could sneak by without proper documents of his own. The clerk at the inn, however, upon discovering the ruse, asked them both to leave the premises. When the pair refused to comply, the clerk called the police. As the incident unfolded, Captain Johannsen became increasingly boisterous, disturbing the inn's other guests, until finally the police forced him to leave.[86] The *Moji shinpō* report of this encounter expressed surprise, perhaps laced with sarcasm, over Johannsen's contemptible behavior, which was less than that expected of someone from an "advanced country." More important than the behavior of such foreigners and their seeming lack of concern for playing by the rules, however, was the fact that the local police had little recourse in dealing with them over even relatively minor transgressions.

85. Ibid., November 1, 1893.
86. Ibid., December 29, 1893.

Local authorities appear to have had more power to intervene when illegal acts were committed by Japanese, most notably in cases of prostitution and smuggling. Port development and prostitution went hand in hand. The former castle town of Kokura, for example, opened brothels as part of the port's reconstruction project of the late 1870s, with the intention to use profits to help offset the cost of reconstruction and to attract more ships.[87] The early coal ports of Wakamatsu and Ashiya received brothel licenses at the start of 1875.[88] Although the town of Tanoura temporarily forbade prostitution in 1872, its brothels reopened in 1882 under revisions of Fukuoka Prefecture's prostitution laws.[89] In Moji, too, prostitution grew with the port. The town established the Uchihonmachi red-light district in 1893, deliberately locating it within easy walking distance of the docks. At the district's peak during the Russo-Japanese War, nearly 2,000 prostitutes operated in Moji, servicing over 90,000 customers, about 1,000 of whom were foreigners.[90] Stories about prostitutes dotted the pages of the *Moji shinpō*, whether they were falling in love, leaving the business, discussing working conditions, or stealing from customers.

In view of the presence of foreign ships at Moji, it is not surprising that the clientele for local prostitutes included foreigners, especially for offshore prostitution (*oki-uri shōgi*). This was a practice in which young women, usually in their late teens or twenties, would offer their services onboard ships. This type of prostitution was the special provenance of the Kanmon Strait, where women called at ships anchored in the offing at either Moji or Shimonoseki. Since these prostitutes, in going offshore, crossed jurisdictions and operated in liminal zones of contact, opportunities for illegal activity increased. Transgressions committed by the prostitutes themselves or by others could range from something minor, punishment for which was only a small fine, to a considerably more egregious act like smuggling women for the international sex trade operating in East and Southeast Asia.[91]

87. *KKS*, 24–27; Stanley, *Selling Women*, 193.

88. *KKSGS*, 14.

89. Chikuhō Sekitan Kōgyōshi Nenpyō Hensan Iinkai, *Chikuhō sekitan kōgyōshi nenpyō*, 1:81; *KKSGS*, 20.

90. Imamura, *Shashinshū*, 114; *Moji shinpō*, August 15, 1893.

91. *Moji shinpō*, September 12 and 27, 1893.

Women and girls from Kyushu's poor farming villages had been forced into prostitution since at least the 1870s. They were often smuggled aboard coal ships, first at Nagasaki and later at special trading ports like Karatsu, Kuchinotsu, and Moji.[92] As ports with international steamer traffic, the special trading ports became main centers where women would be clandestinely taken aboard ships in the offing. Hidden in storerooms, these women would emerge only after reaching their destination, usually at one of the three major entrepôts of Singapore, Hong Kong, or Shanghai.[93]

The *Moji shinpō* reported cases of local infractions as well as those with an international dimension. In one fairly straightforward case, three women (ages eighteen to twenty-two) who worked at a Moji restaurant were arrested for selling sex on the British steamship *Sainan*. Their boss at the restaurant was also arrested for having served as the mediator in this arrangement and for engaging in illegal prostitution on the premises of his otherwise legitimate business.[94] In another case, six prostitutes boarded the British steamship *Kintuck* one evening at Shimonoseki. A return ferry reportedly failed to pick them up at the designated time. When they were found early the next morning in Kobe, they claimed that they had been unable to disembark before the ship weighed anchor.[95] The article does not indicate whether there was any more to the story but, given the regularity with which women were smuggled through the port, it is likely that the six intentionally traveled to Kobe, perhaps with yet another destination in mind.

A more obvious case of trafficking in women occurred on September 17, 1893, when the Moji customs police raided the British steamship *Benlawers* while it sat at anchor to load coal. Onboard they found six kidnapped women, ages eighteen to twenty, from Nagasaki, Yamaguchi, and Shimane Prefectures. Police immediately arrested Shida Hirosaburō, a twenty-six-year-old from the city of Nagasaki. Shida had up to six other accomplices—four from Kobe, as well as his twenty-two-year-old mistress and a fifty-six-year-old man from Yamaguchi Prefecture—in taking these women. Apparently, the traffickers had paid a British crewman

92. Mihalopoulos, *Sex in Japan's Globalization*, 20–25; Ng, "Making of a Japanese Community," 119–21.

93. Shimizu and Hirakawa, *Japan and Singapore*, 30.

94. *Moji shinpō*, November 7, 1893.

95. Ibid., January 24, 1893.

185 yen for each woman that he allowed onboard for passage to Hong Kong, the ship's next destination.[96]

In addition to the cases of prostitution and the illegal trafficking of people recorded in the *Moji shinpō*, Nagasaki Customs logged a number of times when Japanese individuals smuggled import and export goods. During the last decade of the nineteenth century, the customs house recorded several instances in the treaty port of Nagasaki and at the special trading ports under its jurisdiction (Izuhara, Moji, Hakata, Karatsu, Kuchinotsu, Sasuna, and Naha). During this period, the number of annual cases reported was fairly small, between five and twenty-eight, perhaps reflecting the difficulty of catching suspected perpetrators. The majority of infractions occurred at Nagasaki and Moji, the busiest of the seven ports. The import and export goods confiscated by customs officers were mostly foodstuffs, including sake, white rice, soybeans, wheat, fish (the largest haul contained 7,500), sugar, vegetables, and Korean ginseng. Other seized cargo included tobacco, coal, and seven head of cattle.[97]

Together, these stories and statistics document that Japanese law enforcement at both the local and national level struggled to maintain order in the ports. Beyond cases that involved just a few individuals, there were also those that turned into major international incidents. Such events highlight the limits of Japan's control over its waterways as the country's stakes in a complex system of international trade grew and of its ability to find recourse in international law under the unequal treaties when trouble arose.

A Question of Maritime Sovereignty: "Who Says There Is No Inland Sea?"

Collisions between ships at harbor and in the sea lanes were quite common.[98] The high volume of traffic and disparity in the types of ships in use (size, power, level of mechanization, and building materials) contributed to the chaos of busy ports and waterways. The possibility of

96. Ibid., September 17, 1893.
97. *NZE*, 229–45.
98. The quotation "Who says there is no Inland Sea?" comes from the title of a newspaper article covering the legal proceedings (*Moji shinpō*, November 14, 1893).

accidents rose when ships operated at excessive speed or at night when visibility was poor.[99] In cases of collision, crews might be courteous to each other, as when a German steamer rescued twelve Japanese shipwreck victims. But there were also cases of indifference. One steamer did not even stop after it struck a smaller boat in the Kanmon Strait.[100] Small incidents like these happened frequently at the special trading ports. But problems could also take place farther from shore in the crowded maritime zones that served as throughways between East Asia's treaty ports. One such incident captured newspaper headlines around the country, and Moji's citizens paid close attention. The collision of two ships in the Inland Sea led to a years-long court battle between the British and the Japanese over questions of judicial and territorial jurisdiction, the results of which could have ramifications for everyone involved in Japan's maritime enterprises.

In late December 1892, the *Ravenna*, a British merchant ship with twenty-three passengers traveling between the treaty ports of Kobe and Yokohama, accidentally collided with the *Chishima*, a brand new, uninsured, Japanese warship making its maiden voyage home from England, where it had been built on commission for Japan. The warship was sunk, killing seventy of its crew. The Japanese government, listing the emperor as owner of the *Chishima*, sued the *Ravenna*'s owner, the P&O, for 850,000 yen in damages and compensation to the families of the deceased.[101] Under the terms of the Anglo-Japanese Treaty of Amity and Commerce (1858), which granted extraterritoriality to Britain, the case went to the British Court located in Yokohama.

The *Chishima-Ravenna* case raised an important question of Japan's territorial integrity: namely, whether the Inland Sea belonged to Japan or comprised part of the international high seas. This was a significant question on the eve of treaty revision. The controversy arose when the P&O filed a 100,000-yen counterclaim against the Japanese emperor for damages sustained by the *Ravenna* in the collision. The Japanese inadvertently raised the issue of territoriality when arguing that the counterclaim should be denied since the accident had taken place in Japan's

99. See, for example, *Moji shinpō*, January 15 and November 5, 1893.

100. Ibid., March 3 and September 1, 1893.

101. Japan's Naval Court and the Court at Nagasaki handled decisions about the responsibility of both captains. The *Ravenna*'s pilot, Mr. Kitano (his first name is not given), was found guilty of involuntary manslaughter and fined 200 yen. The captain of the *Chishima*, who was also Japanese, was acquitted.

territorial waters and thus should be heard in Japanese, not British, courts.[102] The Court's Judge Robert Anderson Mowat agreed, denying P&O the right to sue for damages in his court.[103]

The debate intensified when the counterclaim went to Shanghai on appeal. Her Britannic Majesty's Supreme Court for China and Japan allowed the appeal based on Chief Justice N.J. Hannen's view that the collision took place not in Japanese waters but on "the highway of nations," which in his opinion meant that "it occurred at a spot which . . . must be considered as the high seas."[104] Hannen's ruling brought the status of the Inland Sea into heated debate.

Back in Tokyo, Lower House representative Hatoyama Kazuo vehemently refuted two arguments supporting the Shanghai Court's position that the collision site did not constitute Japanese territorial waters. The first argument held that the Inland Sea, lying directly on navigation routes for ships traveling between China's eastern coast and the West Coast of the United States, had been used as a "highway of nations" since the signing of the unequal treaties in the 1850s. Hatoyama declared this argument "mistaken in its facts," claiming it a "falsehood" to say that the Inland Sea had become a public passage between China and the United States. Were it not for calling at treaty ports, he insisted, all ships could use the open sea rather than the Inland Sea to reach the United States from Shanghai and Hong Kong.

Looking at the situation according to international law, which holds that 3 miles from shore is within the territorial jurisdiction of any given country, or "the distance a cannonball can reach from land," the British Foreign Office librarian, Sir Edward Hertslet, found the Inland Sea to be Japan's territorial waters since the strait leading into it is less than 6 miles wide.[105] But he found this neither precluded it from being used as a "highway of nations" nor ensured that all portions of this body of water, including where the accident occurred (just about 3 miles off Shikoku), were international waters.[106]

102. *Moji shinpō*, November 15, 1893.
103. Marston, "British Extra-Territorial Jurisdiction," 228.
104. Chief Justice N.J. Hannen, quoted in Marston, "British Extra-Territorial Jurisdiction," 231.
105. Herstlet, quoted in ibid., 234. The *Moji shinpō* cites a Japanese proclamation of August 29, 1870, that declared foreign seas lie approximately 3 *ri* (1 *ri* is 2.44 miles) from shore (November 14, 1893).
106. Marston, "British Extra-Territorial Jurisdiction," 233.

The Foreign Office legal adviser, W.E. Davidson, concurred with Herstlet. Although foreigners had treated the Inland Sea as a highway, he stated, Japan "has never consented to such use and is consequently not estopped [sic] from now protesting against it when claimed as a matter of right." While agreeing that Japan was able to freely protest use of this passage, Davidson also managed to leave open the question of Japan's territorial right to the Inland Sea. The fact that Japan "under the pressure of superior force . . . has permitted vessels to pass on sufferance cannot be treated as an abandonment by Japan of the right to treat the sea as an inland sea, *if that right otherwise exists.*"[107] Davidson's comments also raised doubts over how willing a participant in international law Japan was as a country with compromised sovereignty.

The second, related argument that Hatoyama made similarly looked to precedent by bringing up the Shimonoseki Incident. When Western ships attempted to pass through the Inland Sea by way of the Strait of Shimonoseki in 1863, forces from Chōshū domain, in protest against the foreign presence and the opening of treaty ports, fired upon them and prevented access to the strait. After a joint foreign fleet attacked Chōshū and reopened the waterway, the Tokugawa shogunate signed the Convention of October 22, 1864, at Yokohama, agreeing to settle the matter by paying an indemnity of $3 million. The Shanghai Court's view was that Japan paid the indemnity because it had obstructed use of the Inland Sea, thereby conceding that it was indeed a public passageway.

In considering the Shimonoseki Incident, Hatoyama asserted that the court "very clearly twisted the historical meaning." Japan did not pay the indemnity on the grounds that it was illegal to obstruct others' rights of passage to the Inland Sea; to suggest otherwise was to intimate Japanese "ignorance."[108] Payment of the indemnity meant only that Japan, under threat of military force, had chosen the lesser of two evils: a fine or the opening of another treaty port.

This debate over the Inland Sea's status during the *Chishima-Ravenna* case brings into focus the maritime context of informal empire. The Ansei Treaties regulated only land-based interactions; they did not touch upon those that transpired on the water. The treaties specified that foreign subjects were allowed to move freely on land for a distance of 24.4

107. Quoted in ibid., 235. Italics added.
108. *Moji shinpō,* November 16, 1893.

miles (10 *ri*) in any direction from an open port unless otherwise indicated.[109] But as far as restrictions on travel by water were concerned, the treaties stated only that harbor regulations were to be mutually arranged at each site. Maritime space as a site of interaction was indeterminate, and the original treaties did not explicitly address Britain's underlying consideration in the Inland Sea debate: namely, free access to the treaty ports.

Even though the ability to navigate along the Inland Sea made travel among all five treaty ports considerably easier, only Kobe lies directly on that waterway. According to Sir Thomas Barclay, a member of the Institut de Droit International, who advised the Japanese government during the *Chishima* case, foreign vessels had right of access to Kobe via the Inland Sea as long as Kobe was a treaty port, "and to this extent only the Inland Sea can be properly described as a Highway of nations." Otherwise, he averred, the Inland Sea "is under the law of Japan."[110]

Throughout these discussions, the treaty ports, the Inland Sea passage, and rights to Japan's national waterways were integrally connected. The special trading ports also became part of this system. Moji's development and the rapid expansion of Japan's coal industry both depended on the British empire in Asia, and both profited from foreign ships traveling between the continent and Japan's eastern treaty ports by way of the Inland Sea. After all, the vast majority of foreign ships arriving at Moji stopped there when traveling between Kobe and Hong Kong.

Moreover, the cooperation of business entities that operated out of treaty ports and special trading ports were predicated on good diplomatic relationships. In transmarine East Asia, there were always multinational perspectives to consider, and balancing those interests was always tricky. A *Moji shinpō* article published on November 21, 1893, provides an example of the multipolar nature of international relations in the region. The article in question framed the *Chishima* Incident as a "good opportunity" for bettering Russo-Japanese relations. Private correspondence from Japanese living in Vladivostok revealed that these overseas residents were "secretly pleased" by the way that Japan was standing up to Great Britain. Since proceedings began, Russians had been treating them "all the more kindly" and commiserating with them about "Britain's insatiable greed." Further, they had offered the Japanese residents support

109. Yunesko Higashi Ajia Bunka Kenkyū Sentā, "Treaty of Peace."
110. Quoted in Marston, "British Extra-Territorial Jurisdiction," 236.

in the face of both British injustice and what were apparently "sneering" articles in Yokohama's English-language newspapers about how the Japanese press was covering the case.[111] This informal and rhetorical support would have been welcome at a time when the case and its treatment only fueled the Japanese desire for treaty revision.

At the same time, however, the Japanese press clearly indicated that they were not willing to relinquish any territory beyond that already lost to extraterritorial provisions. An article published just days prior to Hatoyama's comments went beyond international law in declaring the Inland Sea a part of Japan not simply on the basis of long-standing practice and political documentation but by *waga shinsei naru shuken* (divine sovereignty).[112] Such a view attempted to move the issue outside the reach of international law. This invocation of an inherent sovereignty to legitimize a claim to the Inland Sea was in keeping with broader efforts to demarcate Japan's borders in this period of nation-building, a project designed at once to resist imperialist encroachment and to lay claim to new territory.

In settling the *Chishima* Incident, neither side invoked international law to formalize its position nor did either side have to relinquish its views. The British Judicial Committee of the Privy Council in London that reviewed the case set aside the Inland Sea dispute, ruling that the P&O's counterclaim would exceed British treaty rights. In September 1895, nearly three years after the accident, the Japanese government accepted an offer of just 90,000 yen, a fraction of the original claim of 800,000 yen, and settled out of court.[113] The British court made no final decision on the territorial status of the Inland Sea and did not pursue the matter further. Even though the Japanese government maintained that the Inland Sea was unequivocally part of Japan, it took no further steps to formalize this position in international law.[114] Fighting for a higher settlement at this point was not in the country's best interests. Even though the final verdict in the *Chishima* case was reached after Japan signed a

111. *Moji shinpō*, November 21, 1893.
112. Ibid., November 14, 1893.
113. This amount is from Chang, "The Chishima Case," 604.
114. Marston, "British Extra-Territorial Jurisdiction," 237–40. Marston writes that as late as the 1970s, international law did not clearly define internal waters and the Japanese government continued to declare the Inland Sea territorial waters based on historic precedent.

new treaty with Great Britain, it would not go into effect until 1899. Balancing the need to maintain territorial integrity with the long-standing commitment to end the unequal treaties remained a central concern.[115]

Conclusion

The *Chishima* case reveals two important things about Japan's position in the mid-1890s on the eve of treaty revision. First, Japan's sovereignty was still precarious. This case targeted waters that were not otherwise endangered, highlighting the ongoing threat to Japan's independence, even decades after the Shimonoseki Incident. Moreover, East Asia involved an increasingly complex set of international relations with direct bearing on Japan's security. Second, Japan's navy continued to rely heavily on the Western powers for its warships. Even as it continued to fight for its relevance and value in competition with the army, the Japanese navy had to purchase its capital ships, at considerable cost, from Western countries, and the *Chishima* was not the first that failed to make it home.[116]

Even at the end of the century, Japan continued to negotiate the costs and benefits of being a participant in commercial and military activities defined by the environment of informal imperialism that still reigned in East Asia. The paradox of informal imperialism permeates the relationships and events discussed in this chapter. Certainly, Japan faced military dangers. At a disadvantage when it began trading in the world economy, Japan had weak naval and commercial fleets, requiring them to share resources to carry out their respective missions. For the first three decades of the treaty port era, Japan remained in a precarious position with limited control over its waterways and coastline. Moreover, it had to contend with the ongoing issue of legal, and social, subordination to the Western powers.

Yet Japan's integration into the nineteenth century world order as a semisovereign state carried advantages as well. Throughout the treaty port era, the Japanese made effective use of the Western presence in Asia,

---

115. Chang also makes this point and further indicates that incurring even greater costs than they already had in investigating and trying the case was not a desirable option ("The Chishima Case," 609–10).

116. Ibid., 595.

especially as seen in the reliance on foreign shipping at Moji. By the 1880s, the turn toward stability at home reaped significant changes. Opening the special ports of export created new sites of national integration and global encounters, especially at ports of significant transactions like Moji. These encounters represent legal activities as well as illegal ones, such as smuggling goods and women, that often crossed national boundaries. At the same time, the government focused new attention on maritime districting and security, channeling authority to local sites for help in managing the arrival of foreign vessels. These moves came as Japan continued its efforts to remove the unequal treaties while securing its influence in the region.

Even as the *Chishima* case was being tried, Japan at last gained the treaty revision that it had sought for so long. At the same time, it tested its position in East Asia, as well as its military and diplomatic power, by going to war against China. With Japan's victory in 1895, the world of East Asian informal imperialism shifted decisively. Taking Taiwan as its first formal colony raised Japan's international standing to that of a formal empire at the same time that its defense perimeter expanded. The war not only tested the mettle of its ground and naval forces but also put Japan's system of ports to new use. The country's wartime imperial headquarters were located in Hiroshima, with nearby Ujina serving as the main port of operations for the war effort. This arrangement turned the Inland Sea into a vital military passage, placing Moji directly on the main sea route to the warfront on the continent.

PART III

Moji in the Empire

FIVE

The Sino-Japanese War Comes Home

The Sino-Japanese War of 1894–95 brought prosperity and the beginnings of global recognition to the port of Moji. Mojiites followed this conflict—from the dispatch of troops to Korea in early June to the signing of the peace treaty the following April—with a keen awareness of the ways in which events on the continent directly affected the port city's day-to-day operations. As hostilities escalated, Moji immediately began to function in support of the war effort, especially as an anchorage and distribution site for warships and *goyōsen* (ships requisitioned for military transport and supply) making roundtrips to Korea and China. The militarization of the port disrupted its ongoing function as a special port of export only temporarily; before long, local self-interest converged with rising nationalism as Moji's identity became integrally tied to Japan's growing military and commercial project in Asia.

The months leading up to the war were a period of anticipation and uncertainty for the Japanese government and ordinary citizens alike. In addition to a new, final round of treaty revision negotiations with Great Britain, the intensification of the Tonghak Rebellion in Korea led China and Japan to send troops to the peninsula at the beginning of June. These two distinct processes—treaty revision and escalating tension between China and Japan—were joined through the changing geopolitics of informal imperialism in the region, and both resulted in decisions that, coming just two weeks apart, had decisive consequences for East Asia and its balance of power.[1] After nearly forty years under the unequal treaties, the Meiji oligarchs finally completed the treaty revision that had been so elusive, signing the Anglo-Japanese Treaty of Commerce and Navigation on July 16, 1894. On August 1, Japan formally declared war against China. The timing does not appear to be incidental.

Although Japan's return to full sovereignty already appeared more certain by mid-1894 than it had been at any time in the preceding half-century, the general threat to East Asian security was simultaneously rising. China and Japan's decade-old rivalry over which gained influence in a turbulent Korea was accelerating at the same time that Russia's involvement was also growing. In particular, the launch of construction on the Trans-Siberian Railway in 1891 signaled that the Russian empire planned to strengthen its foothold in the region. This step concerned all parties with a stake in East Asian stability. In addition to heightening local rivalries, the Russian initiative also brought long-standing tensions between Russia and Great Britain eastward, which accelerated the latter's interest in reinstating Japan's sovereignty.[2] These "reconfigurations of interempire competitions" also presented Japan with a new opportunity to take charge of its fate.[3]

The citizens of Moji had a front-row seat to the larger events and activities that accompanied this moment. Their willing, often eager, participation in the war effort sprang largely from concern over the port city's own prosperity, which developed in tandem with a rising sense of service to the nation.[4] Moji's promoters believed in the promise of the port city and its future, which was being rhetorically and materially linked to treaty revision, military initiatives, and a continuing dependence on

1. Hiyama Yukio argues that this war destabilized East Asian relations in the long run, calling it the start of the "fifty-year war" with China ("Nisshin sensō no rekishiteki ichi," 16).

2. Nish, *The Anglo-Japanese Alliance*, 10. Nish also points to Britain's concern over opposition to the treaties within Japan that could gain momentum and make trade more difficult if they did not sign revisions. See also Paine, *Sino-Japanese War*, 100.

3. Burbank and Cooper, *Empires in World History*, 306. In this quotation they are arguing, in effect, that the existence of informal imperialism depends on competition among empires and can also be eliminated or turned to formal empire by such competition.

4. On the interconnected nature of local identity and rising nationalism during the Russo-Japanese War, see Shimazu, *Japanese Society at War*.

access to treaty ports throughout East Asia.[5] These linkages are especially clear in relation to the port's wartime coal trade, its media reportage on the conflict, and the ways in which the war—and its spoils—came back home to Moji.

War, Coal, and Transport

By the second week of June 1894, Moji and its surrounding areas had already become caught up in early preparations for war. Local recruits reported for inspection at centers like Shimonoseki and Fukuoka before taking up positions as sailors, stokers, cooks, and torpedo hands. Senior officials at the Kokura Battalion headquarters met to prepare for the impending conflict. Rice prices rose as the Tonghak Rebellion interfered with Japanese imports from Korea and at least twenty police officers were dispatched to protect Japanese residents living in Korean treaty ports.[6]

Since commercial shipping firms owned the tonnage needed for wartime transport, they curtailed their regular routes, or hired foreign ships to cover them, while the government refitted their steamships: occasionally as torpedo boats or armed intelligence ships but most often for the transport of troops, horses, and supplies.[7] Suddenly, many of the ships arriving at Moji were warships and *goyōsen* rather than commercially operated steamers. Nearly two months before the war, two OSK steamships were assigned to conduct transport between Moji and Korea, immediately linking the port to the center of action just across the Korea Strait.[8] As growing numbers of commercial ships were diverted from regular service, without sufficient provision for replacement

5. As Katherine G. Morrissey says about the people of the Pacific Northwest's Inland Empire, "what . . . shaped their regional identity was not so much a consensus of opinion; it was not that everyone agreed. Rather they held in common ways of thinking, a stake in meanings associated with their place, and a vision of the future" (*Mental Territories*, 11).

6. *Moji shinpō*, June 6–9, 1894.

7. Nippon Yūsen Kabushiki Kaisha, *Voyage of a Century*, 31. A total of 136 ships were requisitioned during the war, 66 of which belonged to NYK (Kizu, *Nippon Yūsen senpaku*, 65).

8. *Moji shinpō*, June 9, 1894.

vessels, Japan's flow of goods began to come to a halt, and coal shortages became prevalent at home and across transmarine East Asia.[9]

The shortage of vessels intensified, forcing the NYK to end its run between Yokohama and the special trading port of Otaru. The absence of this service prevented Hokkaido coal from reaching its regular destinations, increasing demand for already taxed supplies of Kyushu coal. Factory owners and manufacturers in Kyoto, Osaka, and Tokyo reported insufficiencies, sparking a coal panic at home.[10] Japanese coal was hard to acquire in China as well, leading to greater purchases of Cardiff coal for military use. Ongoing shortages at Shanghai left at least five Chinese warships stranded at port, unable to answer orders to set sail for Korea.[11]

Labor shortages in Moji and Chikuhō were also reported as more stevedores and miners were needed to handle suddenly high demand. Large numbers of applicants came to Kanmon in the hope of being hired as laborers. Meanwhile, Chikuhō's previous troubles with reckless mining resurfaced as "extreme abuses" of illegal, haphazard mining in areas outside the *shakku* concession system grew, and new coal sellers petitioned to set up shop in Moji. The Mitsui group planned to buy up any available coalfields in Chikuhō.[12]

The shortages of transportation and labor, concerns over coal supplies, and higher than usual demand—which at this early stage was largely a result of stockpiling by the Army and Navy ministries, naval bases, and public railroads—led to a general state of agitated buying and soaring prices. The panic had widespread effects, as seen when a British warship bought up all remaining coal at Nagasaki one day in mid-June.[13] For some, however, the heavy demand was a boon, leading to exceptionally large profits for Moji's coal sellers and an enhanced profile for the port. Editors at the *Moji shinpō* marveled when just three days of coal sales topped 17,000 tons. For them, this "giant total" was a first and served to confirm the centrality of Moji as a coal market, one that now seemed

9. Insufficiencies continued despite attempts to offset them, such as when NYK purchased six extra ships from overseas to help (ibid., June 12, 1894).

10. Ibid., June 12–15 and 28, 1894.

11. Ibid., June 29–30, 1894. The Chinese also increased production at the Kaiping colliery (ibid., August 1, 1894).

12. Ibid., June 21–27 and July 1, 1894. See also *KKSS SK*, 1:87–88.

13. *Moji shinpō*, June 14–20, 1894.

certain to become well known at home and abroad.[14] Similarly, sales were brisk at the special trading port of Karatsu, where coal miners and merchants, along with restaurateurs catering to shippers loading at port, soaked up the profits.[15]

By mid-July, however, this heady run on coal was replaced with new realities and worsening business conditions. A sharp downturn in sales meant that roughly half of Moji's 4,000 stevedores no longer had enough to do.[16] As war looked increasingly likely, Japanese coal mine owners and sellers recognized the need to temper desires for short-term profits with a responsibility to protect the country's coal supply and keep it out of enemy hands.[17] Mitsui Bussan stopped selling coal to Chinese buyers at its various branch offices and dismissed all Chinese workers from its ships. Members of the CSKK and other coal wholesalers agreed that they would not sign new contracts with Chinese nationals.[18] Such measures, however, remained insufficient since coal could pass to China through foreign or even Japanese individuals. And putting the country before personal gain did not appeal to everyone. In one scandal, two Nagasaki locals plotted to secretly transfer nearly 1,000 tons of coal to a Chinese man in the foreign settlement who managed to ship it out to Shanghai.[19] Even after the government banned all overseas coal exports, problems with illegal sales remained, including transactions taking place on board vessels in Moji's offing.[20]

The sudden reversal from unusually strong sales to safeguarding the coal supply augured Moji's reconfiguration as a wartime port geared toward government service. Profits thereafter followed the vicissitudes of the war. Certainly, the city's fortunes were tied to the contraction and expansion of overseas export markets and purchases of coal by the Japanese military. But they also followed the movement of the country's military convoys, which anchored at Moji en route to the continent from

14. Ibid., June 23, 1894.

15. Ibid., July 7, 1894.

16. Ibid., July 10, 1894.

17. The same logic applied to rice exports and the need to reserve sufficient supplies of the grain to feed Japan's military personnel (ibid., July 21 and September 4, 1894).

18. Ibid., June 30 and July 22–24, 1894.

19. Ibid., July 1 and July 8, 1894.

20. Ibid., August 22, 1894.

the hastily erected Imperial Military Headquarters (Dai Hon'ei) and its naval base at Ujina.

The anticipated declaration of war came on August 1 leading to a dramatic rush of activity at Moji, which saw an "unceasing arrival of ships" as the country mobilized its sailors, soldiers, and weapons. When large vessels dropped anchor, smaller launches made trips to collect supplies from shore, bringing a significant amount of commerce to local businesses. The *Moji shinpō* described the sounds of whinnying war horses and the bustle of restaurants, ice shops, and candy stores. Crowded inns had no rooms left to rent, and shopkeepers handled the heavy flow of customers with smiles on their faces.[21] This was the first in a series of business surges at the port that came as Japan's military transported troops and supplies in advance of major battles.[22]

The rhythm of war became Moji's rhythm. Again in October, as the military pushed into the Liaodong Peninsula ahead of brutally taking Port Arthur, Moji hummed with life. Restaurants doubled the number of regular patrons while sake merchants, dry-goods dealers, and haberdasheries took in unusual profits.[23] Once more, in January 1895, during the lead-up to the major offensive at Weihaiwei, a "grand spectacle" appeared along Moji's waterfront. The newspaper described the scene: "Yesterday, from morning to evening, [nineteen of] our *goyōsen* arrived from the east and gathered at Moji . . . all with flags flying high on their masts. . . . Several of their commissariat steam launches made continual trips to shore and back, offering a view that makes Moji's wide harbor seem narrow." A similar level of commotion ensued on shore, where military police made their rounds as 2,000 extra laborers hauled cargo that was "piled everywhere" on the streets of Kaigan-dōri and Sanbashi-dōri. When each ship started its engines to leave port, a round of fireworks acknowledged its departure.[24]

These battles may have been fought in distant locations, but the war comprised a fundamental part of Moji's daily affairs. The port's role in supplying and loading coal on government ships was essentially a

21. Ibid., August 4, 1894.

22. Roughly 240,000 Japanese were mobilized for the war and about 174,000 of these "were employed on the battlefield." All troops heading to the continent left from Hiroshima Prefecture (Lone, *Japan's First Modern War*, 52–53).

23. *Moji shinpō*, October 13, 1894.

24. Ibid., January 12, 1895.

correlative function of the special trading port. The war proved at once beneficial and disruptive to commercial operations, and local businesses remained concerned about their own bottom lines. Local groups generated quantitative reports assessing the short-term impact of the war on coal markets as well as more speculative reports about prospects for coal sellers over the next year or two. News of large-scale troop departures was punctuated by regular updates on the ever-changing situation in overseas coal markets, especially in Hong Kong and Shanghai, which sat so close to the theaters of war. Coal prices and supplies at home, with regard to Chikuhō and Moji in particular, were followed intently. Worries over the long-term effects of the wartime ban mounted as piles of stored coal rose higher and higher.[25]

Coal industry leaders in the three Kyushu prefectures of Fukuoka, Nagasaki, and Saga petitioned the central authorities to lift the ban on coal exports. Businessman Yasukawa Keiichirō traveled to Tokyo to represent the industry in the halls of power. The Ministry of Finance, in discussion with the Home Ministry, decided that banning coal exports harmed Japan's economy more than it helped in the war against China. The lack of Japanese coal in East Asian markets meant that the British were importing Australian coal to China instead, thus eliminating the strides that the prewar Japanese coal industry had made, without keeping fuel out of Chinese hands. The ministers rescinded the ban for these three prefectures, allowing export from the top mines and coalfields at Takashima, Miike, and Chikuhō. Local coal dealers resumed work with renewed optimism for their prospects.[26] Regardless of who was buying, coal remained Moji's life blood and had to keep flowing. The circulation of information about the coal industry and the war itself also became vital to the port's operations at this time.

"Unrivaled" War Reportage

Newspapers comprised one industry that did exceptionally well throughout the war. Nationwide, editors were just starting to allow reporters the freedom to pursue their own leads, a development that coincided with readers' growing fascination with and demand for first-hand information

25. Ibid., September 4 and November 22, 1894.
26. *KKSS SK*, 1:87–88; *Moji shinpō*, October 21–29, 1894.

about the fighting. The stationing of overseas correspondents was a relatively new phenomenon that came of age with the Sino-Japanese War. During the nearly eight months of combat, a total of 66 newspapers sent 114 correspondents, in addition to artists and photographers, to the continent and to the Imperial Military Headquarters in Hiroshima.[27]

As the war remade the landscape of Japan's news, in both content and coverage, Moji correspondents found themselves literally on the frontlines. By dispatching correspondents to battle sites abroad and by interviewing passengers returning home from the continent, the *Moji shinpō* kept readers continuously engaged with the war effort and its impact on the port. Like many newspapers around the country, the *Moji shinpō* focused much of its coverage from June 1894 to April 1895 on news concerning the conflict. But this local daily also chronicled the state of East Asian transportation and coal markets, connecting each to the port's pivotal role as a wartime transportation hub and fueling station. The newspaper's commitment to a pioneering style of reportage continued unabated throughout the conflict and drew an unprecedented number of readers.

In keeping with its interest in building a strong paper and informing its audience, the *Moji shinpō* sent its first overseas correspondent, Kawata Masazō, to Korea even before war had been declared. He was dispatched just days after Japanese troops took Korea's King Kojong hostage in a radical move designed to force reforms and sever its formal ties with China.[28] Kawata was a native of Kiku County and a well-traveled "adventurer," whose lived experience provided exciting tales of bravado if not the qualifications to interpret military operations and events in Asia for the reading public.[29] As a young naval recruit stationed in Korea, Kawata had participated in battles supporting Kim Ok-kyun's 1884 Kapsin coup attempt in Seoul. After leaving the navy, he had worked in the Ogasawara Islands manufacturing salt under businessman Tanaka Tsurukichi. While there, he befriended Kim, who was exiled in Japan.[30] Next, after spending time aboard a whaling vessel in

27. Huffman, *Creating a Public*, 197, 208.

28. Paine, *Sino-Japanese War*, 121–22.

29. *Moji shinpō*, June 27, 1894.

30. Kim Ok-kyun was assassinated in Shanghai in March 1894 after having been lured there under false pretenses. Despite Japanese requests to take custody of Kim's remains, the Chinese government delivered it instead to Korea, where it was

the Arctic and visiting the United States, Kawata gained military experience in 1891 as a soldier in Chile's revolutionary army, fighting for that country's freedom "amidst a shower of bullets."[31]

Just months after returning home to northern Kyushu for the first time in years, Kawata departed for Korea in the *Moji shinpō*'s employ. His first series of reports appeared as a regular column from the end of June through October, often featured as the paper's lead story, in which he described his personal experiences and the situation in Korea in vivid detail. Moreover, his ability to speak foreign languages, including English and some Spanish, Chinese, and Korean, indicate his penchant for immersing himself in new situations and communicating with the people around him. This penchant, together with his use of phrases from classical written Chinese, ensured that his submissions would contain rich, reflective vignettes about life and death as well as authoritative accounts of encounters with native populations. Additionally, his own military experience surely informed his explanations of battlefield tactics. Highlighting the immediacy of his reports, the *Moji shinpō* declared it would, with celerity, bring the "flash of swords and roar of bullets" from the combat zone to its readers, and accordingly gave Kawata's fifty-one installments a dramatic flair by titling them "Gun Smoke and Flashing Swords."

Kawata soon received a license from the Imperial Military Headquarters allowing him to become a *jūgun kisha* (war correspondent with official permission to "follow the army").[32] As Japanese forces advanced and the arenas of battle pressed northward—first across Korea and then into Manchuria—the paper sent additional correspondents to cover all

---

decapitated and dismembered. His assassin, by contrast, received a hero's welcome in Seoul. The brutal treatment of Kim's remains served to rally Japanese public anger against both Korea and China, playing an important role in the rise of tensions among the countries that led to war that summer (Paine, *Sino-Japanese War*, 96–99). Kawata ruminated on their friendship and Kim's death—even considering going to Shanghai to claim his remains—in a short series of *Moji shinpō* articles published April 8–25, 1894. Kim's remains did not reach Korea until April 12, 1894.

31. *Moji shinpō*, June 27 and 30, 1894.

32. *Moji shinpō*, August 3, 1894. Ōta Takeshi was the second journalist dispatched to Korea and he left Moji aboard the *Yodogawa Maru* in late July (ibid., July 27, 1894).

major campaigns.[33] By early September it had assigned three correspondents to cover events in Seoul, Inchon, and Pusan. Although Japan did not initially have a codified system for reporters on the frontlines, the government soon issued emergency regulations allowing war correspondents to operate under military supervision and requiring them to subject their work to Home Ministry censorship.[34] At the end of October, just as Kawata's first series ended, the paper sent a second *jūgun kisha*, Hagihara Hayanosuke, to the continent to cover the latest battles.[35] Later, in January 1895, as Japanese troops advanced deeper into Manchuria from the east and the Japanese launched their attack on Weihaiwei with the ultimate goal of reaching Beijing, the paper kept pace and enhanced their coverage, sending five special correspondents into these advancing combat zones.[36]

On the home front, the *Moji shinpō* also dispatched correspondents to domestic sites of military preparation and operation, stationing one at the Sasebo naval station and sending the coal industry expert Kōnoe Kitarō to Hiroshima, where he arrived just in time to witness and report on the arrival of the emperor at the new military headquarters.[37] The paper supplemented such first-hand accounts with news obtained through interviews with diplomats, army and navy officers, former expatriates, and other knowledgeable observers and insiders.

This newspaper's correspondents compared favorably to those of some of the country's most prominent papers, including the *Yomiuri shinbun* and the *Ōsaka mainichi shinbun*, each of which sent four reporters to the continent. Although it could not compete with the numbers of correspondents sent by such giants as the *Minyūsha* (30 correspondents), *Asahi shinbun* (over 20 correspondents), or *Tōkyō nichi nichi* (12 correspondents),

33. Correspondents were named specifically to cover major battles at Pyongyang, Port Arthur, Weihaiwei, and Niuzhuang. See also note 31.

34. Huffman, *Creating a Public*, 206. Foreign reporters, on the other hand, could not follow the Japanese army until after its victories at Pyongyang and the Yalu River in mid-September. Foreign reporters did not accompany Chinese forces during the war (Paine, *Sino-Japanese War*, 189–90).

35. *Moji shinpō*, October 26, 1895.

36. Ibid., January 20, 1895.

37. Ibid., September 18, 1894.

the *Moji shinpō* held a key advantage over even these competitors: its office's proximity to the sites of battle.[38]

By taking advantage of Moji's strategic location, the paper quickly made a name for itself and, for the first time since its inception, turned a profit with innovative accounts of the war delivered at unrivaled speed. As Moji lay "along the main transportation artery for the war," ships making roundtrips to the front, "from the east and from the west, all gather[ed] at Moji," creating an opportunity for the paper's editors to get the latest information out to readers expeditiously.[39] On the eve of the war, the paper published a list of thirteen ports in China and Korea and their distances from Moji, effectively placing the port at the center of an expansive network and highlighting its vital, expanding links to continental ports.[40]

Since returning warships, *goyōsen*, and commercial ships alike typically made their first stops at Moji on the way to and home from the continent, they provided the paper with two ways to obtain the latest news. First, these ships often carried written stories being sent in by overseas correspondents. These stories appeared in the local press immediately, allowing the *Moji shinpō* to scoop its competitors in cities farther from the action. At this time, not only were telegraph services often disrupted due to sabotage and fighting, but the cost of transmission was expensive enough to prevent transmitting whole stories in this manner.[41] Second, local journalists were able to row out to returning ships anchored at Moji and interview their passengers and crews, thus setting this paper apart from others of the day. As printed in its own pages, "out of hundreds of papers in this country, the *Moji shinpō* is unparalleled" in bringing its readers "the latest warnings and strange tales about Japan and China

---

38. Huffman, *Creating a Public*, 208. As Stewart Lone shows through the *Gifu nichi nichi*, local papers used different methods to connect their readers to the war, such as publishing letters written by local troops fighting on the front (*Japan's First Modern War*).

39. *Moji shinpō*, January 2, 1895.

40. Ibid., June 16, 1894. The ports and their distances in miles are listed as follows: Inchon (n/a); Wonsan (388); Cheju (210); Port Arthur (642); Taku (now Dagu) (791); Chefoo (608); Hong Kong (1,182); Pusan (124); Port Hamilton (190); Weihaiwei (557); Niuzhang (781); Shanhaiguan (736); Shanghai (565).

41. See Huffman, *Creating a Public*, 209.

200 MOJI IN THE EMPIRE

in Korea."[42] Not surprisingly, the editors regularly emphasized these distinctive features of their paper's reportage, claiming that they could print news from the front within five days of military action, if not sooner. This was a fast turn around given that lag times generally spanned at least a week, if not two or more.[43]

The *Moji shinpō* had also begun conducting shipboard interviews just prior to the declaration of war. On June 27, the editors announced that this would become a "distinctive feature," and indeed, this method of reportage proved quite appealing to readers.[44] Exactly one month later, a printed announcement touted the addition of three reporters as *hōmon kisha* (interviewers) to call on ships and "learn the latest information" about the places from which its passengers were returning. With a sensationalistic spin, they advertised that "however strange the tales, you will know about them from the vivid reports in our pages."[45] The war, in other words, offered a rare, close-up look at Korea and China, lands that had long been off-limits and were still exotic to most Japanese citizens in the late nineteenth century. It also provided an unfolding drama in which every victory provided an opportunity for the government and its growing patriotic associations to instill in the population a sense of pride in Japan. Newspapers played an integral role in fostering both patriotism and a Japanese identity that was distinguishable from that of other Asians.

Importantly, however, the war also provided a chance to promote local agendas and identities. With continual refrains about the uniqueness of their port—based on its strategic location both within the country and in East Asia, coupled with its important wartime functions— the *Moji shinpō* centered its worldview on the place it represented and upon which it depended. In a sense, the paper did not simply write about Japan's war from the point of view from Moji; it wrote about Moji's war. The rest of the archipelago was but a backdrop to that story.

During the intense months of fighting, hundreds of ships in military service stopped at Moji as they plied an increasingly well-worn path to and from the continent. More than thirty ships, however, became regular features in the harbor. Visiting Moji on repeated occasions, either

---

42. *Moji shinpō*, June 27, 1894.
43. Ibid., September 8, 1894; Huffman, *Creating a Public*, 209.
44. *Moji shinpō*, June 27, 1894.
45. Ibid.

en route to regular destinations—as was the case for the *Tatsutagawa Maru*, *Yodogawa Maru*, and *Higo Maru*—or as requisitioned ships arriving from various battlegrounds—including the *Takasago Maru*, *Genkai Maru*, and *Yokohama Maru*—these ships formed recognizable notes in the rhythms of Moji's war each time they appeared at port. Even as assignments changed, such as when private company vessels entered into or rotated out of military service or when previously fixed routes were redirected to accommodate shifting battle locations and transport needs, these ships remained known entities.[46] NYK's *Genkai Maru*, for example, would stop at Moji on its regular Tientsin route before it began calling as a requisitioned vessel in the country's service. The OSK's *Shirakawa Maru* followed the opposite path, anchoring at Moji as a *goyōsen* before being assigned to a new commercial route running between Moji and Inchon.

The *Saikyō Maru* provides a remarkable example of a vessel whose changing fortunes reflected Moji's shifting wartime networks. Local reporters first interviewed passengers aboard this ship in July 1894, when it was in service to NYK's Yokohama-Shanghai route. In August, reporters again boarded the ship while it was anchored at Moji on its new Yokohama-Nagasaki route. Both times the paper published stories about the latest conditions in Shanghai (in August it had picked up passengers at Nagasaki who had just returned from Shanghai aboard another ship).[47] By late September, the *Saikyō Maru*, which had just become the warship *Saikyō-gō*, limped back to Moji as a damaged naval intelligence ship that had drawn fire during the famous maritime Battle of the Yalu. The *Moji shinpō* reporters interviewed its military crew and captain about their experiences and about the conflict itself, which had ended in a major victory for Japan. This battle-hardened vessel became legendary, attracting reverent passengers after being repaired and returned once again to NYK's Shanghai route.[48]

Starting in July and continuing through the first months of combat, information from shipboard interviews appeared almost daily in the *Moji shinpō*. The stories often appeared in two or more installments, occasionally comprising up to half the paper's daily content, and many issues

46. Ibid., July 8, 18–19, and November 21, 1894.

47. Ibid., July 25 and August 8, 1894.

48. Ibid., September 28–30, 1894, and Nippon Yūsen Kabushiki Kaisha, *Voyage of a Century*, 16. The ship would later be requisitioned once more for service in the Russo-Japanese War of 1904–5.

contained interviews from multiple ships at anchor. The frequency of
these testimonies emphasized Moji's physical proximity to the continent and kept developments continuously in front of readers. The paper
gave a new account from a different ship nearly every day in July (covering thirty-one ships in twenty-six days), and during August all but three
issues carried news from approximately thirty-five ships. After these
first two months, the number of shipboard interviews and their appearance in the paper declined to about a dozen each during September and
October. And even though the totals dropped off to ten or less for the
months between November 1894 and March 1895, the paper continued
to highlight this signature method of reportage even after the war ended.
These features were central; the *Moji shinpō* did not contain the same
kinds of stories about hometown war heroes that were characteristic of
many other local newspapers.[49]

The information gathered from shipboard conversations would be
published the next day in summarized form, so sources, typically referred
to simply as "passengers," were usually multiple and anonymous to readers.[50] When the paper did identify its sources, it might name reporters
from other papers, the crew of a ship or its officers, Japanese citizens
aboard a foreign ship, well-known individuals or officials (such as Ōtori
Keisuke, then minister to Korea, or Foreign Secretary Katō Takaaki), or
someone whose business was integral to the story being told (such as a
Japanese merchant resident in Korea or commercial sailors in Taiwan).[51]

For the most part, passengers discussed conditions in the region from
which they were returning and what they knew of either the broader war
or events that they had personally witnessed. These might include battle
descriptions, troop movements, the location of warships, and soldiers' living conditions.[52] Some of the most thrilling battle stories came at the
start of the war. The NYK's *Higo Maru* had been at anchor in Inchon's
harbor when Japan famously attacked the *Kowshing* in nearby waters. Since

49. See Huffman, *Creating a Public*, 211.

50. At times, however, these reports would be delayed so they could be processed by government censors before publication.

51. *Moji shinpō*, July 20 and October 29–30, 1894. Ōtori fought against the new
Meiji government's forces alongside Takemoto Enomoto in Hokkaido at the end of
the Meiji Restoration. He later became part of the Meiji government and was the
legation minister in Korea during the Sino-Japanese War.

52. For example, see ibid., July 17–27 and August 7, 1894.

this British steamer was carrying Chinese military personnel at the time, its sinking led to the formal declaration of war. Upon their return to Moji several days later, the *Higo Maru*'s passengers, which included 160 Japanese citizens who were being evacuated from their residences in Seoul and Inchon, described their experiences to reporters. Their animated tales were soon followed by those from passengers aboard the *Tatsutagawa Maru*, who had spotted corpses in the water as they were en route between Pusan and Inchon. These were undoubtedly the bodies of Chinese soldiers who had died when the *Kowshing* foundered in the opening salvos of the war.

Over the next several months, passengers returning from the continent talked to local correspondents about a wide variety of issues. Many shared their personal observations, relayed facts, or repeated hearsay. They offered information about foreign political situations and diplomatic figures, including Li Hongzhang, who orchestrated the war for China, and General Yuan Shikai, who led troops in Korea (and would later be instrumental in overthrowing the Qing, becoming the first leader of the Republic of China). Others discussed Japanese victories or relayed numbers of casualties. Returnees also provided information regarding the content of local newspapers, the reliability of telegraph lines, blockaded transportation routes, and business conditions at different ports. Many also provided stories about the lives of Japanese expatriates still residing in the treaty ports of China and Korea, with special attention to how the war was affecting them. Some Japanese, for example, had turned to dressing as Koreans in order to blend in.[53]

A few interviews touched on more subjective topics like comparisons between Japanese and Chinese people, but these did not play a significant role in the coverage. The *Moji shinpō* did print derogatory terms, such as "pigtails," to refer to the Chinese, but their use was occasional rather than ubiquitous.[54] In one case, a reporter describes "Chinese people with blue eyes and disheveled hair" to emphasize the special danger presented by Westerners helping to conduct the war for China.[55]

53. Ibid., July 20, 1894.
54. Huffman, Lone, and Paine have all pointed out that Japanese newspapers readily used derogatory comments regarding other Asians at the time. See also Saya, *Nisshin sensō*. In the *Moji shinpō*, China was also often referred to as simply *tekikoku* (enemy nation).
55. *Moji shinpō*, August 9, 1894.

Overall, though, even beginning in the early months of the war, the paper reflected a strong belief in Japan's ability to win, taking stock of the day-to-day logistics of fighting without resorting to significant name-calling.

The manifold narratives coming out of the shipboard interviews provided local readers with an awareness of Japan's standing in the war. Important to Moji's identity as Japan's closest port to the conflict was the fact that these stories also helped generate a very immediate sense of residents' own proximity to the fighting, something that was both thrilling and frightening. One story may have brought an explanatory comparison too close to home by likening the geographical position of China's northern naval bases at Port Arthur and Weihaiwei to the twin ports of Moji and Shimonoseki. The reporter pointed out that both sets of ports sat on opposite sides of a strait that was vulnerable to sneak attacks by torpedo boats.[56] The fact that the Chinese ports were just across the Yellow Sea would not have been lost on them. More generally, though, the consistency with which ships from the continent came into Moji's harbor emphasized its direct connection to events across the Korea Strait but did not cause undue anxiety. As expressed by the paper's editor, "it is as if the steamships that weave together our Kanmon with Korea and China were established as communications ships for the *Moji shinpō* and their passengers are our correspondents."[57] In this light, the location of the war suited the paper, and the port, quite well.

From the War Front to Moji

As the conflict progressed ever more clearly in Japan's favor, the ships calling at Moji began to bring home very tangible results of the fighting in the form of wounded soldiers, military laborers, prisoners of war, and booty from the front. Journalists increasingly boarded anchored ships carrying prisoners of war and tried to speak with them. In late November, the *Kagoshima Maru*, arriving from Pyongyang by way of Inchon, carried 500 sick and wounded Japanese soldiers and coolies from both of these locations. It also held seven Chinese prisoners below deck, all of whom had been captured by Japan's First Army during the battle at Jiuliancheng. All had gunshot wounds to their legs. A *Moji shinpō* reporter gained

56. Ibid.
57. Ibid., July 27, 1894.

permission to enter their "gloomy" and "stinky" room in an interior part of the lower deck and attempted to communicate with them through "brush writing." Since the prisoners were all common soldiers with low education levels, even written communication proved difficult, limiting the exchange. The reporter disembarked with only basic information, such as the prisoners' names and those of their superior officers.[58]

A month later, after battles at Jinzhou and Port Arthur, the *Izumi Maru* arrived at Moji carrying 219 wounded soldiers of Japan's Second Army plus 179 prisoners captured by it. During the ten hours that the ship remained anchored at Moji to take on coal and water, a correspondent went aboard. He relayed that all the prisoners were healthy and being held in a room on the lower deck. They were, however, kept in what he deemed an uncomfortable proximity to injured Japanese soldiers, who were being transferred from the army hospital at Port Arthur. In this case, everyone aboard the *Izumi Maru* traveled on to the port of Ujina for further treatment and detention. Sometimes, however, wounded soldiers disembarked at Moji so that they could be transported to the nearby Kokura Army Reserve Hospital.[59] When the *Kumamoto Maru* called at the port with 444 injured soldiers, for example, 123 men came ashore at Moji while the rest headed on to Ujina.[60]

In addition to the wounded soldiers and prisoners passing through Moji, a significant amount of plunder came to the port as well. Much of it was offloaded and stored in newly built warehouses designated specifically for military use. Moji's stockpiles contained, for instance, flags, clothing, and hats, in addition to such things as donkeys captured by the Army's Fourteenth Regiment, and an abundance of items that were described simply as literary, artistic, and technological goods.[61] Beyond these relatively nondescript items, however, were those much less ordinary. During several days in March, for example, Moji saw a dramatic procession of victor's spoils. Months after the Battle of Port Arthur, where an easy Japanese victory turned savagely violent as soldiers massacred civilians, *gōyōsen* ships anchored at Moji "one after another" to offload enormous cargoes of plunder taken from the town. Many of these

58. Ibid., November 23, 1894.
59. Ibid., December 25, 1894.
60. Ibid., February 24, 1895.
61. Ibid., January 1 and May 11, 1895.

confiscated items were armaments of one kind or another, including guns, rifles, and cannon.[62] Moji was the chosen destination for these items since they could be repaired at its newly built weapons station.

The arrival of the largest war trophy, impressive in its own right, also heralded China's imminent surrender. On March 2, at four o'clock in the afternoon, a large, dark gray battleship with tall masts entered Moji's harbor from Weihaiwei. With much anticipation, thousands of people—the elderly with stooped postures, suckling infants, "women and girls who left their housework behind," and reporters there to fulfill their "responsibility" to record the moment—lined both shores of the Kanmon Strait, arriving from "east, west, south, and north" and "defying a bitter wind" to witness the approach of the surrendered Chinese warship. According to the *Moji shinpō*, the sight evoked, as it undoubtedly also instilled, the "great patriotism of Japan's imperial citizens." The magnitude of this spectacle inspired the paper's editors to devote nearly a full page to describing the ship and recapitulating the clash that had compelled its surrender.[63]

Following the signing of the peace in May, more of Japan's troops began returning home from the warfront via Moji. True to its now-seasoned role as a principal reception center, Moji emerged as "the welcome place for all of Fukuoka." Townspeople turned out to greet the triumphant return of brave veterans and fete military units with grand receptions. Preparations to receive Fukuoka's soldiers from the Sixth, Twelfth, Fourteenth, and Twenty-Fourth Divisions were under way several days ahead of their return from Port Arthur. Throughout the town, flags were flown and lanterns lit in greeting. The centrally located Ishida Ryokan served as the prefecture's welcome office and Governor Iwamura Takatoshi, as well as heads of each county, city, and town, lodged there.[64]

Some of the military personnel were coming full circle. Soldiers of the Sixth Division, for example, had boarded the requisitioned *Nagato Maru* in Moji the previous January before heading to Port Arthur. Four months later, when they returned to their original point of departure, they took in "an unprecedented spectacle" that was replete with shouts

62. Ibid., March 31, 1895.
63. Ibid., March 3–5, 1895.
64. Ibid., May 22–30, 1895.

of "banzai," a military parade, and a variety of celebrations taking place along the waterfront. For the majority of those returning from the war-front, Moji was not their final destination. As they headed on to places like Kokura and Hakata, other welcoming committees would greet them in similar fashion.[65]

Although news and spectacle formed an important part of the war effort for those who did not go to the battlefield, Moji's citizens did more than just read about military exploits and occasionally brave the cold to acknowledge victories, witness a parade, or cheer safe home-comings. Many also performed actions that supported the war. As in other locales around Japan, citizens joined patriotic associations and bought war bonds. Beyond such overt demonstrations of support, Mojiites often furthered the war effort just by doing their jobs. People who piloted steamships and small harbor vessels, worked on the docks or in the offing, sold coal to the navy, and tallied shipping invoices helped advance local and national agendas during this period.[66] In their everyday lives, Moji's citizens were directly linked to Japan's military pursuits.

The importance of their daily activities for the good of the country was rhetorically reinforced in the pages of the *Moji shinpō* throughout the war. When the paper published a brief piece concerning "Fukuoka Pre-fecture and the countries of China and Korea" two and a half months into the fighting, its contributors were not the only ones to find Moji central to national efforts. This piece called attention to Moji's locational and functional significance but from the perspective of someone not based there. Japanese Consul Nose Tatsugorō, who resided in Inchon but was temporarily in Moji aboard the *Higo Maru* en route from Naga-saki to Kobe, granted the paper an interview concerning the Korea trade.

Starting with the basic assertion that Japan's war goal was "to gain rights in Korea and China for our citizens," in what he interestingly viewed as a "trade war" in East Asia, Consul Nose identified Moji as Ja-pan's most promising spot for trade with the continent. "Within Japan the closest location . . . to these two countries is Kyushu; within Kyushu,

---

65. Ibid., May 25–26, 1895.
66. See Gluck, *Japan's Modern Myths*; Hall, *Civilising Subjects*; and Harland-Jacobs, *Builders of Empire,* for discussions on how practices and ideologies influence indi-viduals' identities.

Fukuoka is the most important; and within Fukuoka, Moji occupies the top position nationally in terms of beneficial trade." He went on to declare that once China and Korea "started on the path of civilization," a view clearly fueled by the imperialist rhetoric of the day, their industries and businesses would require coal from Chikuhō's mines. Thus, he concluded, "in the future, Moji stands apart with the brightest prospects as the place at the heart of Tōyō trade."[67]

Consul Nose was certainly not the only person who believed in Moji's promise within this new environment. The recently completed treaty revision made Moji's position "all the more important," even leading to a rush of people coming to the port to buy land.[68] At this juncture, the war caused the Japanese to turn their attention more fully toward the continent and consider their country's place in East Asia. From this vantage point, locals and central officials alike recognized that Moji's location was key. Moreover, treaty revision and the war against China together brought new military and commercial installations to the port, creating physical markers of Moji's new prominence.

War and Progress Inscribed on Moji's Landscape

Throughout the war, along with accounts of Japan's victories, the *Moji shinpō* reported various milestones reached by the town itself. These included the building of a new customs house, the Mitsui Weapons Station (*heiki shūrijo*) warehouses, a new wharf, and the Moji Coal Exchange. All these projects were followed in the pages of the daily paper as Japan's war against China was being fought. Some had been in the works since before the signing of the revised treaties; others were a direct result of the conflict. Regardless of their origin, several such markers of the town's progress came to fruition during the war, revealing how Japan's commercial and military activities began to permanently inscribe themselves onto Moji's physical space.

---

67. *Moji shinpō*, October 16, 1894. Tōyō can be translated as the East, but as a region and category of trade that was being deliberately targeted at this time, using Tōyō is preferable. In an editorial that appeared a year earlier, the "so-called Tōyō trade" was described as "a new field" (ibid., October 21, 1893). See Tanaka for a discussion on the idea of Tōyō (*Japan's Orient*, esp. 3–12).

68. Ibid., August 30, 1894.

Even before the conflict with China erupted, officials impressed by Moji's capacity to export coal authorized the construction of a new two-story, Western-style brick building to house its customs agency. The surge in traffic being handled by the port meant that the existing customs facilities had been quickly outgrown, and the events of the war magnified the sense that Moji would only continue to expand its operations. The new building would be considerably larger and situated "optimally to handle maritime affairs" right at the port's jetty. Construction was completed in just nine months despite delays caused by the war. Planners designed the inauguration ceremony not merely "to commemorate the new customs building, but also to acknowledge the port's development," which was "directly related to the cooperation of its coal industrialists and citizens."[69]

There was no shortage of hype surrounding this grand opening. The ceremony took place on a clear morning in an open lot adjacent to the new building. The event brought together some 400 regional notables, including Governor Iwamura, Diet representative Tsutsumi Michihisa, the county heads of Buzen Province, members of the prefectural assembly, commissioned officers of Moji's garrison, and the Kokura court judge, along with police chiefs and employees of various companies from Moji and the towns of Kokura, Wakamatsu, and Shimonoseki.[70] Watanabe Itaru, the chief of Nagasaki Customs, gave the keynote address. He stated that the impressive scale of the new edifice "reveals the great hopes the government holds for Moji." Following all the speeches, customs personnel had their picture taken with the chief in front of the new building before heading to local restaurants, where multiple banquets sustained the celebration.[71]

In an extended interview published in the *Moji shinpō*, which likely incorporated remarks made during the ceremony, the chief elaborated that "this new agency is an extremely grand structure and may seem exorbitant compared to Moji's current exports, but when we deeply consider Moji's future, this building anticipates the needs of this office and so we have built it. . . . Moji will fulfill its promise . . . and is making remarkable strides." Watanabe also tied both treaty revision and the war

69. Ibid., June 14 and December 5, 1894.
70. Ibid., March 1, 1895.
71. Ibid., March 6, 1895.

into his view of Moji, asserting that our "citizens' dignity advances with each victory in battle." He went on to argue for the importance of having open ports that were not treaty ports, something he believed essential for "the national economy" and lay at the core of the country's "sovereign rights."[72] Further, Watanabe predicted that future peacetime trade with China would form a strong part of "Japan's commercial seas" (*Nihon shōgyōkai*) and went on to sketch the postwar trade scene, considering potential imports and exports of everything from thread and flour to salt and coal. The new Customs House represented these hopes.

At the other end of the harbor, another meaningful structure had also just been erected. Three months into the war, the Mitsui family donated to the country what at the time was called a munitions factory (*gunki seizōjo*). Although initial reports located its future site near the naval base at Kure (Hiroshima Prefecture), Moji would quickly be named instead.[73] An editorial about the port's progress placed this facility in the following light: "Moji's future is not limited to Kyushu's mining areas since its aim is not only to import and export coal. . . . Moji will gradually become an industrial area."[74] Plans for the new munitions factory put it at the naval coal storage site along Moji's eastern coast and turned coal warehouses over to the Army Ministry, which also built a gunpowder storage facility nearby.[75] During the six months of the factory's construction, readers got regular updates covering, for example, land reclamation for the building site, assembly of the boiler, creation of finishing and woodworking rooms, and the installation of machinery. By May 1895, the facility had been renamed and the Mitsui Weapons Station, ironically, began operation just as soldiers were returning from the warfront in large numbers.

The launching of two coal industry organizations also signaled Moji's growth. The first was the Moji Coal Sellers Association, incorporated in March 1895, which moved into the former customs house after it was vacated in May. The association's goal was to bring together

72. Ibid., March 2, 1895.

73. Ibid., October 30–31, 1894.

74. Ibid., November 13, 1894. Northern Kyushu did soon become one of the country's major industrial centers, especially after the Yahata Steel Works began production in 1901, and it remains so today.

75. Ibid., November 29, 1894, and January 8, 1895.

coal sellers to communicate and cooperate for the mutual advancement of their businesses. Unfortunately, little is known about its operations or fate, especially after it was reorganized in 1900.[76] The Moji Coal Exchange would complement the functions of the association. Businessmen, three directors, and thirty-eight investors created the exchange to help regulate coal transactions. Centrally located on San-bashi Street—in front of the train station, with two brokerage houses on the right and the Moji Chikkō office on the left—the exchange opened to great fanfare in late October. Despite its auspicious start, the exchange proved a short-lived affair, lasting just two years before going bankrupt.[77] Continual claims of the port's progress notwithstanding, not all steps taken by Moji's boosters and investors had forward momentum.

Another plan that did not reach fruition was a sensational structure called Kanmon's Triumphal Bridge. In mid-September, Japan's back-to-back victories—first in Pyongyang and then at the Battle of the Yalu—generated a swell of excitement and prompted discussion over how Moji could commemorate the huge victories. The *Moji shinpō*'s editors echoed national expectations and hyperbole in saying that the "unprecedented land war" and "maritime battle of a kind not to be seen again" would be followed by the taking of Beijing.[78] Since Moji would then sit at the center of Japan's empire, they believed, it should have a monument to commemorate the victories that would thus situate the city. An iron bridge across the Kanmon Strait, spanning it from Moji to Shimonoseki, was to be built of the great cache of metal from Japan's war spoils. Mention of the bridge appeared in the paper as late as June 1895, when a series of articles suggested that despite having some fervent supporters, the expensive project did not yet have sufficient funding. It never materialized. Construction of a bridge across the strait

---

76. Ibid., March 2, 1895.

77. Ibid., February 5, March 13, and April 12, 1895.

78. The Japanese military stood poised to take Beijing (an original goal of the war), but then used its threatening position to get China to sign the Treaty of Shimonoseki on April 17, 1895. Whether they might have made good on the threat, or if the international community would have tolerated such a move, was another question. See Paine, *Sino-Japanese War*, ch. 7.

would wait eighty years until 1973, when engineers built the Kanmon suspension bridge, even then considered a feat.

Moji and the Shimonoseki Peace Talks

A final way that the war came home to Moji was through the peace talks held at Shimonoseki. Moji shared in the logistical planning for and the excitement of this weeks-long event. The Meiji government had originally considered conducting the talks at Ujina, near the Imperial Military Headquarters, but ultimately deemed it "extremely inappropriate" to have Chinese diplomats at such a sensitive location.[79] The final choice of location was a boon for Moji. The talks took place right across the strait in a building just offshore and up a steep but small hill. Before the talks began, the *Moji shinpō* anticipated that with "Tōyō's great diplomats" in Shimonoseki—Li Hongzhang (who had first tried to avert war before leading China's forces against Japan), along with Japan's Prime Minister Itō Hirobumi and Foreign Minister Mutsu Munemitsu—the world's attention will be on "our Kanmon."[80]

This major event sent an influx of reporters, police, and dignitaries into Moji for the duration of the negotiations.[81] The *Moji shinpō* seized the opportunity to promote its own role, promising readers that they would know immediately if the talks were successful. In the days preceding the arrival of delegations for each side, the Moji police station hired extra officers to patrol the coastline from both land and water. The neighboring ports of Kokura and Wakamatsu also added patrols to their zones of jurisdiction. When the Japanese warship *Yaeyama* anchored in the Kanmon Strait during the latter part of negotiations to guard the area, Moji's mayor Maeda Masaharu and town council member Tsugawa Ikuzō called on the officers of the vessel and presented them with a barrel of fine sake in thanks for the protection that they provided. Captain Hirayama Tōjirō, who had not been on board during the visit, promptly sent a letter of thanks to the town.[82]

79. It had been earlier rumored that the headquarters itself might move westward to Kanmon, at least partly for its warmer weather, but this did not happen (*Moji shinpō*, February 23, 1895).

80. Ibid., March 13 and 19, 1895.

81. Ibid., April 5, 1895.

82. Ibid., April 9–10, 1895.

When Li Hongzhang's steamship approached Moji on March 19, it first stopped at the narrow entry to the Kanmon Strait before anchoring in the offing by Moji's new customs house.[83] The next day, tens of thousands of spectators gathered "like a fog" to watch Li come ashore at Shimonoseki with his delegation. According to reports, Japanese people everywhere had been hearing and repeating Li's name throughout the war and were keenly interested to finally learn about his personal appearance and bearing. The paper described him as a man who seemed younger than his seventy-three years and appeared to be in good health. Overall, he had "a look of greatness."[84] The next day Li's ship moved and anchored in the offing by Moji's customs house as the peace talks opened in Shimonoseki.

Less than a week after negotiations had begun, as Li left a meeting in a palanquin, he was shot in the face at close range. The headline— "Madman Shoots Li Hongzhang with a Pistol"—topped an extra edition of the *Moji shinpō*, which also contained a rough diagram of the streets where the incident took place. Details indicated that the would-be assassin, Koyama Toyotarō, a twenty-six-year-old man from Tokyo, hid in the doorway of Emura Nitarō's shop (located, ironically, next to a military police station and across the street from a police box); he leaped into the street to fire on Li as Li passed by.[85] A man named Tomiyoshi Yoshigorō ran from the police box to capture the shooter and recover the weapon, by then tossed to the ground. Officers arrested Koyama and immediately escorted him to the military police station. Although he carried a photograph of statesman Itagaki Taisuke and a fifteen-page tract from the Jiyūtō (Liberal Party) on his person, the connection of these items to the assassination attempt was unclear.[86] Authorities in Tokyo acknowledged their responsibility for the embarrassing security failure, and to ensure justice was swift in this diplomatic fiasco, sentenced Koyama to life in prison before the week was out.[87]

---

83. Paine states that two steamships brought Li and his entourage of 100 people (*Sino-Japanese War*, 260).

84. Ibid., March 20–21, 1895. A realistic sketch of Li accompanies the text about his arrival.

85. The paper first reported the madman's name as Koyama Rokunosuke, but he had recently applied to have it legally changed to Toyotarō (ibid., March 31, 1895).

86. Ibid., March 25–31, 1895.

87. Paine, *Sino-Japanese War*, 264.

In the meantime, Japanese officials and citizens from around the country sent letters of sympathy and apology to Li. Of the more than 10,000 letters that he received, those from Mayor Maeda, writing on behalf of the town's citizens, and the Moji Coal Sellers Association were among the first delivered. The Meiji emperor also offered a gesture of sympathy and regret by granting China a three-week armistice, something that Japan had until then been reluctant to do. Despite his close brush with death and with a bullet still lodged in his cheek, Li soon returned to the negotiating table.[88] Approximately three weeks later, Li and Itō signed the landmark Treaty of Shimonoseki, which gave Japan its first formal colonial territories of Taiwan, the Pescadores, and the Liaodong Peninsula, as well as an indemnity of more than 300 million yen, and China's recognition of Korean independence. The treaty additionally awarded Japan new commercial and manufacturing rights, which included most favored nation status, and access to the Yangtze and Wusung Rivers (the latter giving access to Shanghai) and four treaty ports (Shashi, Chungking [Chongqing], Soochow [Suzhou], and Hangchow [Hangzhou]).

The security regulations that had been in force on both sides of the Kanmon Strait for the duration of the peace talks ended on April 21 after the accord was signed and delegates had departed.[89] The Japanese believed their victory to be complete. Just two days later, however, Russia, Germany, and France challenged Japan's rights to the strategic Liaodong Peninsula in what is known as the Triple Intervention. This unexpected insult immediately prompted a sudden increase in the number of foreign warships cruising Japan's coastal waters and sitting at anchor in its ports. Japan's navy watched Russian vessels with particular concern. Authorities at Kobe, for example, issued a directive forbidding sailors on three anchored Russian warships from coming ashore. At Nagasaki, officials monitored four Russian warships and three torpedo boats in the harbor. In early May, Mojiites watched as three Russian warships anchored in the Kanmon Strait for a few days while American and British warships passed by their shores.[90] Despite this flurry of nervous activity that came just as Japan's first modern war had drawn to a close, peace

88. *Moji shinpō*, March 25–31, 1895.
89. Final ratification of the treaty took place in Chefoo on May 8, 1895.
90. Ibid., April 26 and May 5–10, 1895.

would be maintained for almost a decade before Japan met Russia on the battlefield and at sea to secure influence in Korea and Manchuria. Japan's 1905 victory allowed it to take back the Liaodong Peninsula and sign its possession into law in the Treaty of Portsmouth.

Conclusion

The First Sino-Japanese War was unequivocally a turning point in East Asia, as Japan displaced China as the region's leading power. It also, however, bridged long-term processes that started earlier and persisted beyond these remarkable months of fighting, signifying often-unrecognized continuity in Japan's industrialization, imperialism, and identity formation. All three processes culminated at the special trading port of Moji, which, as this chapter demonstrates, stood ready at the vanguard of Japan's first modern war.

With regard to industrialization, the conflict added momentum to ongoing efforts, especially in capital-intensive heavy industries such as steelmaking and shipbuilding, which would decrease Japanese reliance on imports from the West.[91] China's indemnity, for example, helped pay for the establishment of the Yahata Iron and Steel Works.[92] But the war neither launched nor completed the country's needs for this stage of industrial advancement.

Second, the war gave Japan its first formal colonial holdings, if the Ryukyus and Hokkaido are removed from this categorization. Taking Taiwan was not Japan's ultimate aim; rather, it was a compromise that the navy pursued at the end of the war. This territory provided Japan with access to additional resources, such as coal and even bananas, which were first imported to Japan by way of Moji. The NYK immediately opened new routes to Taiwan, expanding the sets of networks traveling through the special trading ports. This new territory, combined with the added commercial privileges in China, including the opening of new treaty ports there, greatly enhanced Japan's international standing as a modern state.

Finally, the war increased Japanese citizens' sense of affinity to the nation—being part of a community distinguished from others by history,

91. Gordon, *Evolution of Labor Relations*, 17.
92. Moji had also been under consideration as a possible site for this facility.

race, culture, and, at this moment, belonging on the winning side of a war fought on the world stage. But Japaneseness was not the only identity in the spotlight. This event also had an impact on specific localities within Japan where people interpreted the war and its happenings—preparations, battles, sacrifices, victories, and spoils—in the context of their village, town, or city. In the case of people living in Moji, as reflected in the pages of the *Moji shinpō*, they viewed the war in relation to its effect on the sounds, sights, and activities of their everyday lives. The situation at Moji demonstrates how the local interacted directly with the global. A keen awareness of their position in larger processes, as will be seen in Chapter 6, comes out even more fully in the Open Ports Movement, which unfolded in the final years of the nineteenth century in preparation for the return of Japan's sovereignty in 1899.

SIX

Securing Status

Sovereignty and Open Ports

In the final years of the nineteenth century, the geographical contours of Japan's port system solidified, taking the basic shape that it would maintain through World War II.[1] The ports that were opened to international trade in 1899 with the enactment of the revised treaties had all been special trading ports, with the sole exception of Taketoyo. The former treaty ports together with the former special trading ports, now collectively known as "open ports," would be the hubs for the country's international trade, most notably serving as the primary links between the home islands and Japan's growing Asian empire.

The same two events—the building of the Trans-Siberian Railway and treaty revision—that brought diplomatic instability to East Asia and helped spark the First Sino-Japanese War also brought new commercial opportunity to Japan. Although foreign diplomats had long requested opening additional ports to foreign commerce since they considered those

1. This refers to ports in Japan's home islands and does not include those added across the empire after 1899. Over the next decade, seven other ports would become open ports at home—Aomori (1906), Itozaki (1900), Miike (1908), Nagoya (1907), Nemuro (1910), Suminoe (1906), and Wakamatsu (1904) (Ōkurashō Shuzeikyoku, *Nihon kanzei, zeikanshi shiryō*, 3:17–91). Japan Unyusho, *Principal Ports in Japan,* covers the country's twenty-six main ports in 1952. Of these, seven are the former treaty ports and open cities; three are the naval bases of Kure, Sasebo, and Yokosuka; eight are former special trading ports—Fushiki, Hakata, Moji, Muroran, Otaru, Shimizu, Shimonoseki, and Yokkaichi; and seven are those opened to foreign trade after 1899—Aomori, Kamaishi (1934), Kawasaki (1926), Nagoya, Shimotsu (1948), Tsukumi (1934), and Wakamatsu.

in operation insufficient for their needs, especially given Niigata's lack-luster performance, the oligarchs would not do so ahead of treaty revision.[2] The opening of more ports to Western trade was an important bargaining chip that Tokyo resolved to hold onto tightly until the new treaties were enacted.

In the meantime, however, other important changes were taking place within the country that would enable treaty revision and aid the country in its transition to full sovereignty, including the promulgation of a constitution in 1889 (and its provision for the creation of a national assembly) and the issuance of the 1890 Japanese Commercial Code. Amid these developments, local boosters quickly proved adept at lobbying through the Lower House of the Diet to expand their own trade privileges. In fact, the potential for new trade that would come with revised treaties—the first, signed with Great Britain in 1894, promised a long-sought equality in commercial transactions—and the 1891 start of construction on the Trans-Siberian Railway—slated to connect the Sea of Japan to Korea, China, and Russian Asia while creating a new route to Europe—prompted a scramble among Japan's ports to gain greater opening.

The last set of ports that had opened on the eve of these significant legislative milestones and international developments were the special ports of export in 1889.[3] In keeping with Tokyo's strategy, the oligarchs did not fully open any ports until the revised treaties were enacted in 1899. They were, however, pushed to begin preparing for Japan's new commercial relationships as the shifting tenor of relations in East Asia prompted citizens and leaders to weigh their opportunities and challenges anew. During the final decade of the nineteenth century, amid considerable debate weighing pros and cons in the Diet, the oligarchs granted new privileges among existing special trading ports while also increasing their number. The Japanese public used their collective voices in the Diet to push for change even as the oligarchs—with a combination of optimism and caution—awaited the enactment of the revised treaties.

2. See, for example, *Moji shinpō*, October 7, 1893.
3. Kushiro (1890) and Muroran (1894) were added shortly after the nine original special ports of export. Muroran gained this status in order to handle Hokkaido's increasing coal production.

Two waves of new special trading port designations came in the 1890s. The first swell came in 1893 and 1894 as three ports—Miyazu, Fushiki, and Otaru—were granted allowances for restricted trade with Russia and Korea in anticipation of commercial relationships to come after the laying of the Trans-Siberian Railway. The second, more dramatic wave of openings took place during the three years following the signing of the first revised treaty in 1894. Ten ports, half of which already had special export status, gained position as "world ports," able to import and export goods with no built-in limits concerning trade partners or commodities. These were different from treaty ports and the later "open ports" since this trade could only be conducted on Japanese-owned vessels and did not contain provisions for foreigners to come ashore.

In all, these designations represented a sea-change in the Meiji government's trade restrictions. Whereas the first wave mirrored earlier special ports in being quietly selected by the government, the second wave took on a new character entirely as it arose from locally generated campaigns, which I call the Open Ports Movement. This movement had begun gathering momentum as early as 1893. It really took shape, however, in January 1895, when businessmen and politicians first collectively petitioned the government and argued their cases in the Lower House.

Passionate voices from around Japan joined forces on behalf of their ports. Diet members crossed geographical and party affiliations to bring about this movement, which continued through the rest of the decade. Although some ports gained new status quickly, others tried, and failed, multiple times. Of those that ultimately succeeded— and not all did—Moji faced one of the toughest battles. Through sustained effort, local representatives spoke to their own concerns while linking their movement to national-level campaigns for trade liberalization. In Tokyo, they found a ready advocate in Taguchi Ukichi, a prominent champion of economic reform and editor of the economics magazine *Tōkyō keizai zasshi*. Taguchi chaired the committee sponsoring the Open Ports Bill (*Kaikō hōan*). Together, these waves represent the steps that Japanese citizens and officials alike took in advance of the 1899 enactment of the revised treaties to better position their cities and towns for extended commercial relations across the

East Asian region and to make their country more competitive in the global economy.

Eyeing the Tōyō Trade

In Moji, local boosters saw fresh possibilities for their port in these changing domestic and international environments and first launched a major civic initiative to raise public bonds for urban development in March 1893. This announcement heralded a new stage in efforts to increase Moji's trading privileges as the town's elite, who held visions of ever greater prosperity, found its special trading status unnecessarily restrictive. Their longer-term goal was to make Moji an open trade port with full privileges to export and import a broad range of goods. In order to achieve this goal, they knew that they "must establish the foundations of the future now," building a port infrastructure able to handle a growing population and evolving commercial transactions. One urgent need that they identified was to improve public health and safety services, including better drinking water, hygiene, hospital facilities, and disease prevention. The last was crucial since outbreaks of cholera were frequent, and thousands upon thousands of people passed through Moji annually in transit on ships and trains. Ensuring health and safety was a must for maximizing Moji's role as a trade and transportation hub. Additionally, residents targeted education as an area requiring advancement and even suggested teaching English in local schools so that citizens would be more worldly.[4] Importantly, such advances would also help raise Moji's standing in the national port hierarchy.

As the town continued to enrich Moji's infrastructure, a lobbying drive for greater trade privileges also got under way as ports around the country began seeking enhanced trade status. Shimonoseki, for example, applied to the Home Ministry to become a special export-import port just as Moji was launching its development drive.[5] By September, the Moji Club, an elite group of local businessmen, drafted a bill to elevate Moji's trade status to allow it to import goods and geographically

4. Ibid., March 4–10, 1893.
5. Ibid., March 9, 1893.

expand its commercial partners.[6] These initiatives came as treaty revision negotiations (still underway at this time) were intensifying and other ports began obtaining designations that Moji's residents coveted. At this early stage, however, the bill's originators had no idea how long and arduous a battle they would face.

In mid-October, a *Moji shinpō* editorial delivered a strong response to the Diet's sanction for the port of Miyazu to trade with Vladivostok and Korea. Part exhortation to achieve more and part disbelief that Miyazu would be selected for this commercial expansion over Moji, the three-part article, titled "Moji Must Become a Trade Port for China, Korea, and Vladivostok," argued that Moji's centrality to domestic railroads and East Asia's maritime networks meant that its port should not only be allowed to trade with Vladivostok and Korea (like Miyazu) but trade directly with Singapore, Bombay, and Manila as well. Extending the argument further still, the editorial considered the time and expense routinely wasted in making roundtrips to Kobe and Nagasaki from other parts of Asia, suggesting that by expanding Moji's trade, ships would no longer bypass it on these longer routes. In sum, the article asserted, "there are a hundred needs for an open port and a thousand reasons that fast-moving water heads for Moji's harbor."[7] The same kind of fervent rhetoric for, if not belief in, a single port's promise could be found in statements being made in other parts of Japan, too. After all, Moji's residents were not the country's only boosters promoting their port by claiming its centrality to Japan's developing Tōyō trade.

MIYAZU

The Diet's approval for Miyazu to trade with Russia and Korea, marking this port's first designation for overseas commerce, was met with envy at the same time that it gave hope to others seeking trade allowances. Although the edict that sanctioned Miyazu's opening held forward-looking goals, it rested on procedures established a decade earlier, when Izuhara, Shimonoseki, and Hakata were named for the Korea trade. Miyazu gained the same level of permission that these earlier designees had to conduct

6. Ibid., September 22, 1893. The editor-in-chief and future president of the *Moji shinpō*, Mōri Yasutarō, was one of the bill's authors.

7. Ibid., October 14, 20, and 21, 1893.

trade but was restricted to domestically owned vessels.[8] The main difference in trade privileges was locational; the impetus in 1883 was to encourage trade in Japan's informal empire in Korea whereas a decade later,
although further access to the Korea trade sweetened the deal, the main
target was Russia, reflecting the latter's heightened presence in East Asia.

Although gaining these allowances signified an important milestone
for Miyazu, it also proved to be just the beginning of that port's ambitions. Its boosters continued to push for greater opening for the rest of
the decade, competing with many of Japan's ports—especially those, like
Moji, that already had a satisfying taste of international trade as special
ports of export. And like Mojiites, Miyazu's citizens believed that its port
was most deserving of a higher rank. A written opinion by supporter
Konishi Yasubei detailed why Miyazu was the best port along the Sea
of Japan to become the region's international trading port. His principal concern was to develop the "Tōyō trade." He argued that trade
through Miyazu would be convenient for the whole country and enable
Japanese merchants to take advantage of Russia's dual position in Europe
and Asia.

In support of his argument, Konishi evaluated the Sea of Japan ports
that he perceived would be most competitive with Miyazu. The seven
other places that he identified, in geographic order along the coast from
southwest to northeast, were: Yuya (in Nagato), Setozaki (Nagato), Maizuru (Kyoto), Obama (Fukui), Tsuruga (Fukui), Nanao (Ishikawa), and
Shinagawa (Akita).[9] Konishi appraised each harbor in terms of its shoreline, water depth and seabed quality, convenience for anchorage and
loading, inland transportation, space for future coastal development, lighthouses, dangers such as reefs and shoals, and restrictions, especially ones
owing to military needs. Assigning numbers to quantify how the ports
fared in each category, he generated a mathematical formula in which
Miyazu landed in second place behind Tsuruga, its prime competition.[10]

8. KR, vol. 17 (1893), no. 34: Kōtsū 1, "Miyazu-kō ni oite Urajiosutoku-kō nado
bōeki ni kan suru . . . ," March 14, 1893.

9. These ports may have been under scrutiny by the government, or among
those most considered to have potential; Aoki Chōnosuke evaluated the same set of
ports in his *Tsuruga-kō kaikōron*, 9. Of these seven ports, only Tsuruga and Nanao
would contend for and gain greater opening by 1899. Maizuru would become a
naval station in 1901.

10. Konishi, *Miyazu-kō*, 10.

Konishi then went on to explain that although Tsuruga's main advantages over Miyazu were its inland transportation networks and lighthouses, Miyazu already had permission to build two lighthouses and planned (pending approval) to lay a railroad connecting Miyazu to Kyoto. The line, to form an extension running directly through Maizuru, would be completed in three or four years, thus giving the edge to Miyazu.[11]

Despite Konishi's admirable efforts, his calculations could not outmaneuver Tsuruga; this rival would become a "world trade port" in 1896, but Miyazu would not. Even after Miyazu gained open port status in 1899, it struggled to succeed.[12] A full decade later, in 1909, Diet member Okada Taizō lamented the fact that even though sixteen years had passed since its initial designation as a trade port, Miyazu still was not prospering. Despite being in close proximity to Vladivostok, which he called the "headquarters of the commercial war" on the Sea of Japan, it fared poorly compared to the other international ports then open in Ura Nihon, namely, Niigata, Fushiki, Nanao, Tsuruga, Sakai, and Hamada.

With reasoning that echoed the problems suffered by Kyushu's port of Misumi in the mid-1890s, Okada attributed the lack of growth to the fact that Miyazu did not yet have the railroad extension that it needed to link the port directly to Kyoto and Osaka. To punctuate his argument, Okada used Tsuruga as a point of contrast, claiming that it was the most prosperous of the Sea of Japan ports. Turning Konishi's earlier argument on its head, Okada stated that since it did serve as a rail hub, Tsuruga had ample inland transportation and could therefore develop rapidly, whereas Miyazu could not.[13]

Both Konishi's and Okada's comments, however, are somewhat puzzling since Miyazu actually bested all these other ports in total value of both domestic trade and combined trade (nearly 22 million yen), including Tsuruga (at 20.5 million yen). In this light, their remarks appear disingenuous. When considering only the value of foreign trade, however, they are harder to dispute. Miyazu's foreign trade was indeed paltry, at under 82,000 yen, with only Nanao faring worse, at little more than 25,000 yen. The authors' concerns lay directly with the lack of

11. Ibid., 19.
12. To ensure they would receive this designation, however, Miyazu's townspeople did form a 500 member *kiseidōmei* association in 1898 to lobby for becoming a commercial port (*shōkō*) (*Yomiuri shinbun*, February 1, 1898).
13. Okada, *Nihon kai to Miyazu-kō.*

overseas commerce, especially with Vladivostok, which locals believed should be much higher. Compared to Shimonoseki's 13 million yen in foreign trade and its combined trade of nearly 70 million yen, or Moji's roughly 30 million in overseas trade and combined total of over 45 million yen, all of Ura Nihon's foreign returns were small.[14] Miyazu was certainly not alone in its disappointment that results did not meet expectations, something also found in neighboring Fushiki.

FUSHIKI AND OTARU

The next two ports to gain permission to trade with Russia and Korea were Fushiki and Otaru, in 1894. Both had already been active as special ports of export, the former drawing from a significant rice hinterland and the latter serving the Hokkaido coal trade. The stated reason for choosing this pair as special ports for Korea and Russia was that Otaru would best serve commercial transactions with the Russian coastal territories and Sakhalin while Fushiki would be suitable for trading with these areas plus Korea as well.[15] A key point in selecting these two locations over others along the Sea of Japan was that customs facilities were already there, making start-up costs considerably lower than at sites without any prior special trading status.[16]

These particular assets notwithstanding, however, their locations on the Sea of Japan placed them at a general disadvantage with respect to Japan's transportation networks. Nishi Moromoto published his 1893 tract *On Building Fushiki Port* (*Fushiki chikkōron*) with the aim of presenting an effective bid for port development, which he argued, would then help it gain open port status. Unlike Konishi and Okada, however, he tended to favor cooperation over competition in the region. Nishi wrote just before Miyazu's designation when Fushiki was still the only special trading port along the Sea of Japan coast. His strategy was to emphasize that the region did not have as many special trading ports as other parts of Japan.

14. Naimushō Dobokukyoku Kōwanka, *Dai Nihon teikoku kōwan tōkei*.

15. KR, vol. 18 (1894), no. 38: Kōtsūmon-shi, "Iburi-no-kuni Muroran-kō wo tokubetsu yushutsukō ni tsuika . . . ," May 21, 1894. It was at this same time that the Ministry of Finance added Muroran to the list of special ports of export and granted Naha permission to trade with China.

16. The *Moji shinpō*'s three-part editorial suggested that the start-up costs for Miyazu combined with an unknown ability to generate income were a cause for worry (*Moji shinpō*, October 20, 1893).

Compared to five ports in Kyushu, two in Hokkaido, and two in other parts of mainland Honshu, he argued that the Sea of Japan lagged behind. In adding the treaty ports to the picture, he further enhanced the profile of harbors in Honshu and along the Inland Sea, highlighting the geographical imbalance even more.[17]

Nishi then proceeded to identify four things needed for future growth along the Sea of Japan. Each element was directly related to changes that would come about with treaty revision: the end of extraterritoriality, tariff autonomy, the extension of foreign residence outside treaty ports, and free transactions with foreign merchants anywhere in Japan. But even after these changes were addressed, he argued that the Sea of Japan ports still faced additional difficulties since Japan's ongoing weakness in long-distance shipping meant that foreign vessels handled most of the trade with North America and Europe, leaving this commerce primarily in the hands of foreign merchants. Given these circumstances, which could not be easily remedied, Fushiki could best earn revenue by trading on Japanese ships with the opposite coast (*taigan bōeki*) of the Sea of Japan. Here he believed that Siberia constituted the most desirable market.[18]

Perhaps Nishi's arguments helped convince decision makers, for in May of the next year, Fushiki gained permission to trade with Korea and Russia. The sole stipulation was that only vessels owned by Japanese citizens could haul its cargo. In addition to expanding the locations with which Fushiki could trade, the new designation had two other immediate results. First, the port was no longer limited to the five special export-port commodities of coal, rice, sulfur, wheat, and wheat flour but could both import and export a variety of goods. Second, this designation shifted existing trade patterns on the coast, leading to a precipitous decline in trade at Niigata's proxy port of Ebisuminato by the following summer.[19] Despite arguments to the contrary, expanded trade had clear limits, at least for this part of Japan.

Miyazu and Fushiki performed comparably following their 1893 and 1894 designations as special trading ports for Korea and Russia, consistently falling in the bottom third in trade value among Japan's ports

17. Nishi, *Fushiki chikkōron*, 18–19.

18. Quotation from Nishi in Fushiki Kōshi Hensan Iinkai, *Fushiki kōshi*, 307. A key early promoter of Fushiki, Fujii Nōzo, envisioned making the Sea of Japan the "future Mediterranean of Asia" (Lewis, *Becoming Apart*, 206).

19. Fushiki Kōshi Hensan Iinkai, *Fushiki kōshi*, 311.

handling international commerce through the end of the Meiji era. They ranked ahead of only two other Ura Nihon ports, Nanao and Hamada, and the Kyushu port of Misumi.[20] Additionally, more than half of Fushiki's early trade consisted of imports, primarily salted fish, while its exports were rice and salt.[21] Despite this poor performance, Fushiki's backers would continue to fight for its development over the long term. In 1911, the Fushiki Chamber of Commerce applied to have regular steamship service to Vladivostok, a route that was finally approved almost a decade later. And with Japan's 1932 conquest of Manchuria, Fushiki contended for privilege within Japan's expanding empire by creating business associations to promote commerce in northern Korea, Manchuria, and Mongolia.[22] Overall, the Sea of Japan ports did increase their trade with these areas plus the Russian Maritime Province during the early 1930s, when, on average, Fushiki and Tsuruga, just behind Niigata, outperformed the others.[23]

Otaru, which also gained permission to trade with Russia and Korea in 1894, handled considerably more trade than either Miyazu or Fushiki.[24] This is partly attributable to the fact that it was designated primarily to export coal, which accounted for the majority of its transactions and traded at higher levels than rice.[25] Otaru also, however, had special privileges that enabled it to export additional products from its hinterland. Even before gaining permission to trade with the Russian territories, Siberia, Sakhalin, and Korea, Otaru had received unique permission in 1891 from the Ministry of Finance to export *kombu*, timber, and wooden boards.[26] Furthermore, five years later, local shipowner

20. *NZE*, 426–67; Ōkurashō Shuzeikyoku, *Nihon kanzei, zeikanshi shiryō*, 3:17–91.

21. *DNGBN*, 1894.

22. Lewis, *Becoming Apart*, 206–11; see also Young, *Japan's Total Empire*, 192, 207, and 262, on efforts in Toyama, Niigata, and other Ura Nihon prefectures to engage with new opportunities in Manchuria.

23. Naimushō Dobokukyoku Kōwanka, *Dai Nihon teikoku kōwan tōkei*, 1932–35.

24. *DNGBN*, 1899.

25. Total amounts for rice and coal exports across the special ports of export for 1893 indicate that coal sold at three times the value of rice (roughly 3 million compared to 1 million yen) (Yokkaichi-shi Kaigisho, *Yokkaichi shōkō kaigisho hyakunenshi*, 107).

26. Otaru became a special port of export in 1889, gained this unique export permission in 1891, and then was designated to trade with Russia and Korea in 1894. It further qualified for the next five goods added for special ports of export in July 1898 before becoming an open port in 1899.

Ōtsuka Shichihei received an annual government subsidy of nearly 23,000 yen (increased to more than double that amount just two years later) to run his ship, patriotically named the *Aikoku Maru* (Love of Country), on regular routes to the ports of Hakodate, Otaru, Sakhalin, Niigata, and Vladivostok.[27] This special dispensation likely originated from the government's ongoing concern over developing Hokkaido, bolstered by its newer interest in promoting the Russia trade.

Beyond those ports that did gain permission to enter the potentially lucrative Russia trade, there were others that also wished to do so but were not successful in their bids. Most notably, inhabitants of Aomori attempted to gain special export status to trade with Russia, submitting an application to the Diet in January 1895. Despite great local interest and an ardent campaign, their request was rejected largely due to the port's militarily strategic location.[28] In this mix of competition and cooperation, and success and disappointment, for harbors poised to trade with Russia, the next round of campaigns—by which port boosters sought open port status so as to import and export without geographic or commodity restrictions—also produced variable results. Whereas earlier Diet decisions considered ports on a case-by-case basis, the next wave of designations grew on a nationwide campaign to open the country's harbors in anticipation of the return of Japan's full sovereignty in 1899.

The Open Ports Movement

In late December 1894, as Japan was still preoccupied with the war in China, the Yokkaichi Chamber of Commerce met to investigate the issue of expanding Japan's international trade ports. Although the chamber's primary concern was Yokkaichi, which failed to trade even once during the five years that it had been a special port of export, it advocated change for the country's ports more broadly. Within two weeks of its first meeting, it had drafted a proposal, submitting it to the Upper and Lower Houses of the Diet as well as to the Ministries of Finance and of Agriculture and Commerce. It also sent the proposal out to ports around the country asking for their cooperation and support.

The chamber's main platform stated that current trade did not contribute sufficiently to the generation of national wealth. Considering that

27. Takabatake, *Otaru kōshi*, 186–87.
28. SGS, no. 21, February 1, 1895, 329–30.

the war—which it referred to as the "sei-Shin jiken" (conquer China incident), mirroring the name of the 1873 "sei-Kan ron" (conquer Korea debate)—appeared to be winding down and the revised treaties would soon be enacted, it argued that it was urgent to create long-range plans for Japan's international commerce. If Japan waited to act until after the system of extraterritoriality ended and the interior was "thrown open" to foreigners, it would be too late. After sympathizing with a country exhausted from war, it exhorted its audience not to rest, for "as the nation's dignity advances and its military becomes known throughout the world," it must now attend to foreign trade.[29]

The proposal compared Japan's commerce to that of thirty-eight other countries and placed it in an unacceptable twentieth place. Its solution for becoming more competitive was to open more ports, placed optimally around the country to access production hinterlands, and to establish suitable markets overseas. Notably, however, it was not seeking more special ports of export since it found them to be severely flawed. Arguing that only three of the eleven special ports of export—Shimonoseki, Kuchinotsu, and Moji—produced effective results, it listed three major problems with them: first, they were permitted exports but not imports, "which is contrary to the principle rules of trade"; second, the range of permitted export goods was excessively narrow; and, third, these restrictions proved inconvenient to foreign trade partners.[30] These criticisms turned into negatives the terms that Finance Minister Matsukata Masayoshi crafted very precisely six years earlier to enable what was then a welcome expansion of exports while still protecting the country against unwanted foreign ingress into that trade. These regulations, however, now seemed unnecessarily prohibitive to many, as the signing of revised treaties continued with the various powers and a newly vociferous public demanded Japan create a more up-to-date formula for expanding its commercial relationships.

After the proposal had circulated widely, its proponents rewrote it as a bill and submitted it to the Diet in January 1895. This Open Ports Bill bore the signatures of five Diet members who crossed party lines. Suzuki Mitsuyoshi (a Jiyūtō representative from Mie Prefecture), together with four representatives from Tokyo, Sudō Tokiichirō and the well-known free trade advocate Taguchi Ukichi (both members of

29. Yokkaichi-shi Kaigisho, *Yokkaichi shōkō kaigisho hyakunenshi*, 109.
30. Ibid.; see also *Moji shinpō*, January 22, 1895.

Taguchi's Imperial Financial Reform Party (Teikoku Zaisei Kakushintō), as well as Takagi Masatoshi and Tsunoda Shinpei (of the Constitutional Reform Party, or Rikken Kaishintō), submitted the bill.[31] They had the backing of several other Diet members, including Fukuoka Prefecture's Jiyūtō representative, Fukue Kakutarō, and its Kokumin-ha (Nationalist faction) representative, Tsutsumi Michihisa, who together would lead Moji's fight.[32]

The Open Ports Bill named six ports—Moji, Shimonoseki, Tokyo, Shimizu, Yokkaichi, and Otaru (all but Tokyo and Shimizu were already special trading ports)—that were seeking allowance to "export our country's special products and to receive commensurate imports." They would not be special trading ports but open ports. The bill demanded that these open ports be allowed to accommodate foreign residence in the service of trade. A main difference with the treaty ports, however, was that foreigners would not be permitted to own property in these new locations and would require a special license to come ashore and stay the night as long as extraterritoriality was in force.[33] The bill claimed that these six ports were optimal locations for achieving the otherwise vague goals of developing trade and contributing to the national treasury.

On being given the floor in the Lower House on January 18, 1895, it was Taguchi Ukichi who presented the bill, stating clearly that it aimed to remedy the limitations of the current port system. He quickly turned to address the special ports of export, arguing that their inability to import was a primary problem that created two further disadvantages. First, it left them able to conduct only a kind of half-trade, greatly reducing the volume of commodities, including the export of key goods, that they could handle. Second, ships cruising without return cargo had unusually high transportation costs, cutting the profitability of exports.[34] Focusing specifically on Yokkaichi, Taguchi added that the limit of five export commodities unnecessarily reduced the trade that this port could conduct with Korea and Vladivostok, especially by preventing the reexport of foreign goods.[35]

---

31. Discussions about making Tokyo an open port in late 1890 failed to produce tangible results (Taguchi, *Teiken Taguchi Ukichi zenshū*, 4:373–74).

32. Noguchi, "Meiji chūki Moji-kō," 167.

33. *Moji shinpō*, January 20, 1895.

34. SGS, no. 11, January 18, 1895, 162.

35. Ibid., 163.

More generally, Taguchi went on to address the state of Japan's econ-omy. Setting up a pointed contrast, he expressed pride in the military's newfound strength before lamenting that the nation's finances were not equally strong. Contending that commerce is the best way to generate money, he compared the sums secured by maritime customs taxes in Japan with those in countries like England and France to make the point that even though Japan's revenues had increased during the Meiji era, they were still low. The situation could be quickly remedied, he continued, by acting immediately to open these ports. After throwing this opening pitch, Taguchi next fielded a series of questions about the bill's provisions and the logistics of their implementation.[36]

Representative Suehiro Shigeyasu, for example, raised concern over how foreign settlements would function in these locations. Tagu-chi dismissed the matter, saying that opening foreign settlements was not even on the table.[37] Suehiro further questioned why none of the proposed ports were on the Sea of Japan, especially considering the po-tential for trade with Korea and Vladivostok and given that only Niigata handled overseas trade along that coast. In response, Taguchi channeled the query back to his main point, stating that Niigata's lack of dealings suggested that another port would have to be allowed to import but would first have to ensure it could turn a profit. Representative Obata Gentarō, however, intervened to correct Suehiro's comment by stating that Miyazu and Fushiki could also handle foreign trade, having re-cently gained permission to trade with Korea and Russia. He then sug-gested also considering Tsuruga, a significant port that could perform well because of its rail connections to the transportation routes of the old Tōkaidō road connecting Tokyo and Kyoto.

Reassessing the ports under consideration was not Taguchi's aim. The sponsors of the Open Ports Bill had tried to address the choice of the six sites in their original statement of reason, using the ports' effec-tive transportation infrastructures, especially direct access by railroad, as a key rationale. With regard to Moji and Shimonoseki, which already had rail junctions, the statement indicated they would be able to receive

36. Ibid.
37. Taguchi makes the same point during later deliberations in response to a similar question from Representative Kawashima Atsushi (ibid., no. 21, February 1, 1895, 325).

exports from and imports heading to a wide area across Japan's Sanyō, Kyushu, Shikoku, and Chūgoku regions. Awarding these two ports broader privileges would make shipping through the Inland Sea more convenient. Further, Shimonoseki, together with Yokkaichi and Otaru, already had permission to trade with Vladivostok and Korea, so any increase in expenses from a status change would be small.[38] The *Moji shinpō* reported that Taguchi Ukichi, perhaps in frustration over the questioning, had explained the choice of the six ports by stating simply they "are the most advantageous places." He reiterated this point in the Diet when he replied to Amano Isaemon's query about sites with the assertion that direct consultation with the localities was the best way to ensure selection of the best ones.[39]

The bill also parried the concern that allowing more places to handle trade would diminish the treaty ports already in operation. Its drafters adhered to the idea that Japan's ports were not in competition with one another since all traded for the prosperity of the country as a whole. Any losses incurred by a particular port would in essence be a sacrifice to the greater good of the country.

Although competition between ports certainly existed, as evidenced throughout the naming process, and may well have pulled trade from existing ports, as seen in Nishi's discussion of Fushiki and Ebisuminato, the bill offered historical examples aimed to underscore the more palatable idea that greater opening would improve the commercial prospects of all ports, thus giving the sense of an unlimited potential for trade.

> In earlier times, our open ports were first limited to Nagasaki and then extended to four other ports, which conducted prosperous trade and now we see two hundred million yen in imports and exports. This has decidedly not weakened Nagasaki's trade. The situation in China is also the same. In olden days they traded through Canton . . . but then Shanghai and other ports opened and today they flourish. These decidedly did not weaken Canton's trade. Recently in Korea the two ports of Inchon and Wonsan opened . . . these decidedly did not weaken Pusan's trade. . . . Opening new ports does not diminish older ports.[40]

The fact that this account of successful ports only listed treaty ports in East Asia, including those that Japan forced open in Korea, reflected

38. *Moji shinpō*, January 22, 1895.
39. Ibid., January 20, 1895; SGS, no. 21, February 1, 1895, 326.
40. *Moji shinpō*, January 20, 1895.

the reality of trade under informal imperialism. Taguchi addressed this point by saying: "Our country's treaty ports were opened at a time when we unavoidably had to accept foreign demands." He then took this familiar refrain to spin it in an unexpected direction, arguing that as a result, "several of our domestic ports of importance still have not become open ports."[41] In other words, treaty ports may have flourished, but they were by no means the only ones that could do so. With treaty revision, not only would Japan have greater latitude to make its own choices about which ports to open but there were better choices to be made.

Not everyone was convinced. Representative Obata raised the specific concern that if the port of Tokyo were to become profitable, it would cause some decline at a now-thriving Yokohama. Taguchi replied that the opposite would happen, as the two ports would complement each other. They would, for example, handle different kinds of shipping and cargo, with Tokyo in a position to use pack horses and barges while making better use of the Sumida River, which runs through the city to Tokyo Bay. Elaborating on this idea, he optimistically asserted that Tokyo could become a great East Asian marketplace, calling it "Tōyō's London."[42]

During the Diet session on February 1, 1895, the debate over the Open Ports Bill resumed in a congenial manner but soon became heated. Taguchi once again started the discussion, conversing with the Diet members present over some of the same issues discussed previously, like locations and concessions, while also raising new ones. Representative Hoshi Tōru, former chief of the Yokohama Customs House, asked whether opening these ports would invite problems with foreigners becoming involved in Japan's coasting trade. Undoubtedly, Taguchi would recognize this as a legitimate concern, knowing that it was a historical soft spot, but he unequivocally declared that it would never be permitted.[43] This pat retort likely did not allay Hoshi's legitimate fears, but the discussion nonetheless moved forward.

Midway through the meeting, Megata Tanetarō, director-general of the Tax Bureau and member of the committee hearing the bill, inquired about the logistics of these openings since they encompassed more than

41. Ibid.
42. SGS, no. 11, January 18, 1895, 163.
43. Ibid., no. 21, February 1, 1895, 326–27.

the ports themselves and would set in motion extraordinary change. Yet to be convinced that additional "doors" for trade were necessary, Megata cautioned that any such openings would at the very least require careful preparations and very clear rules.[44]

The reluctance shown at the Diet session did not thwart Taguchi and the bill's other advocates. They held their ground, in part, because they knew that broad support for their proposal did exist. Whereas the Open Ports Movement grew directly out of the revised treaties and an interest in planning for the 1899 opening of the country, it also tapped into longer-standing conversations that had been taking place between the country's protectionist and liberal factions. Even before the process of signing new treaties began, Taguchi had championed efforts to eliminate the export tax on overseas trade. The idea had won a high level of support among business leaders, gaining the endorsement of nearly 450 local business groups in 1892.[45] The delegates in Tokyo who foiled these aspirations countered, in part, with the argument that treaty revision had to be accomplished first.[46] At that time, revision was not guaranteed, making it an easy way to delay further discussion. Now, as this major obstacle to trade liberalization was being removed, some issues previously deferred came under more serious discussion.

Kawashima Atsushi, for example, asked for clarification on how these new open ports would relate to the treaty ports after revision, saying that Taguchi only claimed that there would be no relation between the two. But, he continues, after enactment, more foreigners will come to these sites to conduct trade. In Tokyo, for example, renovating the port would be costly and require building warehouses, establishing customs houses, and the like. Kawashima stated his clear opposition to the bill's sponsors and ended by trying to discredit them over their "delusions" about "turning the Sumida River into an open port."[47]

---

44. Ibid., 328.

45. The movement to abolish the export tax, as Miles Fletcher describes it, bears strategic similarity to the Open Ports Movement. In particular, both took pains to publicize their proposals and turned to news media in general and Taguchi Ukichi specifically, to gain greater support as they took their ideas to the national assembly (Fletcher, *The Japan Spinners Association*, 62). See also Taguchi, *Teiken Taguchi Ukichi zenshū*, 4:412–28.

46. Fletcher, *The Japan Spinners Association*, 63.

47. SGS, no. 21, February 1, 1895, 329.

Suzuki's rebuttal closed the debate. After thanking Kawashima for his kind recommendation that they withdraw the bill, he attempted to allay any remaining apprehension over opening these ports to international trade. Taking time to emphasize that there was no reason to be worried about foreigners accessing the coasting trade—essentially arguing that as a sovereign state, Japan could prohibit it—he then concurred that, naturally, some new laws would have to be put in place concerning how these ports operate.[48] He then revisited the issue of why these six ports were on the table, suggesting that other promising ports, such as Atsuta (renamed Nagoya in 1907), might one day be opened as well. In the meantime, however, more suitable locations, such as the Kanmon ports of Moji and Shimonoseki, had already proven their value and were already conducting foreign trade. With regard to the idea that there was no rush to open additional ports, he dismissed it as something that one could always argue. Finally, while conceding that these openings would cost money and problems would surely arise, he declared the relevant question to be whether profits would make up for them and, for these six ports, contended that they would.

Despite the strong arguments made in support of the Open Ports Bill, the House rejected it that same day. In a detailed account of the proceedings published over the course of four days, the *Moji shinpō* delineated the reasons behind the Lower House's decision. Among the objections cited were the basic and prohibitive administrative costs of placing structures like warehouses and personnel such as customs officials, police officers, and, in some cases, soldiers, in these ports. In particular, Moji and Shimonoseki would require added defenses, which included the installation of batteries and barracks. Deputy Minister of the Navy Itō Toshiyoshi had asserted that opening six additional sites would have large ramifications for the navy since it would have to be able to protect these sites as well as their major shipping routes. Such trading ports might also hinder military preparations and thus would require more elaborate investigation. He concluded with what was likely the final straw for the bill: the continuing war with China made taking such a step at this time unwise.[49]

48. Ibid., 330–31.
49. *Moji shinpō*, February 6–9, 1895; Noguchi, "Meiji chūki Moji-kō," 169; SGS, no. 21, February 1, 1895, 329–30.

Looking at the Open Ports Bill from the specific vantage point of Moji reveals a clear tension at work between Japan's commercial and military interests. Because it had already been carrying out both functions, Moji's boosters believed that an expanded role for the port during the war would help its bid for greater opening. In fact, when the bill was first proposed in the Diet, the *Moji shinpō* touted how beneficial Moji had been for a country at war and concluded that it was thus a perfect choice for an open port. After all, its military operations had earned it "official national recognition," and it had already effectively, "silently," become an open port for the military, fulfilling its needs by handling cargo and accommodating ships making roundtrips to Korea, China, and Vladivostok. As a result, Moji could readily combine its military and commercial roles to become a "great economic and military base . . . at the heart of Tōyō trade."[50] Clearly, they did not foresee that the Navy Ministry would point to Moji's very same wartime role as the primary reason to block its attempts for greater opening.

Revised Ambitions

The rejection of the Open Ports Bill did not, however, stop the people of Moji and Shimonoseki from trying again, for they quickly submitted a new joint resolution to the Lower House. Fukue and Tsutsumi signed the legislation again on behalf of Moji and Representatives Kajiyama Teisuke and Kawakita Kanshichi signed on behalf of Shimonoseki.[51] This time around, they set their sights somewhat lower, petitioning to become world trade ports instead of fully open ports. Although they were proposed together, Moji and Shimonoseki were not the only ports on the Diet's agenda. In February and March, the Lower House deliberated on six separate bills, submitted by sponsors from the ports of Tsuruga, Aomori, Moji and Shimonoseki (jointly), Hakata, and Sakai and Hamada (jointly), as well as Karatsu. All eight ports primarily sought permission to engage in the Tōyō trade, including Korea, China, the Russian Maritime Province, the Siberian coast, Sakhalin, and for Moji and Shimonoseki, even the British territories of India.[52] Perhaps surprisingly after the failed

50. *Moji shinpō*, January 22, 1895.
51. Noguchi, "Meiji chūki Moji-kō," 169.
52. *Moji shinpō*, February 7, 15, 21, March 8 and 12, 1895.

attempt the previous month, all quickly received initial approval on March 8, 1895, in the Lower House. The *Moji shinpō* announced the welcome news in large print and followed up two days later with a message from Representative Fukue indicating they would have official permission to trade with Tōyō on April 1 after the bill passed the Upper House. However, Fukue's prediction did not bear out since the bills were rejected by the Upper House before its session ended at the end of the month.[53]

Despite the rejection of this second attempt, Moji's supporters remained optimistic about their future chances for greater opening since they had at least gained approval in the Lower House. Nonetheless, some months passed before their efforts regained momentum. Peer pressure may have helped prod Mojiites to action once again. The *Moji shinpō* reported at the end of August that in the port of Misumi, then a special port of export that had not yet joined the struggle, agitated citizens were meeting to discuss gaining open trade status.[54] Over the next couple of weeks a flurry of articles came out assessing Moji's position in relation to Shimonoseki and other Kyushu trade ports, including Misumi. Some called for Moji's citizens to wake up and fight for the future position of their port.[55]

In October 1895, the *Moji shinpō* published a report comparing the trade levels of ports around the country (see Table 2). Using Ministry of Finance data for 1894, the newspaper highlighted the improving performance of both Moji and Shimonoseki, which ranked highly in Japan's port hierarchy, giving them the edge over all other special trading ports.[56] The article does not indicate how the war may have affected these totals. Combining the totals of Moji and Shimonoseki under the heading of Kanmon helped Moji statistically. By looking at Shimonoseki and Moji separately, Shimonoseki ranked fifth and Moji by itself ranked seventh, trailing Kuchinotsu only slightly.

Breaking down the numbers, Yokohama and Kobe together accounted for a striking 91 percent of Japan's total trade. Third-place Nagasaki traded at almost twice the rate of fourth-place Osaka. The trade of Kanmon as a combined port followed closely behind Osaka at

53. Ibid., March 10, 12, and 23, 1895; Noguchi, "Meiji chūki Moji-kō," 173.

54. *Moji shinpō*, August 28, 1895.

55. Ibid., August 28 and 29, September 4, 7, 14, and 29, and October 1, 3, 4, and 10, 1895.

56. These statistics correspond to those in *DNGBN* for 1894.

Table 2
Japan's Foreign Trade, 1894

Foreign Trade Ports	Total Value (yen)
1. Yokohama	123,463,000
2. Kobe	86,349,000
3. Nagasaki	8,972,000
4. Osaka	4,779,000
5. Kanmon[a]	4,198,000
(5) Shimonoseki	(2,780,000)
(7) Moji	(1,418,000)
6. Kuchinotsu	1,568,000
8. Hakodate	724,000
9. Karatsu	253,000
10. Otaru	200,000
11. Izuhara	45,000
12. Niigata	44,000
13. Muroran	29,000
14. Fushiki	28,000
15. Misumi	22,000
16. Hakata	19,000
17. Shishimi	16,000
18. Sasuna	13,000
19. Miyazu	500
TOTAL	230,722,500

SOURCE: Adapted from *Moji shinpō*, October 10, 1895.
[a] The entry for Kanmon records the combined total for Shimonoseki and Moji; if the two were ranked separately, Shimonoseki would rank fifth and Moji seventh, after Kuchinotsu.

fifth place.[57] Further, both Moji and Kuchinotsu ranked ahead of the treaty ports Hakodate and Niigata. Yet, as these numbers show, the special trading ports carried only about 3 percent of the country's nearly 231 million yen worth of trade. Looking at just the export of Japanese products gives the special trading ports closer to 5 percent. Despite the dominance of Japan's two major treaty ports, however, special trading port designations were generating significant changes in many, but not all, of the places that had received them.

57. *Moji shinpō*, October 10, 1895.

Of the sixteen special trading ports that had been designated by 1894, only three did not appear on this list—Yokkaichi, Kushiro, and Naha. An earlier article stated that Kushiro and Yokkaichi "have not as yet exported a single time," even though they had each been open for five years (Naha, by contrast, had just opened). The article explained this failure in terms resonant with the arguments made in favor of the Open Ports Bill. The problem was not a lack of export cargo or interested businesses. Rather, exports were hampered because the ports were not permitted to import.[58] Indeed, trade ratios would begin to change after port boosters won more of the privileges that they sought.[59]

In early December, interested parties held a meeting in Kokura to discuss two pending matters. The first was a new world trade port application for Moji, and the second was attracting the nation's new steel plant to the area. Representative Fukue Kakutarō met with local bigwigs, including Shimizu Yoshimasa, Kumagai Naoyoshi, Morinaga Katsusuke, as well as some members of the prefectural assembly, county heads, Moji's mayor Maeda, and approximately twenty concerned citizens from Kokura and Moji.[60] They selected the mayor as their delegate to Tokyo and he sailed for the capital at 9 PM on December 1.[61]

Although *Moji shinpō* readers did not hear much from the mayor during his extended absence, he did have the paper print a Tokyo address so that citizens could correspond with him, and at the end of the month, he sent his regrets that he could not offer proper New Year's greetings from so far away.[62] Mayor Maeda was apparently quite busy during his time in Tokyo, however, as he worked with another envoy from Kiku County, Aoyagi Shirō, to figure out how best to gain support for another bill. They consulted with others from Fukuoka, including former governor Yasuba, and met with Fujii Saburō at the Foreign Ministry's Commerce and Industry Department to learn more about official positions on the matter. Fujii's comments suggest that he was still lukewarm about Moji's greater opening, stating that "treaty revisions have still not been completed with two foreign countries, and in this present situation, it is

58. Ibid., March 7, 1895.
59. *DNGBN*, 1894–1928.
60. *Moji shinpō*, November 5, 1895.
61. Ibid., December 1, 1895.
62. Ibid., December 17 and 28, 1895.

difficult to give a definitive reply as to how we can take decisive action on this."[63] Although the Foreign Ministry continued to have its concerns, the Ministry of Finance as well as the Army and Navy ministries would also need to be convinced.[64]

On January 21, 1896, Representatives Sudō and Taguchi submitted a new Open Ports Bill on behalf of nine ports: Moji, Shimonoseki, Tokyo, Shimizu, Yokkaichi, Aomori, Tsuruga, Kagoshima, and Otaru. They cited many of the same reasons presented the previous year, emphasizing that these ports were "pivotal for the homeland" and opening them was necessary to bolster the country's wealth.[65] At the same juncture, other ports were also trying to boost their own trade by submitting a variety of bills and petitions to the Lower House. Obata Iwajirō and eight others proposed a different bill seeking permission for foreign ships to serve the Tōyō trade in the eight ports of Tsuruga, Sakai, Hamada, Shimonoseki, Hakata, Moji, Karatsu, and Aomori.[66] Four of these ports (Tsuruga, Shimonoseki, Moji, and Aomori) were named in both new pieces of legislation. Additionally, advocates for Hamada separately applied for permission to handle cargo for the Korea trade while those for Nanao applied to establish a single large port that would serve both military and commercial needs on the Sea of Japan, especially with regard to trade with Russia and Korea.[67]

By the end of March, the new bills had been rejected with the explanation that because "two or three countries" had still not signed revised treaties, the government could not acquiesce to these requests.[68] The repeated pressure from so many sites, however, may at last have

---

63. Noguchi, "Meiji chūki Moji-kō," 175.

64. *Moji shinpō*, February 1, 1896.

65. Ibid., January 25, 1896.

66. SGS, no. 29, March 3, 1896, 434–35, and no. 33, March 10, 1896, 490–92; *Moji shinpō*, March 1 and 3, 1896.

67. SGS, no. 25, February 27, 1896, 376. The people of Hamada began their bid for more trade in May 1892 when they applied to the Ministry of Finance to send goods to Shimonoseki, having them go through its customs house before being shipped overseas. This source does not clarify if the request was granted. This example, however, does raise the important question as to whether other domestic ports attempted to or had to get explicit permission to conduct foreign relay trade by way of the special trading ports' customs agencies. See also KGS, no. 38, March 19, 1896, 485; Rakusei, *Hamada kōshi*, 95.

68. SGS, no. 46, March 26, 1896, 814–15.

had an impact, for in late April, both houses approved a general statement agreeing to name four or five world trade ports.[69] A month later, the Diet confirmed that shipping allowances would be expanded to enable "foreign trade outside the open ports" and would issue a separate edict indicating which ports would be selected for this trade. Another announcement quickly followed, explaining that with the enactment of the revised treaties in 1899, those ports named as "world trade ports will become open trading ports."[70] The measure marked a huge step forward in the Open Ports Movement, but it meant that in order to become an open port in 1899, sites like Moji would first have to somehow gain import privileges. This information helped them channel their efforts in a very specific direction.

Moji's Extended Campaign

Although Moji's determined movement for greater opening contributed to these strides for the country's ports and their merchants, its strategic location and military function continued to complicate its own battle. For "Moji alone" the opinions of the civil administration and the army differed, and as a result, its appeals for designation as a world trade port continued to be turned down. The military's objection rested on Moji's position "at the entrance to our territorial waters and at the strategic junction of Kyushu and Sanyō." Since "it would be a serious matter to have foreign ships enter and leave the harbor of this natural stronghold by day and night," the Imperial Military Headquarters opposed opening this port to international trade.[71] This analysis, however, failed to indicate that the port had already been accommodating hundreds of foreign ships, including occasional warships, every year since its special trading port designation in 1889.

Earlier that year, Fukuoka governor Iwamura Takatoshi outlined what it would mean in military terms for Moji to function as an open port. "The day Moji becomes an open port" will be the day that "foreign warships can anchor at Moji." It has to be "ready to temporarily deal with the matters of foreign countries, . . . to conceal the movements and secrets

69. *Moji shinpō*, April 24, 1896.
70. Ibid., May 26, 1896.
71. Ibid.

of the military" and "to conduct foreign trade amidst military and national defense realities."[72] The governor, however, did not offer information on exactly how Moji's readiness for these responsibilities would be determined. Indeed, it is unlikely that any kind of clear formula for such preparedness existed or could be easily created.

Within just a few weeks, news and rumors trickled in about which ports the government had chosen for world trade status. On June 11, the paper reported that six places had been selected, and "we have reliably heard that two ports in Kyushu other than Moji" were among them.[73] They would have to wait nearly four months for definitive word that Matsukata Masayoshi, now prime minister, had signed the edict designating the new world trade ports. Hakata, Karatsu, and Kuchinotsu—all in Kyushu—were named, as were Tsuruga, Sakai, and Hamada—all on the Sea of Japan.[74] Of those ports named in the bill for the Tōyō trade, five of the original applicants, in addition to Kuchinotsu, had been selected while Moji, Shimonoseki, and Aomori had not. Although they may have anticipated this result, Moji's supporters were of two minds. On the one hand, the government demonstrated a new level of willingness to expand the geography of Japan's trade, which should have been good news for Moji. On the other hand, they lost out on this opportunity and now had to contend with nearby ports holding privileges that might put their more restricted commerce at risk.[75]

These selections did not satisfy Taguchi Ukichi either. He continued to have doubts about the wisdom of the special trading ports and opposed the restrictions they placed on trade partners and commodities, especially barriers on imports. Even though the newly named world trade ports differed from true commercial (*tsūshō*) ports by not allowing for foreign ships and residence, he could at least view them as a step in the right direction. The bigger problem that Taguchi had with this announcement was the choice of three Sea of Japan ports: Tsuruga, Sakai, and Hamada. An obvious strike against them, Taguchi contended, was

72. Ibid., February 7, 1896.

73. Ibid., June 11, 1896.

74. Sakai was long known as a shipbuilding and repair station, which may have contributed to its appeal (Sakai Shōkōkai, *Sakaiminato annai*, 25). In 1902, it gained a railroad line, making it an effective hub connecting land and sea transport (Omotani, *Sakaiminato yōran*, 3).

75. *Moji shinpō*, October 6, 1896.

that NYK's lack of routes to and from these ports meant that they would still not prosper. He strongly advocated that three ports on the Pacific coast be opened to trade instead, nominating Tokyo, Shimizu, and Yokkaichi to take their place (all three of which were named in the most recent Open Ports Bill).[76] The next year, he would get part of his wish when Shimizu and Yokkaichi, together with Nanao, would join the list of world trade ports in 1897.[77] Tokyo, however, would not be among them.

Following their failure to win approval that fall, Moji's advocates had gone back to work drawing up a new application. This time they expanded the geographical range of the movement even farther into Chikuhō. They formed the Moji World Trade Port Realization Committee, recruiting members from such institutions and businesses as the Eighty-Seventh National Bank, branches of the Japan Trade Bank and Japan Commercial Bank, Moji's Coal Association, and Moji's Wholesale Association, which was run by Ishida Heikichi. Others who were involved in this broad effort included Yasukawa Keiichirō and the Shimonoseki shipping agent Uriu Hajime, as well as the heads of counties, towns, and villages. In all, more than seventy people gathered to discuss a renewed initiative to win special status for Moji. Together, they decided to launch a vast campaign that would canvass all the towns and counties throughout the entire region influenced by Moji's trade.[78]

In the meantime, the *Moji shinpō* played an important role in generating interest in this movement through its detailed chronicling of the port's ongoing efforts.[79] The paper closely followed and often emphasized the progress of its home port, frequently comparing it to competing ports to demonstrate its successes and prod its readers to believe that they could achieve more. Assessments of the port's progress in both numerical and rhetorical terms expose the geographical hierarchies in which Moji was embedded. The general tenor of such reports reveals

76. Taguchi, *Teiken Taguchi Ukichi zenshū*, 4:510–12.

77. Nanao had been under consideration to be named a naval base (*gunkō*) in late 1895 (*Yomiuri shinbun*, November 27, 1895). Nanao seems an unlikely choice given its close proximity to Fushiki. Its citizens had, however, submitted an application to the Diet to be named an open port, and with comparatively little fuss, gained approval in 1897 (Ishikawa-ken, *Ishikawa-ken Nanao-kō yōran*, 3–4, 40).

78. *Moji shinpō*, November 11, 1896.

79. *KKSS*, 123.

the competitive worldview from Moji and also helps put the success of this port into a national perspective. This newspaper undoubtedly helped the regional movement continue to grow over the next several months as it gained crucial support across a wider portion of northern Kyushu.

The ongoing and intensive efforts of Moji's boosters over the course of six long years began to bear fruit in early July 1898. An imperial ordinance decreed new regulations for the ports that would open following the enactment of the revised treaties, and Mojiites still hoped to be included among them.[80] More directly, the government added five more goods—charcoal, cement, manganese ore, sulfuric acid, and bleaching powder—that Moji could export.[81] The Open Ports Movement, in all of its guises, proved effective at last with the *Moji shinpō's* July 13, 1899, announcement that both Kanmon ports, Moji and Shimonoseki, would soon become fully open international ports of trade. On the eve of Japan's return to sovereignty, the government had finally listened to the large contingent of regional voices supporting Moji and its bid for a higher level of commercial activity.[82]

Place, Nation, and Empire after 1899

From the inside, Moji's fight was about the port and its prosperity, but the nationwide Open Ports Movement meant something different to its various stakeholders. The oligarchy's first concern lay with ensuring that treaty revision progressed smoothly in order to regain the country's sovereignty and prestige. The military, especially the Navy Ministry, had its own interests in protecting strategic sites throughout the archipelago, and Kanmon in particular occupied a vital chokehold. People from different port locales saw each other as both allies and competitors who helped call attention to their own battles for advancement but might also cause their defeat. Other crusaders, like Taguchi Ukichi, at least partly engaged the open ports question in conjunction with a larger ideological fight over how Japan would operate in the world, especially as a sovereign country with freer trade choices.

80. KR, vol. 22 (1898), no. 26: Kōtsū 2, Kōshin 2, "Kaikō kōsoku wo sadamu," July 7, 1898.

81. Moji Shiyakusho, *Moji shishi,* 887.

82. *Moji shinpō,* July 14, 1899.

Taguchi was by no means the only journalist addressing the situation or the only one who believed that the government could proceed differently. Ishii Kashigorō, a reporter at *Jiji shinpō*, published *Nihon no kōwan* (Japan's harbors), a compilation of his recent articles on the subject. These investigative reports on Japan's port system (or, from his perspective, the lack thereof) had already appeared in the paper over a thirty-day span, deliberately mirroring the previous year's successful series "Tetsudō ron" (On railroads). Ishii claimed that this earlier series brought considerable attention and reform to the country's railroads, and he now wished to show that, as the end of the unequal treaties rapidly approached, Japan had to pay more attention to its ports.[83] He was less anxious about port locations than he was about port operations.

Ishii was particularly miffed by "the government's indifference" to creating effective links between land and sea transport. He saw this need in physical terms—such as the establishment of proper anchorages and landings—and in logistical ones—coordinating the timing of ship and railroad schedules—with a mind to ensure convenience and profit while minimizing the loss of sitting cargo. Further, he argued that without clearly demarcated passageways, foreign and domestic ships arbitrarily dropped anchor, which only encouraged their crews to conduct themselves with rudeness and arrogance. Since appropriate channels were not in place to report problems, people subject to such misbehavior had no official recourse against it. For reasons like these, Ishii maintained that Japan lacked a true system of ports, unnecessarily hampering its trade.[84]

Since Japan was in essence a maritime country, Ishii continued, as many ports as possible should be open. He reasoned that the "territory of countries is small, but the territory of commerce pervades the world." Anything blocking it "will be destroyed as civilization progresses. . . . Those countries that put soldiers at national boundaries, close strategic harbors, anchor battleships, tax imports, burden sailors with quarantines, etc., are continuing feudal customs."[85] In arguing against allowing Japan to operate in this closed way, Ishii was criticizing the government's protectionist tendencies. He did not think that the government was taking re-

---

83. Ishii, *Nihon no kōwan*, preface.
84. Ibid., 1–12.
85. Ibid., 135–36.

sponsibility for strategically protecting the country while ensuring its prosperity and modernization. As Ishii—and those who sponsored the Open Ports Bill—soon found out, the revision of the unequal treaties was not the final goal that needed to be achieved in order to bring prosperity to the country's ports.

The open ports differed wildly in the level of success that they found from 1899 into the 1940s. For the rest of the Meiji era, which ended in 1912, some of them accommodated quite large volumes of trade while others barely handled any trade at all (see Table 3). Many of the ports along the Sea of Japan continued to fare poorly even after becoming open ports. Limits of transportation—whether in railroads or shipping—remained a problem especially for this area. Tsuruga and Fushiki outperformed the other Sea of Japan ports until the end of World War II. These were followed by Sakai and Nanao, and then by Hamada and Miyazu, neither of which rose above their Meiji totals.[86] Of the Kyushu ports, Misumi would begin to perform at higher levels after 1912. Kuchinotsu would decline precipitously as Miike began to overtake its role in exporting coal whereas Karatsu would steadily rise in the 1910s before dropping off by 1930 as the country began to import greater amounts of coal from the Chinese mainland. On Honshu, Yokkaichi continued to handle high amounts of trade, besting Shimonoseki by the end of the Meiji era.

In the end, none of the former special trading ports did as well as Moji, a fact that was heightened when it was statistically combined (which happened whenever convenient) with Shimonoseki to comprise the port of Kanmon. During the late Meiji era, Moji handled an average amount of 27 million yen in foreign trade per year. The amount rose to an average annual total of nearly 90 million yen during the 1910s and 1920s and over 200 million yen from 1937 to 1945.[87] Shimonoseki's numbers for these same periods were also significant—coming in at just above 6 million yen (1899–1911), over 25 million (1912–26), and more

---

86. Ōkurashō Shuzeikyoku, *Nihon kanzei, zeikan shi shiryō*, 3:17–91.

87. The former treaty ports of Yokohama, Osaka, and Kobe continued to outperform other ports but the ratios of their trade began to even out. For example, in 1934 Yokohama handled only about twice as much trade as Moji. That year Yokohama tallied just over 1.5 billion yen of Japan's total 16.5 billion yen in trade while Moji held its own at close to 850 million yen. Naimushō Dobokukyoku Kōwanka, *Dai Nihon teikoku kōwan tōkei*, 1934.

Table 3
Foreign Trade Averages of the Open Ports, 1899–1911

Japan's Foreign Trading Ports	Late Meiji Era, 1899–1911 (in 1,000 yen)
1. Yokohama	306,125
2. Kobe	273,779
3. Osaka	54,112
4. Moji	27,208
5. Nagasaki	18,179
6. Yokkaichi	7,209
7. Shimonoseki	6,171
8. Kuchinotsu	3,860
9. Hakodate	3,795
10. Shimizu	2,858
11. Otaru	2,618
12. Muroran	1,947
13. Taketoyo	1,928
14. Tsuruga	1,643
15. Karatsu	1,445
16. Niigata	1,079
17. Izuhara	513
18. Hakata	307
19. Kushiro	226
20. Sakai[a]	187
21. Misumi	187
22. Fushiki	158
23. Hamada	117
24. Miyazu	90
25. Nanao	35

SOURCE: Adapted from *Nihon kanzei, zeikanshi shiryō*, 3:17–91, and *DNGBN*.
[a] Sakai and Misumi tied for twentieth place.

than 37 million (1937–45)—but nowhere close to Moji's totals. Even taking into account that Shimonoseki's significant Korea trade became domestic trade instead of foreign trade after 1910, statistics still put Moji's total trade at roughly twice Shimonoseki's by 1935.[88]

88. Ōkurashō Shuzeikyoku, *Nihon kanzei, zeikan shi shiryō*, 3:17–91; *DNGBN*, 1899–1928; Naimushō Dobokukyoku Kōwanka, *Dai Nihon teikoku kōwan tōkei*, 1909–40.

The rapid establishment of administrative institutions in these twin ports soon after their full opening indicates their readiness to operate as international ports. Within two years of the end of the treaties, in 1901, the British stationed a consulate in Shimonoseki to function for both ports. The reasons given for choosing this site directly related to the convenient location and facilities of these twin ports, which provided access to international shipping routes, domestic railways, and steady supplies of coal. As British consul Frank W. Playfair of the Shimonoseki and Moji Consular District wrote in his 1901 annual report, "There is no doubt that this is a most convenient port for vessels, other than mail steamers, loading coal, being on the direct route from Yokohama to Shanghai, Hong Kong, and Singapore. Coal is cheap and abundant and loading very expeditious."[89] The Japanese government must have agreed, for when, in 1909, it decided to replace the previously closed customs house in Niigata, Moji was named the sixth national customs house, joining those in Yokohama, Kobe, Osaka, Nagasaki, and Hakodate. And, indeed, its selection was partly based on its location in relation to a greatly increased continental trade.[90] By 1912 the United States was making arrangements to place a consulate in Moji, but World War I disrupted its plans.

The scale of Moji's growth as an industrialized city can be seen in the following description from a 1920s travel guide geared to the American touring public. It characterized Moji as "a sort of Japanese Pittsburgh" that "is not unattractive just after the rains come from heaven have washed its smudgy face." The American author's extended portrayal offers a sense of the port's activities from an outsider's perspective:

> There is an air of suppressed restlessness and energy about the place strangely out of keeping with its Japanese aspect. Immense power plants, scores of factory chimneys, clouds of sooty smoke, and all the unhandsome attributes of a manufacturing Occidental city are features of it, and the inhabitants seem determined to level all the surrounding hills and make of the spot a Kyushu metropolis. The train seems glad to get away from the dingy port, and it hurries out through the noisy suburbs to the shore of the undefiled sea where one may breathe pure air and feast the eyes on the

89. PRO FO 797/4, F.W. Playfair to the minister in Tokio, May 20, 1902. In speaking of "this port," he is referring to Kanmon, meaning both Moji and Shimonoseki.
90. Ōkurashō Zaiseishishitsu, *Ōkurashō shi,* 1:497.

inspiriting sight of hundreds of ships of all classes—steamers, fore-and-aft and square-rigged sailors, medieval junks with bellying sails like the dorsal fins of huge sea-creatures, sampans, luggers, and what-not, standing in or out of the narrow strait and betimes courtesying to the strong tide-rip that ruffles its surface.[91]

Moji appears in this guidebook because it functioned as a stop on Western travel routes, and the mood of surprise at the level of Moji's industrialization in this passage, aside from its discriminatory overtones, suggests that at least to an observer, it ranked among the world's more significant industrial cities. The city's own citizens continued to tout it in their local *Moji shinpō* as the showcase port for Japan's successful transition to industrialized modernity.

Conclusion

The years-long Open Ports Movement came at a crucial juncture in Japan's drive for equality with the Western powers. It reveals that the people and the government did ultimately work together in the service of both local and national goals. Negotiations that had taken place under duress in the 1850s set the stage for Japan's entry into the global economy. Nearly half a century later, the Japanese demonstrated a significant level of readiness to take greater control of their commercial relations. The government took clear steps to establish the legislative, military, and transportation infrastructure necessary to expand the number of locations handling foreign trade. But the real story here is the degree to which local sites around the country did all that they could—individually and in partnership with one another—to convince officials in Tokyo that they were ready and eager to engage in global commerce.

The system of special trading ports had put more trade in the hands of Japanese merchants around the archipelago, allowing them to gain not just revenue but vital experience as they worked to establish their businesses and their ports. In contrast to the treaty ports, where the vast majority of trade was conducted by foreign merchants (around 80 percent in Yokohama during the 1890s), the special trading ports generally kept at least 90 percent of trade in Japanese hands. It is difficult to know whether these trends continued into the twentieth century, as these

91. Terry, *Terry's Guide*, 650.

figures stopped being published in national statistics soon after 1899.[92] Although the timing of these openings was directly related to the treaty revision with the Western powers, the special trading ports represent the shift toward greater trade with East Asia that had been taking place in the closing two decades of the nineteenth century. The foreign trade of both Kanmon ports was conducted almost exclusively within East Asia.

Moji, in particular, continued to perform extremely well, rising to rank in the top four, behind only Yokohama, Kobe, and Osaka. As boosters predicted, Moji did, in fact, become central to the Tōyō trade, maintaining its key role as a fueling base and coal exporter. Other ports would open to accommodate foreign trade across the next few decades, including some of those that made earlier attempts, including Aomori, Kagoshima, and Nagoya. Tokyo, by contrast, would not open to foreign trade until 1941. Of those selected, none had their privileges revoked, although the trade of some, like Kuchinotsu, steadily decreased over time. In the end, the Open Ports Movement and the various local improvements, site investigations, and debates that accompanied it served the country well in its transition to full sovereignty. By the time that Japan was "thrown open" to foreign trade, Japanese merchants, officials, and politicians had all spent years preparing for that decisive moment. The former treaty ports and special trading ports would remain the primary nodes in Japan's system of foreign trade, increasingly linking the country to its growing Asian empire in the decades to come.

92. *DNGBN*, 1890–1901.

CONCLUSION

The situation of informal imperialism that existed throughout East Asia during the second half of the nineteenth century generated serious challenges and great opportunities for Japan. Ports were the first sites targeted in the opening of the country, and they remained the most significant locations in Japan for its interactions with the outside world for the rest of the Meiji era. The proximate maritime spheres with which Japan engaged under this system—the places where its ships and merchants most often traveled and conducted trade—made up transmarine East Asia and rapidly gave rise to extensive regional trade networks that intersected wider circuits of global commerce.

Attending to this system of ports was crucial in managing Japan's extended transition into the modern world of nation-states. Although such major end-of-century occasions as victory in the First Sino-Japanese War and the enactment of the revised treaties proved to be watershed moments for the country's military, industrial, and commercial development, they cannot alone explain Japan's rapid rise as an independent imperialist power. The special trading ports demonstrate that deep changes were taking place throughout Japan—in fiscal stability, transportation infrastructure, local development, and international exchange—to reveal a much longer trajectory and a much broader geography of Japan's modern integration into the world order.

This integration depended on the extended presence of Western informal imperialism in transmarine East Asia. The competitive and cooperative environment of informal imperialism simultaneously demanded

Japan's entry into the modern system of nation-states and provided the matrix in which it would modernize and become an imperialist power. The special trading ports in particular reveal how Japan worked within the system of informal imperialism to meet its own needs while working to regain its sovereign status. The Japanese understood that the empires on their waterfront represented both danger and opportunity. The launch of Japan's own empire was a constituent part of these larger efforts to gain geopolitical security, commercial power, and equality in the system of modern nation-states. The special trading ports offered one means by which Japan could pursue these goals.

The creation of Japan's port system tells us much about the Meiji era from the local to the national to the global. The history of Japan's ports reveals the multiple layers of interest involved in their creation—from local visionaries who drew up plans and scrounged for financing to prefectural assembly members and wealthy business owners who helped bring early dreams to fruition. For a port to function well, it also had to connect to national and international transportation systems. Since these broader networks provided access to hinterlands and markets alike, the people and the state had to work together to bring success to ports after they received permission to trade. Developing the smooth functioning of this infrastructure engaged local and state actors in a national dialogue about the direction of Japan and its trade. Significantly, though, local actors in the special trading ports also had to manage their direct involvement in global processes, whether in the conduct of business, politics, wartime responsibilities, or journalism.

The state also had to negotiate complex geopolitical realities to keep Japan safe from further predation while working toward the creation of a "rich nation." Pinpointing how and when Japan moved from being a semicolony to an imperialist country is no simple task and may well be a fruitless endeavor. As Martin Dusinberre states, "the slippery, contradictory processes of modernization and imperialism were two sides of the same coin."[1] The function of the special trading ports, especially as seen at Moji, confirms this view. Moreover, Japan—which operated under unequal terms of interaction at the same time that it received tremendous assistance—was able to draw on the growing system of informal imperialism within East Asia, making particular use of commercial

---

1. Dusinberre, "Janus and the Japanese Empire."

and transportation networks, to establish itself. The environment and apparatuses of imperialism were part and parcel of Japan's modernity, as seen throughout the five acts outlined in Chapter 1.

The curtain rose in the first act with the unbidden arrival of the Western powers on Japan's waterfront in the mid-1850s. Under the threat of force, the Japanese *bakufu* negotiated the unequal treaties that would establish the basic framework for Japan's international relations over the next half-century. These treaties opened five ports and two cities to foreign residence and trade, making them Japan's primary sites of international contact. These openings required Japan to alter the "four gates" that had been in place throughout most of the Tokugawa era. Importantly, the treaties did not preclude the use of other ports under Japanese jurisdiction for international trade, as seen immediately at the port of Izuhara on Tsushima, which remained open to trade with Korea. Over the next few decades, the Japanese chose to slowly open other sites in keeping with their own changing economic and strategic needs. The shift from gates to treaty ports was but the first stage in a much longer period of opening the country as Japan became an increasingly active and independent participant in the world economy. When the revised treaties were enacted in 1899, instead of six international trade ports, Japan proper had twenty-eight ports able to handle foreign trade.

The second act began when the oligarchs, who needed to bring revenue into the financially pressed country, experimented with exporting rice from sites more convenient to production hinterlands. These efforts came just as Japan turned to establishing a modern trade infrastructure—with deepwater harbors, steamships, and railroads—that built on and shifted existing transportation geographies in particular response to high demand for coal and rice, as discussed in Chapter 2. At the same time, Tokyo was also pushing for new diplomatic and commercial relationships with its neighbors, signing a commercial treaty with China, launching an informal empire in Korea, and subsuming the Ryukyu Kingdom and Hokkaido. All these processes had direct bearing on Japan's system of ports. In 1883, the oligarchs opened the ports of Izuhara, Shimonoseki, and Hakata to trade and Sasuna and Shishimi were soon to follow. Not only did these openings encourage local participation in the Korea trade at these sites, but they also deliberately channeled this trade to Japanese merchants; Western merchants were not allowed at these ports. These first two acts emphasized the ways government leaders at the national level handled their new involvement with global processes.

Without time for an intermission, domestic pressure from citizens with increasing political power, a stabilizing economy, and hopes for imminent treaty revision carried the third act. These forces combined to reconfigure regional geographies to allow new enterprises to develop and thrive. Whereas the second act was dominated by top-down processes as the oligarchs intervened directly in the country's markets and the direct export of key products, the third act highlighted the national-to-local dynamics at work in modernizing transportation and industry. As seen specifically in relation to Chikuhō and Moji, deep local involvement was essential to initiating and bringing together the elements—the coal industry, the railroads, and the port—necessary for success. Moreover, the naming of special ports of export gave merchants around Japan the opportunity to create economic opportunity for themselves and promote their local communities while also acting as vital links to national and international trade networks.

Through these channels, miners, industrialists, merchants, stevedores, and others were able to earn a livelihood on shores and in harbors where domestic lighters and foreign steamships operated alongside each other, as examined in Chapter 4. At the same time, the Meiji government also focused new attention on the country's waterways. Even though maritime commerce and naval operations were fully interdependent through the 1880s, Tokyo worked to establish the domestic shipping industry while attending to the development of its naval forces, both for protection at home and excursions abroad. Japan's military and commercial fleets necessarily developed in symbiosis with one another as the country worked to stabilize its economy and modernize its transportation infrastructure.

This process also revealed the paradox of informal imperialism in Japan. On the one hand, Japan operated at a disadvantage under the treaty port system. The country remained in a precarious financial position and a subordinate legal one. On the other hand, the Western informal empires in transmarine East Asia offered it advantages. As seen in the operation of its ports, Japan was able to make effective use of the extensive commercial networks established through informal imperialism as well as the Western ships that served them. These advantages were most notable at the special ports of export, especially Moji, where West-ern ships functioned as primary consumers and carriers of Japan's coal but only Japanese merchants could conduct this trade.

The stage in Act 4 was split in two. On one half, we see East Asia—the sites of battle during the Sino-Japanese War of 1894–95 and "Tōyō," where Japanese merchants set their sights on trade. While keeping the broader region in view, we see that Japan alone fills the other half of the stage. Chapter 5 covered Moji's role as a major hub for the country's military operations during the Sino-Japanese War. This conflict proved to be a major turning point in the East Asian balance of power, in Ja-pan's trajectory toward great power status, and in terms of generating nationalism and strong local identities. Amid the rising nationalism that came with the war effort, citizens of Moji experienced a growing pride in and increased expectations for their port. Japan's war with China be-came Moji's war as the port's daily rhythms changed to meet the military's needs. Moji's activities during the war reveal a newfound importance for the port as well as a strong awareness that this local site was engaging directly with events taking place on a global scale.

After the war, the port's boosters channeled their faith in Moji's sig-nificance and promise into the Open Ports Movement. Although rheto-ric about Moji neatly fits into the strong narrative of Japan's amazing progress during the late nineteenth century, the Open Ports Move-ment demonstrates that its rise was at no time a given fact. This move-ment, as is true of the longer story of the creation of Japan's modern port system, demonstrates a mixture of competition and cooperation, missteps and cunning, and successes and failures along the way. As the Open Ports Movement revealed in Chapter 6, the choice of which ports to favor for development at the national level was often not clear and prosperity was by no means automatic. In many cases, even after local boosters gained national attention for their port development projects, they still did not manage to win the transportation connections or the trade that was so vital for prosperity.

Despite the vicissitudes of their campaigns, local groups fought hard for themselves and their ports, challenging the Meiji oligarchs through the media and the national assembly to heed their calls for greater access to international trade. Boosters at ports around the country were able to envision their potential within both the national hierarchy of ports and global patterns of commerce. In working to secure their own status, these localities came up against the government's attempts to regain the country's sovereignty. Local and national goals—open ports and sovereignty—were not fundamentally at odds but at times they appeared to be so, especially during the decisive years from 1894 to 1899. In the end, local boosters helped push the government toward a greater liberalization of trade at multiple sites throughout the archipelago.

The last scene, Act 5, began with the enactment of the revised treaties in 1899. Celebrations in Moji and other ports in Japan highlighted the progress that the country and these localities achieved in the course of nearly five decades. The ports designated as "open" that summer formed the core of the country's port system and its global connections. From that moment, they became firmly tied to economic and geopolitical developments in transmarine East Asia and thus were the primary sites from which Japan increasingly expanded its control over the region.

At the end of World War II, in an attempt to bring down the Japanese empire, the United States firebombed several of these ports, including Kobe, Moji, Shimonoseki, Tsuruga, Yokkaichi, and Yokohama, precisely because they were among the primary locations used for military transportation and industrial production during the empire's heyday. Although many of these ports were repaired and reopened during the U.S. Occupation and in the postwar period, the end of Japan's empire and the rise of a post-industrial world decisively changed their operations. From today's vantage, though, the original geographical contours of the special trading ports are still visible in the country's twenty-first century port system.

Moji Today

Today Moji's old waterfront has the air of a post-industrial ghost town. The Mojikō Retro Tourist Association, however, does its best to revive the local cultural heritage and generate income by recreating Moji as a tourist town, low-key as it may be, aimed at visitors seeking an authentic experience of the past.[2] Moji's buildings from the late Meiji and Taishō

---

2. See, for example, Robertson, "It Takes a Village," Weisenfeld, "Touring Japan-as-Museum," and Wigen, "Politics and Piety." Sakaiminato is another former special trading port that promotes tourism, in part, through its Meiji-era history. See, for example, http://www.sakaiminato.net/foreign/en/history.html (accessed March 22, 2014).

(1912–1926) eras have been preserved and relocated to create a short-distance walking tour of the historic city. Bicycle rentals and rickshaws for hire are also available for those so inclined. Visitors can choose to have lunch in the dining room of the old Mitsui Club, see the bed where Albert Einstein spent a night in 1922, walk through the former customs house, visit the Kyushu Railway Museum, or enjoy a high-rise panoramic view of the area from an observation deck.[3] One can take a ferry across the rough waters of the Kanmon Strait to Shimonoseki and then stroll to the modest brick building where Itō Hirobumi and Li Hong-zhang signed the 1895 Treaty of Shimonoseki, now a museum commemorating that moment in history.

Another historic tribute comes every autumn when Moji hosts its annual banana festival, the Banachan Taikai. The once-thriving coal business has been downplayed in favor of the entertaining banana trade and its lively auctions.[4] Bananas were first imported into Japan through Moji soon after the country gained possession of Taiwan in 1895 and quickly became a Moji specialty (*meibutsu*). During the festival, the Mojikō Banana Auction Preservation Association (Mojikō Banana Tata-kiuri Hozonkai) reenacts the fast-pitched sales designed to sell ripe bananas as they were unloaded from ships just back from Taiwan. A man in period dress stands in the public square in front of the train station, a Renaissance Revival structure. Bunches of yellow bananas are spread out before him. His loud chanting and rhythmic stick beating attract a crowd. This street auctioneer's words entice onlookers to bid on the once-exotic fruit: "Listen to the history of how these bananas came to Japan. Grown in rural Taiwan . . . they traveled by steamship to the port of Kelung and from there crossed glittering waves of gold and silver . . . to finally reach Moji, this great city of Kyushu. . . . Buy bananas here at the port of Moji while they are still at the peak of flavor."[5] Tourists who successfully compete can walk away with a large bunch of bananas purchased at a very low price.

Most days, however, the old port of Moji is a relatively quiet place offering a quaint and "romantic" stroll through time. A glimmer of the

---

3. A more recently built attraction, which opened in 2003, is the Kaikyō Drama-ship, a high-tech museum overlooking the Kanmon Strait.

4. Today one of Moji's key businesses is the refrigerated shipping of fruit.

5. Nagaki, "Mojikō to banana," 42–43.

city's earlier history is visible through its well-preserved historic buildings and waterfront.[6] The real richness of Moji's history, however, is
missing from today's tourist town: the coal that was once its life blood.

Reminders of the coal trade can be found more readily at the nearby
port of Wakamatsu, where the Wakachiku Construction Company
houses a small museum and library. The company was originally established in 1888 to build Wakamatsu's harbor and remains in the construction and real estate businesses today. The history of coal can also be
found throughout the Chikuhō region. The Asō family mansion spreads
behind a wall at the top of a hill overlooking the area. Even though its
mines are now closed and their entrances boarded up, museums as well
as former miners tell tales of difficult lives. Slag heaps covered with grass
dot the landscape, and population and income levels remain relatively
low. In the heart of Chikuhō, the humble Tagawa City Coal and History
Museum preserves local stories of the coal industry and its miners.

The coal trade's geographical connections between Chikuhō and
Moji and from Moji to other ports in Japan and on the Asian continent
are not easy to find in these highly localized memorials. Also absent from
these histories is a sense of transmarine East Asia's complex relationships. Today's displays of historical Moji present a highly selective view
of the past that tends to erase the imperialism that supported its earlier
vitality, skirting the issue by directing attention to the area's level of
Westernized modernity during that era.

New kinds of ties have replaced Moji's previous networks, but
connections to East Asia remain an important part of the area's identity.
Moji is now a district of the city of Kitakyushu, having been amal-
gamated with four other previously independent cities—Kokura, Yahata, Tobata, and Wakamatsu—in 1963. Today, this city of 1 million,
which just celebrated its fiftieth anniversary with much fanfare, boasts
that it is the "Gateway to Asia."[7] Kitakyushu has a new international
airport with flights to such cities as Shanghai and Vladivostok and it

6. The major port for container traffic, the Hibiki Container Terminal, opened
in Wakamatsu-ku in 2005. The port of Shin Moji to the northeast of the former
Moji primarily serves as a ferry terminal.

7. See, for example, the city's newsletter, *Kitakyushu Bridges*, vol. 27 (September
2006), https://www.city.kitakyushu.lg.jp/files/000085348.pdf; and the city of Kitakyushu's 50th Anniversary Commemorative homepage, http://www.kita
kyushu50th.jp (accessed October 15, 2013).

initiated the establishment of a "pan–Yellow Sea" economic conference to promote development in cities in Japan (Kitakyushu, Fukuoka, and Shimonoseki), South Korea (Pusan and Ulsan), and northeast China. Just before the 2005 opening of the new Hikibi Container Terminal in Kitakyushu (Wakamatsu-ku), the city's English-language newsletter declared that with the establishment of this facility "Kitakyushu will take a big step forward as an international shipping locus." The terminal also planned to offer reduced customs fees in order to draw new business and ensure it would become "attractive as an entry point to Japanese markets."[8]

On the eve of the twenty-first century, Kitakyushu's mayor Kōichi Sueyoshi listed the city's three major assets as "its advantageous location in the heart of East Asia, its great tradition in industry, and its long-established role as a key junction for transportation."[9] These advantages are essentially the same (just change "tradition" to "future promise" and "long-established" to "newly established") as those that first drew people to Moji in the 1880s and helped its boosters gain open port status in 1899. The historical context and the tenor of the waterfront has changed greatly since then, but local boosters in and around Moji continue to promote the significance of this place as a key site in East Asia.

8. *Kitakyushu Bridges*, vol. 25 (September 2005), http://www.city.kitakyushu.lg.jp/english/e20100007.html.
    9. Ibid., vol. 13 (August 1999).

Bibliography

Newspapers Consulted

Japan Gazette
Japan Weekly Mail
Kitakyushu Bridges
Moji shinpō
New York Times
North China Herald
Times (London)
Yomiuri shinbun

Archival Sources

British Public Records Office, Foreign Office Archives, London
Kokuritsu Kōbunshokan (National Archives of Japan) Digital Archive
Kokuritsu Kokkai Toshokan (National Diet Library of Japan) Kindai Digital Library
Kokuritsu Kokkai Toshokan (National Diet Library of Japan) Teikoku Gikai Kaigiroku

Primary and Secondary Sources

Allen, Matthew. *Undermining the Japanese Miracle: Work and Conflict in a Japanese Coal Mining Community.* Cambridge: Cambridge University Press, 1994.

Aoki Kazuo et al., eds. *Nihon shi daijiten.* Tōkyō: Heibonsha, 1992.

Applegate, Celia. "A Europe of Regions: Reflections on the Historiography of Sub-National Places in Modern Times." *American Historical Review* 104, no. 4 (October 1999): 1157–82.

Arano, Yasunori. "The Entrenchment of the Concept of 'National Seclusion.'" *Acta Asiatica* 67 (1994): 83–103.

Arrighi, Giovanni, Takeshi Hamashita, and Mark Selden. "Introduction: The Rise of East Asia in Regional and World Historical Perspective." In *The Resurgence of East Asia: 500, 150, and 50 Year Perspectives*, ed. Giovanni Arrighi, Takeshi Hamashita, and Mark Selden, 1–16. New York: Routledge, 2003.

Auslin, Michael R. *Negotiating with Imperialism: The Unequal Treaties and the Culture of Japanese Diplomacy*. Cambridge: Harvard University Press, 2004.

Barlow, Tani E. "History and the Border." *Journal of Women's History* 18, no. 2 (Summer 2006): 8–32.

———. "Asian Women in Reregionalization." *positions: east asia cultures critique* 15, no. 2 (Fall 2007): 285–318.

Bayly, C.A. *The Birth of the Modern World, 1780–1914: Global Connections and Comparisons*. Malden, MA: Blackwell, 2004.

Beasley, W.G., trans. and ed. *Select Documents on Japanese Foreign Policy, 1853–1868*. London: Oxford University Press, 1955.

———. *Japanese Imperialism: 1894–1945*. New York: Oxford University Press, 1987.

Bentley, Jerry H. "Sea and Ocean Basins as Frameworks of Historical Analysis." *Geographical Review: Oceans Connect* 89, no. 2 (April 1999): 215–24.

Benton, Lauren. *A Search for Sovereignty: Law and Geography in European Empires, 1400–1900*. Cambridge: Cambridge University Press, 2010.

Biersteker, Thomas J., and Cynthia Weber. "The Social Construction of State Sovereignty." In *State Sovereignty as Social Construct*, ed. Thomas J. Biersteker and Cynthia Weber, 1–21. Cambridge: Cambridge University Press, 1996.

Black, Jeremy. *The British Seaborne Empire*. New Haven: Yale University Press, 2004.

Braudel, Fernand. *The Mediterranean and the Mediterranean World in the Age of Philip II*. Vol. 1. New York: Harper & Row, 1972.

Brechin, Gray. *Imperial San Francisco: Urban Power, Earthly Ruin*. Berkeley: University of California Press, 1999.

Broeze, Frank. "Introduction: Brides of the Sea." In *Brides of the Sea: Port Cities of Asia from the 16th–20th Centuries*, ed. Frank Broeze, 1–28. Honolulu: University of Hawai'i Press, 1989.

Brown, Sidney Devere. "Ōkubo Toshimichi: His Political and Economic Policies in Early Meiji Japan." *Journal of Asian Studies* 21, no. 2 (February 1962): 183–97.

Burbank, Jane, and Frederick Cooper. *Empires in World History: Power and the Politics of Difference*. Princeton: Princeton University Press, 2010.

Caprio, Mark E. *Japanese Assimilation Policies in Colonial Korea, 1910–1945*. Seattle: University of Washington Press, 2009.

Cassel, Pär Kristoffer. *Grounds of Judgment: Extraterritoriality and Imperial Power in Nineteenth-Century China and Japan*. New York: Oxford University Press, 2012.

Chaiklin, Martha. "Monopolists to Middlemen: Dutch Liberalism and American Imperialism in the Opening of Japan." *Journal of World History* 21, no. 2 (June 2010): 249–69.

Chamberlain, Basil Hall. "The Luchu Islands and Their Inhabitants: I. Introductory Remarks." *Geographical Journal* 5, no. 4 (April 1895): 289–319.

Chang, Richard T. "The Chishima Case." *Journal of Asian Studies* 34, no. 3 (May 1975): 593–612.

Chida, Tomohei, and Peter N. Davies. *The Japanese Shipping and Shipbuilding Industries*. London: Athlone Press, 1990.

Chikuhō Sekitan Kōgyōshi Nenpyō Hensan Iinkai, ed. *Chikuhō sekitan kōgyōshi nenpyō*. Vols. 1–4. Fukuoka: Nishi Nihon Bunka Kyōkai, 1973.

Conroy, Hilary. *The Japanese Seizure of Korea, 1868–1910: A Study of Realism and Idealism in International Relations*. Philadelphia: University of Pennsylvania Press, 1960.

Cortazzi, Hugh. *Victorians in Japan: In and Around the Treaty Ports*. London: Athlone Press, 1987.

Crawcour, E. Sydney. "Economic Change in the Nineteenth Century." In *Cambridge History of Japan*, Vol. 5: *The Nineteenth Century*, ed. Marius B. Jansen, 569–617. Cambridge: Cambridge University Press, 1989.

————. "*Kōgyō Iken*: Maeda Masana and His View of Meiji Economic Development." *Journal of Japanese Studies* 23, no. 1 (Winter 1997): 69–104.

Cronon, William. *Nature's Metropolis: Chicago and the Great West*. New York: W.W. Norton, 1991.

Deuchler, Martina. *Confucian Gentlemen and Barbarian Envoys: The Opening of Korea, 1875–1885*. Seattle: University of Washington Press, 1977.

Dohi Noritaka. *Kinsei beikoku ryūtsūshi no kenkyū*. Tōkyō: Rinjinsha, 1969.

Domon Ken. *Chikuhō no kodomotachi*. Tōkyō: Shogakkan, 1985.

Dōyashiki Takejirō. *Kitakyūshū no jinbutsu*. Vol. 1. Kokura: Kineidō, 1931.

Dubois, Colette. "The Red Sea Ports During the Revolution in Transportation, 1800–1914." In *Modernity and Culture: From the Mediterranean to the Indian Ocean*, ed. Leila Tarazi Fawaz and C.A. Bayly, 58–74. New York: Columbia University Press, 2002.

Dudden, Alexis. *Japan's Colonization of Korea: Discourse and Power*. Honolulu: University of Hawai'i Press, 2004.

Dusinberre, Martin. "Janus and the Japanese Empire." *Journal of Colonialism and Colonial History* 14, no. 1 (Spring 2013), http://muse.jhu.edu.ezproxy.memphis.edu /journals/journal_of_colonialism_and_colonial_history/v014/14.1.dusinberre .html.

Duus, Peter. "Japan's Informal Empire in China, 1895–1937: An Overview." In *The Japanese Informal Empire in China, 1895–1937*, ed. Peter Duus, Ramon H. Myers, and Mark R. Peattie, xi–xxix. Princeton: Princeton University Press, 1989.

————. *The Abacus and the Sword: The Japanese Penetration of Korea, 1895–1910*. Berkeley: University of California Press, 1995.

Ericson, Steven J. *The Sound of the Whistle: Railroads and the State in Meiji Japan*. Cambridge: Council on East Asian Studies, Harvard University, 1996.

Eskildsen, Robert. "Of Civilization and Savages: The Mimetic Imperialism of Japan's 1874 Expedition to Taiwan." *American Historical Review* 107, no. 2 (April 2002): 388–418.

Evans, David C., and Mark R. Peattie. *Kaigun: Strategy, Tactics, and Technology in the Imperial Japanese Navy, 1887–1941*. Annapolis: Naval Institute Press, 1997.

Flershem, Robert G. "Some Aspects of the Japan Sea Trade in the Tokugawa Period." *Journal of Asian Studies* 23, no. 3 (May 1964): 405–16.

Fletcher, Joseph. "The Heyday of the Ch'ing Order in Mongolia, Sinkiang and Tibet." In *The Cambridge History of China*, vol. 10: *Late Ch'ing, 1800–1911*, ed. John K. Fairbank, 351–408. Cambridge: Cambridge University Press, 1978.

Fletcher, Max E. "The Suez Canal and World Shipping, 1869–1914." *Journal of Economic History* 18, no. 4 (1958): 556–73.

Fletcher, W. Miles. "The Japan Spinners Association: Creating Industrial Policy in Meiji Japan." *Journal of Japanese Studies* 22, no. 1 (Winter 1996): 49–75.

Fox, Grace E. *Britain and Japan, 1858–1883*. Oxford: Clarendon Press, 1969.

Fox, Edward Whiting. *History in Geographic Perspective: The Other France*. New York: W.W. Norton, 1971.

Frost, Peter K. *The Bakumatsu Currency Crisis*. Cambridge: East Asian Research Center, Harvard University, 1970.

Fujimura Toru, Matsukata Mineo, and Okubo Tatsumasa, eds. *Matsukata Masayoshi kankei monjo*. Vols. 2–3. Tōkyō: Daitō Bunka Daigaku Tōyō Kenkyūjo, 1979–2001.

Fukuoka-shi Kōwankyoku. *Hakata kōshi: kaikō hyakushūnen kinen*. Fukuoka: Fukuoka-shi Kōwankyoku Seisaku Gyōsei, 2000.

Fushiki Kōshi Hensan Iinkai. *Fushiki kōshi*. Takaoka: Fukushi-kō Kaiun Shinkōkai, 1973.

Gallagher, John, and Ronald Robinson. "The Imperialism of Free Trade." *Economic History Review* 6, no. 1 (1953): 1–14.

Gluck, Carol. *Japan's Modern Myths: Ideology in the Late Meiji Period*. Princeton: Princeton University Press, 1985.

Gordon, Andrew. *The Evolution of Labor Relations in Japan: Heavy Industry, 1853–1955*. Cambridge: Council on East Asian Studies, Harvard University, 1985.

Grove, Linda, and S. Sugiyama. "Introduction." In *Commercial Networks in Modern Asia*, ed. S. Sugiyama and Linda Grove, 1–14. Richmond: Curzon Press, 2001.

Hall, Catherine. *Civilising Subjects: Colony and Metropole in the English Imagination, 1830–1867*. Chicago: University of Chicago Press, 2002.

Hamashita, Takeshi. "Tribute and Treaties: Maritime Asia and Treaty Port Networks in the Era of Negotiation, 1800–1900." In *The Resurgence of East Asia: 500, 150, and 50 Year Perspectives*, ed. Giovanni Arrighi, Takeshi Hamashita, and Mark Selden, 17–50. New York: Routledge, 2003.

Hane, Mikiso. *Peasants, Rebels, and Outcastes: The Underside of Modern Japan*. New York: Pantheon Books, 1982.

Hane, Mikiso, and Louis G. Perez. *Modern Japan: A Historical Survey*. Boulder: Westview Press, 2009.

Hara Takeshi. *Meijiki kokudo bōeishi*. Tōkyō: Kinseisha, 2002.

Harada Wasaku. *Ōsaka shōsen kabushiki gaisha kōro annai*. Ōsaka: Shinshindō, 1903.

Harland-Jacobs, Jessica. *Builders of Empire: Freemasons and British Imperialism, 1717–1927*. Chapel Hill: University of North Carolina Press, 2007.

Hawks, Francis L., comp. *Narrative of the Expedition of an American Squadron to the China Seas and Japan.* New York: HMS Press, 1967.

Hayashi Eidai. *Kaikyō no onnatachi: Kanmon-kō okinakashi no shakaishi.* Fukuoka: Ashi Shobō, 1983.

Hein, Laura E. *Fueling Growth: The Energy Revolution and Economic Policy in Postwar Japan.* Cambridge: Council on East Asian Studies, Harvard University, 1990.

Hellyer, Robert I. *Defining Engagement: Japan and Global Contexts, 1640–1868.* Cambridge: Harvard University Asia Center, 2009.

Hidemura Senzō and Tanaka Naoki. Introduction to *Chikuhō tankōshi,* by Kōnoe Kitarō. Moji: Kinkodō, 1898. Reprint, Tōkyō: Bunken Shuppan, 1975.

Hiroi Isamu. *Nihon chikkōshi.* Tōkyō: Maruzen, 1927.

Hiyama Yukio. "Nisshin sensō no rekishiteki ichi." In *Kindai Nihon no keisei to Nisshin sensō: sensō no shakaishi,* ed. Hiyama Yukio, 16–34. Tōkyō: Yūzankaku Shuppan, 2001.

Hoare, J.E. "The Chinese in the Japanese Treaty Ports, 1858–1899: The Unknown Majority." In *Proceedings of the British Association for Japanese Studies,* vol. 2, part 1:18–33. Sheffield: University of Sheffield, 1976–86.

————. *Japan's Treaty Ports and Foreign Settlements: The Uninvited Guests, 1858–1899.* Folkestone, Kent, UK: Japan Library, 1994.

Hong, Lysa. " 'Stranger within the Gates': Knowing Semi-Colonial Siam as Extraterritorials." *Modern Asian Studies* 38, no. 2 (May 2004): 327–54.

Hopkins, A.G., ed. *Globalization in World History.* New York: W.W. Norton, 2002.

Horowitz, Richard S. "International Law and State Transformation in China, Siam, and the Ottoman Empire during the Nineteenth Century." *Journal of World History* 15, no. 4, (December 2004): 445–86.

Howe, Christopher. *The Origins of Japanese Trade Supremacy: Development and Technology in Asia from 1540 to the Pacific War.* London: Hurst, 1996.

Howell, David L. *Geographies of Identity in Nineteenth-Century Japan.* Berkeley: University of California Press, 2005.

Huber, J. Richard. "Effect on Prices of Japan's Entry into World Commerce after 1858." *Journal of Political Economy* 79, no. 3 (May–June 1971): 614–28.

Huffman, James L. *Creating a Public: People and Press in Meiji Japan.* Honolulu: University of Hawai'i Press, 1997.

Imamura Motoichi. *Shashinshū Meiji, Taishō, Shōwa Moji: Furusato no omoide 56.* Tōkyō: Kokusho Kankōkai, 1979.

Imano Takashi. "Meiji 20 nen zengo ni okeru Chikuhō sekitan kōgyō—sentei kōku o megutte." *Enerugii shi kenkyū* 12 (June 1983): 9–28.

Inukai, Ichirou, and Arlon R. Tussing. " 'Kōgyō Iken': Japan's Ten Year Plan, 1884." *Economic Development and Cultural Change* 16, no. 1 (October 1967): 51–71.

Irish, Ann B. *Hokkaido: A History of Ethnic Transition and Development on Japan's Northern Island.* Jefferson, NC: McFarland, 2009.

Ishii Kashigorō. *Nihon no kōwan.* Tōkyō: Jiji shinpōsha, 1898.

Ishikawa-ken. *Ishikawa-ken Nanao-kō yōran.* Kanazawa: Ishikawa-ken, 1912.

Jansen, Marius B. "Japanese Imperialism: Late Meiji Perspectives." In *The Japanese Colonial Empire, 1895–1945*, ed. Ramon H. Myers and Mark Peattie, 61–79. Princeton: Princeton University Press, 1984.

Japan Unyusho, ed. *Principal Ports in Japan, 1952*. Tokyo: Japan Port and Harbor Association, 1952.

Jones, F.C. *Extraterritoriality in Japan and the Diplomatic Relations Resulting in Its Abolition, 1853–1899*. New York: AMS Press, 1970.

Kadokawa Nihon Chimei Daijiten Hensan Iinkai, ed. *Kadokawa Nihon chimei daijiten*. Tōkyō: Kadokawa Shoten, 1988.

Kalland, Arne, and Brian Moeran. *Japanese Whaling: End of an Era?* London: Curzon Press, 1993.

Kalland, Arne, and Jon Pederson. "Famine and Population in Fukuoka Domain during the Tokugawa Period." *Journal of Japanese Studies* 10, no. 1 (Winter 1984): 31–72.

Kamen, Henry. *Empire: How Spain Became a World Power, 1492–1763*. New York: HarperCollins, 2003.

Kanmon Kōro Kōji Jimusho, ed. *Kanmon kōro: Rekishi aru kaikyō no nagare*. Kitakyūshū: Kitakyūshū-shi, 1999.

Kasaba, Reşat. "Treaties and Friendships: British Imperialism, the Ottoman Empire, and China in the Nineteenth Century." *Journal of World History* 4, no. 2 (Fall 1993): 215–41.

Katō, Eiichi. "Research Trends in the Study of the History of Japanese Foreign Relations at the Start of the Early Modern Period: On the Reexamination of 'National Seclusion'"—From the 1970s to 1990s. *Acta Asiatica* 67 (1994): 1–29.

Katō, Hidetoshi. "The Significance of the Period of National Seclusion Reconsidered." *Journal of Japanese Studies* 7, no. 1 (Winter 1981): 85–109.

Katsuki Yasuharu. *Ongagawa: ryūiki no bunka shi*. Fukuoka: Kaichōsha, 1994.

Kerr, George H. *Okinawa, the History of an Island People*. Rutland, VT: C.E. Tuttle, 1958.

Kim, Key-Hiuk. *The Last Phase of the East Asian World Order: Korea, Japan, and the Chinese Empire, 1860–1882*. Berkeley: University of California Press, 1980.

Kim, Kyu Hyun. *The Age of Visions and Arguments: Parliamentarianism and the National Public Sphere in Early Meiji Japan*. Cambridge: Harvard University Press, 2007.

Kim, Minkyu. "Revolutions and the Transmutation of the East Asian Interstate System: The Meiji Restoration, the Kapsin Coup, and the Regulation System." Ph.D. dissertation, University of California at Los Angeles, 2006.

Kitakyūshūshi, ed. *Kitakyūshūshi sangyō shi*. Kitakyūshū: Kitakyūshūshi Sangyōshi, Kōgai Taisakushi, Dobokushi Hensan Iinkai Sangyōshi Bukai, 1998.

Kitakyūshūshi Kaikō Hyakunenshi Hensan Iinkai, ed. *Kitakyūshū no kōshi: Kitakyūshūkō kaikō hyakunen o kinen shite*. Kitakyūshū: Kitakyūshū-shi Kōwankai, 1990.

Kitakyūshū Shishi Hensan Iinkai, ed. *Kitakyūshū shishi: kindai gendai, kyōiku bunka*. Kitakyūshū: Kitakyūshū-shi, 1986.

———. *Kitakyūshū shishi: kindai gendai, sangyō keizai*. Vols. 1–2. Kitakyūshū: Kitakyūshū-shi, 1991–1992.

Kizu Shigetoshi. *Nippon Yūsen senpaku 100-nenshi*. Tōkyō: Kaijinsha, 1984.

Knight, Alan. "Britain and Latin America." In *The Oxford History of the British Empire*, vol. 3, *The Nineteenth Century*, ed. Andrew Porter, 122–45. Oxford: Oxford University Press, 1999.

Knight, Franklin W., and Peggy K. Liss, eds. *Atlantic Port Cities: Economy, Culture, and Society in the Atlantic World, 1650–1850*. Knoxville: University of Tennessee Press, 1991.

Kobayashi Shigeru, Watanabe Rie, and Yamachika Kumiko. "Shoki gaihō sokuryō no tenkai to Nisshin sensō." *Shirin* 93, no. 4 (July 2010): 1–33.

Kodama Kota and Kawazoe Shōji, eds. *Fukuoka-ken no rekishi*. Tōkyō: Yamakawa Shuppansha, 1997.

Kokaze Hidemasa. *Teikoku shūgikano Nihon kaiun: Kokusai kyōsō to taigai jiritsu*. Tōkyō: Yamakawa Shuppansha, 1995.

Kokubu Kazuo. *Shittemoraitai Nihon no minato*. Tōkyō: Kindai Bungeisha, 2000.

Konishi Yasubei, ed. *Miyazu-kō wo shite Nihonkai no bōeki-kō to nasu no ikensho*. Kyōto: Konishi Yasubei, 1894. http://kindai.ndl.go.jp/info:ndljp/pid/805576.

Kōno Shōhei. *Yokkaichi chikkō*. Yokkaichi-shi: Yokkaichi Kōwan Kairyōkai, 1908. http://kindai.ndl.go.jp/info:ndljp/pid/846157.

Kōnoe Kitarō. *Moji kōshi*. Moji: Kinkodō, 1897. Repr., Tōkyō: Meicho Shuppan, 1973.

Kramer, Paul A., "Power and Connection: Imperial Histories of the United States in the World." *American Historical Review* 116, no. 5 (December 2011): 1348–49.

Kumabe Mamoru. "Sekitan sangyō hattenki ni okeru Kuchinotsu-kō no seisui." *Jinbun chiri* 24, no. 5 (October 1972): 66–80.

Kutney, Gerald. *Sulfur: History, Technology, Applications & Industry*. Toronto: Chem Tec Pub, 2007.

Larsen, Kirk W. *Tradition, Treaties, and Trade: Qing Imperialism and Chosŏn Korea, 1850–1910*. Cambridge: Harvard University Asia Center, 2008.

Lee, John. "Trade and Economy in Preindustrial East Asia, c. 1500–c. 1800: East Asia in the Age of Global Integration." *Journal of Asian Studies* 58, no. 1 (February 1999): 2–26.

Lewis, James B. *Frontier Contact Between Chosŏn Korea and Tokugawa Japan*. London: Routledge Curzon, 2003.

Lewis, Michael. *Becoming Apart: National Power and Local Politics in Toyama, 1868–1945*. Cambridge: Harvard University Asia Center, 2000.

Lin, Ming-te. "Li Hung-chang's Suzerain Policy toward Korea, 1882–1894." In *Li Hung-chang and China's Early Modernization*, ed. Samuel C. Chu and Kwang-Ching Liu, 176–205. Armonk, NY: M.E. Sharpe, 1994.

Lloyd's Register of British and Foreign Shipping, ed. *Lloyd's Register of British and Foreign Shipping*. London: Cox and Wyman, 1893–94.

Lone, Stewart. *Japan's First Modern War: Army and Society in the Conflict with China, 1894–95*. New York: St. Martin's Press, 1994.

Lynn, Martin. "British Policy, Trade, and Informal Empire in the Mid-Nineteenth Century." In *The Oxford History of the British Empire*, vol. 3: *The Nineteenth Century*, ed. Andrew Porter, 101–21. Oxford: Oxford University Press, 1999.

Marston, Geoffrey. "British Extra-Territorial Jurisdiction in Japan: The Case of the *Ravenna* and the *Chishima*." *British Year Book of International Law* 68 (1997): 219–45.

Masuda Hiromi. *Japan's Industrial Development Policy and the Construction of the Nobiru Port: The Case Study of a Failure.* Tokyo: United Nations University, 1981.

———. "Coastal and River Transport," and "Policy." In *Technological Innovation and the Development of Transportation in Japan,* ed. Hirofumi Yamamoto, 7–15 and 32–44. Tokyo: United Nations University Press, 1993.

Matsukata, Fuyuko. "King Willem II's 1844 Letter to the Shogun: 'Recommendation to Open the Country.'" Trans. Adam Clulow. *Monumenta Nipponica* 66, no. 1 (2011): 99–122.

McClain, James L. "Local Politics and National Integration: The Fukui Prefectural Assembly in the 1880s." *Monumenta Nipponica* 31, no. 1 (1976): 51–75.

McMaster, John. "The Takashima Mine: British Capital and Japanese Industrialization." *Business History Review* 37, no. 3 (Autumn 1963): 217–39.

McPherson, Kenneth. "Port Cities as Nodal Points of Change: The Indian Ocean, 1890s–1920s." In *Modernity and Culture: From the Mediterranean to the Indian Ocean,* ed. Leila Tarazi Fawaz and C.A. Bayly, 75–95. New York: Columbia University Press, 2002.

Metzler, Mark. *Lever of Empire: The International Gold Standard and the Crisis of Liberalism in Prewar Japan.* Berkeley: University of California Press, 2006.

Mihalopoulos, Bill. *Sex in Japan's Globalization, 1870–1930: Prostitutes, Emigration, and Nation-Building.* London: Pickering & Chatto, 2011.

Mitani, Hiroshi. *Escape from Impasse: The Decision to Open Japan.* Trans. David Noble. Tokyo: International House of Japan, 2006.

Mitsui Bussan Kaisha. *Miike Coal, with a Description of the Coalfield, the Quality of the Coal, Testimonials from Consumers, Together with Sailing Directions for the Ports of Shipment, Kuchinotzu and Misumi, Customs Regulations, Telegraph Code, etc., etc.* Shanghai: North China Herald Office, 1893.

Mitsui Mining Department, comp. *The Mining Enterprise of the Mitsui Firm.* Tokyo: Mitsui Mining Department, 1910.

Moji Chikkō Gaisha. "Moji chikkō gaisha teikan." 1886.

Moji Shiyakusho, ed. *Minato to ayunda 70 nen.* Moji: Moji Shiyakusho, 1959.

———. *Moji shishi.* Moji: Moji Shiyakusho, 1933.

———. *Moji-shi tōkei nenpō.* Vols. 1–4. Moji: Moji Shiyakusho, 1911–15.

———. *Shize chōsa shiryō.* Vol. 1. Moji: Moji Shiyakusho, 1904.

Moritake Takahiro. *Sekai ni Shizuoka-ken cha utta otoko: Shimizu-kō kara hajime no chokuyushutsu.* Shizuoka: Shizuoka Shinbunsha, 1993.

Morris-Suzuki, Tessa. "Lines in the Snow: Imagining the Russo-Japanese Frontier." *Pacific Affairs* 72, no. 1 (Spring 1999): 57–77.

Morrissey, Katherine G. *Mental Territories: Mapping the Inland Empire.* Ithaca: Cornell University Press, 1987.

Moulder, Frances. *Japan, China, and the Modern World Economy: Toward a Reinterpretation of East Asian Development ca 1600 to ca 1918.* Cambridge: Cambridge University Press, 1977.

Nagaki Nobufumi. "Mojikō to banana." *Hiroba Kitakyūshū* 3, no. 177 (2001).

Nagasue Toshio. *Chikuhō: Sekitan no chiikishi.* Tōkyō: Nihon Hōsō Shuppan Kyōkai, 1973.

Naimushō Dobokukyoku Kōwanka, ed. *Dai Nihon teikoku kōwan tokei.* Tōkyō: Kōwan Kyōkai, 1909–1940.

Nakamura, Naofumi. *Chihō kara no sangyō kakumei: Nihon ni okeru kigyō bokkō no gendōryoku.* Nagoya: Nagoya Daigaku Shuppankai, 2010.

Nakano Kinjirō. *Kaikyō taikan: Kanmon kaikyō oyobi Kitakyūshū no taigaiteki hatten to sono shōrai.* Moji: Kaikyō Kenkyūjo, 1925.

Ng, Benjamin Wai-Ming. "Making of a Japanese Community in Prewar Period (1841–1941)." In *Foreign Communities in Hong Kong, 1840s-1950s,* ed. Cindy Yik-yi Chu, 111–32. New York: Palgrave Macmillan, 2005.

Nippon Yūsen Kabushiki Kaisha, ed. *Voyage of a Century: Photo Collection of NYK Ships.* Tokyo: Nippon Yūsen Kaisha, 1985.

Nish, Ian Hill. *The Anglo-Japanese Alliance: The Diplomacy of Two Island Empires, 1894–1907.* London: Athlone Press, 1966.

Nishi Moromoto. *Fushiki chikkōron.* Toyama: Hokuriku Seironsha, 1893. http://kindai.ndl.go.jp/info:ndljp/pid/846128.

Nishi Nihon Bunka Kyōkai, ed. *Fukuoka kenshi: Chikuhō sekitan kōgyō kumiai.* Vol. 2. Fukuoka: Fukuoka Prefecture, 1987.

———. *Fukuoka kenshi: Kindai shiryōhen, Chikuhō kōgyō tetsudō.* Vol. 1. Fukuoka: Fukuoka Prefecture, 1990.

———. *Fukuoka kenshi: Tsūshi hen.* Vol. 1. Fukuoka: Nishi Nihon Bunka Kyōkai, 2003.

Nishi Nihon Shinbunsha, ed. *Fukuoka-ken hyakka jiten.* Fukuoka: Nishi Nihon Shinbunsha, 1982.

Noguchi Fumi. "Meiji chūki Moji-kō no tokubetsu yushutsunyū-kō shōkaku undō ni tsuite." In *Kindai Nihon no kigyoka to seiji: Yasukawa Keiichirō to sono jidai,* ed. Manabu Arima, 166–89. Tōkyō: Yoshikawa Kōbunkan, 2009.

Ogino Yoshihiro. "Meiji chūki ni okeru Chikuhō sekitan kōgyō kumiai no soshiki to katsudō: Meiji 18 nen no seiritsu kara Meiji 33 nen koro made." *Enerugii shi kenkyū* 13 (December 1984): 1–32.

Oguma, Eiji. *"Nihonjin" no kyōkai: Okinawa, Ainu, Taiwan, Chōsen, shokuminchi shihai kara fukki undō made.* Tōkyō: Shin'yōsha, 1998.

Okada Taizō. *Nihon kai to Miyazu-kō.* Kyōto: Okada Taizō, 1909. http://kindai.ndl.go.jp/info:ndljp/pid/765864.

Ōkurashō, ed. *Dai Nihon gaikoku bōeki nenpyō.* Tōkyō: Ōkurashō, 1882–1928.

———. *Kōbushō enkaku hōkoku.* Tōkyō: Ōkurashō, 1888.

Ōkurashō Kanzeikyoku, ed. *Zeikan hyakunenshi.* Tōkyō: Nippon Kanzei Kyōkai, 1972.

Ōkurashō Shuzeikyoku, ed. *Nihon kanzei, zeikanshi shiryō.* Vol. 3. Tōkyō: Ōkurashō Zeikanbu, 1958.

Ōkurashō Zaiseishishitsu. *Ōkurashō shi: Meiji Taisho Showa.* Vol. 1. Tōkyō: Ōkura Zaimu Kyōkai, 1998.

Omotani Tomotarō. *Sakaiminato yōran.* Sakai-machi (Tottori-ken): Dai Hachikai Tottori Shimane Ryōken Shūzen Kumiai Rengō Seishuhin Hinpyōkai Kyōsankai, 1917. http://kindai.ndl.go.jp/info:ndljp/pid/958197.

Osterhammel, Jürgen. "Britain and China, 1842–1914." In *The Oxford History of the British Empire*, vol. 3: *The Nineteenth Century*, ed. Andrew Porter, 146–69. Oxford: Oxford University Press, 1999.

————. "Semi-Colonialism and Informal Empire in Twentieth Century China: Towards a Framework of Analysis." In *Imperialism and After: Continuities and Discontinuities*, ed. Wolfgang J. Mommsen and Jürgen Osterhammel, 290–314. London: Allen & Unwin, 1986.

Ōwaki Seijun. *Beikokuron.* Tōkyō: Shōkabō, 1900.

Ōyama Azusa. *Kyūjōyakuka ni okeru kaishi kaikō no kenkyū: Nihon ni okeru gaikokujin kyoryūchi.* Tōkyō: Ōtori Shobō, 1988.

Paine, S.C.M. *The Sino-Japanese War of 1894–1895: Perceptions, Power, and Primacy.* New York: Cambridge University Press, 2003.

Patrick, Hugh T. "External Equilibrium and Internal Convertibility: Financial Policy in Meiji Japan." *Journal of Economic History* 25, no. 2 (June 1965): 187–213.

Peattie, Mark R. "Introduction." In *The Japanese Colonial Empire, 1895–1945*, ed. Ramon H. Myers and Mark R. Peattie, 3–52. Princeton: Princeton University Press, 1984.

Perez, Louis G. *Japan Comes of Age: Mutsu Munemitsu and the Revision of the Unequal Treaties.* Cranbury, NJ: Associated University Presses, 1999.

Pineau, Roger, ed. *The Japan Expedition, 1852–1854: The Personal Journal of Matthew Calbraith Perry.* Washington, DC: Smithsonian Institution Press, 1968.

Pittau, Joseph. "Inoue Kowashi, 1843–1895, and the Formation of Modern Japan." *Monumenta Nipponica* 20, no. 3/4 (1965): 253–82.

Pomeranz, Kenneth. *The Great Divergence: China, Europe, and the Making of the Modern World Economy.* Princeton: Princeton University Press, 2000.

Rafael, Vincente L. "Regionalism, Area Studies, and the Accidents of Agency." *American Historical Review* 104, no. 4 (October 1999): 1208–20.

Rakusei. *Hamada kōshi.* Hamada-machi (Shimane-ken): Rakusei, 1900. http://kindai.ndl.go.jp/info:ndljp/pid/766268.

Rawlinson, John L. *China's Struggle for Naval Development, 1839–1895.* Cambridge: Harvard University Press, 1967.

Rekidai Chiji Hensankai, ed. *Nihon no rekidai chiji.* Tōkyō: Rekidai Chiji Hensankai, 1981.

Robertson, Jennifer. "It Takes a Village: Internationalization and Nostalgia in Postwar Japan." In *Mirror of Modernity: Invented Traditions of Modern Japan*, ed. Stephen Vlastos, 110–29. Berkeley: University of California Press, 1998.

Sakai Shōkōkai. *Sakaiminato annai.* Sakai-machi (Tottori-ken): Sakai Shōkōkai, 1906. http://kindai.ndl.go.jp/info:ndljp/pid/766179.

Sakurai Makoto. *Kome sono seisaku to undō.* Tōkyō: Nobunkyo, 1989–1990.

Samuels, Richard J. *The Business of the Japanese State: Energy Markets in Comparative and Historical Perspective.* Ithaca: Cornell University Press, 1987.

―――. *Rich Nation, Strong Army: National Security and the Technological Transformation of Japan.* Ithaca: Cornell University Press, 1994.

Sasaki, Junnosuke. *Modes of Traditional Mining Techniques.* Tokyo: United Nations University, 1980.

Sawada Yōtarō. *Okinawa to Ainu: Nihon no minzoku mondai.* Tōkyō: Shinsensha, 1996.

Saya Makito. *Nisshin sensō: "kokumin" no tanjo.* Tōkyō: Kodansha, 2009.

Schencking, J. Charles. *Making Waves: Politics, Propaganda, and the Emergence of the Imperial Japanese Navy, 1868–1922.* Stanford: Stanford University Press, 2005.

Schmid, Andre. "Colonialism and the 'Korea Problem' in the Historiography of Modern Japan: A Review Article." *Journal of Asian Studies,* 59, no. 4 (November 2000): 951–976.

Shimazu, Naoko. *Japanese Society at War: Death, Memory and the Russo-Japanese War.* Cambridge: Cambridge University Press, 2009.

Shimizu, Hiroshi, and Hirakawa Hitoshi. *Japan and Singapore in the World Economy: Japan's Economic Advance into Singapore, 1870–1965.* New York: Routledge, 1999.

Shimonoseki-shi. *Shimonoseki shishi.* Vol. 1. Shimonoseki: Shimonoseki Shikyakusho, 1958–1965.

Smith, Thomas C. *Political Change and Industrial Development in Japan: Government Enterprise, 1868–1880.* Stanford: Stanford University Press, 1955.

Smith, W. Donald. "Gender and Ethnicity in Japan's Chikuho Coalfield." In *Towards a Comparative History of Coalfield Societies,* ed. Stefan Berger, Andy Croll, and Norman LaPorte, 204–218. Burlington, VT: Ashgate, 2005.

Society for the Registry of Shipping, ed., *Lloyd's Register of British and Foreign Shipping.* London: Wyman and Son, 1893–94.

Stanley, Amy. *Selling Women: Prostitution, Markets, and the Household in Early Modern Japan.* Berkeley: University of California Press, 2012.

Sugiyama, Shin'ya. *Japan's Industrialization in the World Economy, 1859–1899: Export Trade and Overseas Competition.* London: Athlone Press, 1988.

Sumiya Mikio. *Nihon sekitan sangyō bunseki.* Tōkyō: Iwanami Shoten, 1968.

Sumiya, Mikio, and Koji Taira. *An Outline of Japanese Economic History, 1603–1940.* Tokyo: University of Tokyo Press, 1979.

Taguchi Ukichi. *Teiken Taguchi Ukichi zenshū.* Tōkyō: Yoshikawa Kobunkan, 1990.

Taiwan Jimukyoku, ed. *Taiwan jijō ippan.* Tōkyō-shi Taiwan Jimukyoku, 1898.

Takabatake Yoshikazu. *Otaru kōshi.* Takigawa-mura (Hokkaido): Takabatake Toshiyoshi, 1899.

Takeda Reitarō. *Chikugo hana mushiro Moji sekitan chōsa.* Kurume: Shiritsu Kurume Shōgyō Gakkō Dōsōkai, 1903.

Takeuchi Masato. *Dai Nihon bōekiron: Tokubetsu yushutsu hen.* Tōkyō: Shōshōkai, 1890.

Tanaka Kazuji. *Teikoku no Kanmon.* Ōsaka: Sekizenkan Honten, 1915.

Tanaka, Stefan. *Japan's Orient: Rendering Pasts into History.* Berkeley: University of California Press, 1993.

Tashiro, Kazui. "Foreign Relations during the Edo Period: *Sakoku* Reexamined." Trans. Susan Downing Videen. *Journal of Japanese Studies* 8, no. 2 (Summer 1982): 283–306.

Terry, T. Philip. *Terry's Guide to the Japanese Empire*. Boston: Houghton Mifflin, 1920.

Toby, Ronald P. *State and Diplomacy in Early Modern Japan: Asia in the Development of the Tokugawa Bakufu*. Princeton: Princeton University Press, 1984.

Tōjō Nobumasa. "Chikuhō sekitan kōgyō ni okeru kindaika katei—Asō Namazuta tankō no kikaika wo chūshin toshite." In *Senzenki Chikuhō tankōgyō no keiei to rōdō*, ed. Ogino Yoshihiro, 1–36. Kyōto: Keibunsha, 1990.

―――. "Karatsu kaigun tankō no settei to sono keiei." *Keizaigaku kenkyū* 59, nos., 3–4 (March 1994): 81–109.

―――. "Meiji-ki Nihon ni okeru saisho no Chōsenjin rōdōsha: Saga-ken Choja tankō no tankōfu." *Keizaigaku kenkyū* 57, nos. 3–4 (August 1992): 297–315.

―――. "Nisshin sengo no Chikuhō ni okeru Chōsenjin tankō rōdōsha boshū keikaku." In *Fukuoka kenshi: Kindai kenkyū hen*, ed. Nishi Nihon Bunka Kyōkai, 57–68. Fukuoka: Fukuoka Prefecture, 1987.

Totman, Conrad. *The Green Archipelago: Forestry in Pre-Industrial Japan*. Berkeley: University of California Press, 1989.

Tsuda Koreyasu. "*Moji Shinpō* kabunushi meibo." Kitakyūshū Shiritsu Chūō Toshokan, Kitakyūshū-shi, Fukuoka-ken, Japan, 1892.

―――. "*Moji shinpō* hakkō no shushi oyobi hōhō." Kitakyūshū Shiritsu Chūō Toshokan, Kitakyūshū-shi, Fukuoka-ken, Japan, 1892.

Tsugawa Masayuki. *Ōsaka Dōjima komeshōkaijo no kenkyū*. Kyōto-shi: Kōyō Shobō, 1990.

Uchida, Jun. *Brokers of Empire. Japanese Settler Colonialism in Korea, 1876–1945*. Cambridge: Harvard University Asia Center, 2011.

United Kingdom. Public Record Office. Foreign Office. General Correspondence and Consular Court Records for Japan. 1888–1920.

Vaporis, Constantine Nomikos. *Breaking Barriers: Travel and the State in Early Modern Japan*. Cambridge: Council on East Asian Studies, Harvard University, 1994.

Vlastos, Stephen. "Opposition Movements in Early Meiji, 1868–1885." In *Cambridge History of Japan*, vol. 5: *The Nineteenth Century*, ed. Marius B. Jansen, 367–431. Cambridge: Cambridge University Press, 1989.

Walker, Brett L. *The Conquest of Ainu Lands: Ecology and Culture in Japanese Expansionism, 1590–1800*. Berkeley: University of California Press, 2001.

Weisenfeld, Gennifer. "Touring Japan-as-Museum: *NIPPON* and Other Japanese Imperialist Travelogues." *positions: east asia cultures critique* 8, no. 3 (Winter 2000): 747–93.

Wigen, Kären. "Culture, Power, and Place: The New Landscapes of East Asian Regionalism." *American Historical Review* 104, no. 4 (October 1999): 1183–1201.

―――. "The Geographic Imagination in Early Modern Japanese History: Retrospect and Prospect." *Journal of Asian Studies* 51, no. 1 (February 1992): 3–29.

———. *The Making of a Japanese Periphery, 1750–1920.* Berkeley: University of California Press, 1995.

———. *A Malleable Map: Geographies of Restoration in Central Japan, 1600–1912.* Berkeley: University of California Press, 2010.

———. "Politics and Piety in Japanese Native-Place Studies: The Rhetoric of Solidarity in Shinano." *positions: east asia cultures critique* 4, no. 3 (Winter 1996): 491–517.

———. "Introduction." In *Seascapes: Maritime Histories, Littoral Cultures, and Transoceanic Exchanges,* ed. Jerry H. Bentley, Renate Bridenthal, and Kären Wigen, 1–20. Honolulu: University of Hawai'i Press, 2007.

Williams, Harold S. *The Story of Holme Ringer & Co., Ltd. in Western Japan, 1868–1968.* Tokyo: Charles E. Tuttle, 1968.

Wilson, Noell Howell. *Defensive Positions: The Politics of Maritime Security in Tokugawa Japan.* Cambridge: Harvard University Asia Center, forthcoming.

Wray, William D. *Mitsubishi and the N.Y.K., 1870–1914: Business Strategy in the Japanese Shipping Industry.* Cambridge: Council on East Asian Studies, Harvard University, 1984.

Yamamoto, Hirofumi, ed. *Technological Innovation and the Development of Transportation in Japan.* Tokyo: United Nations University Press, 1993.

Yamashita Naoto. "Nihon shihonshugi seiritsuki ni okeru Higashi Ajia sekitan shijō to Mitsui Bussan: Shanhai shijō wo chūshin ni." *Enerugii shi kenkyū* 8 (June 1977): 83–91.

———. "Higashi Ajia sekitan shijō no tenkai to kōzō." In *Senzenki Chikuhō tankōgyō no keiei to rōdō,* ed. Ogino Yoshihiro, 309–57. Kyōto: Keibunsha, 1990.

Yano Makio. *Sekitan no kataru Nihon no kindai.* Tōkyō: Soshiete, 1978.

Yasuba Yasukichi. "Gaikō kaiun to keizai hatten: sekitan to no kanren wo chūshin ni." *Enerugii shi kenkyū* 8 (June 1977): 43–53.

Yasuba Yasukichi, ed. *Yasuba Yasukazu den, 1835–1899: goketsu, mushi no seijika.* Tōkyō: Fujiwara Shoten, 2006.

Yiengpruksawan, Mimi Hall. *Hiraizumi: Buddhist Art and Regional Politics in Twelfth Century Japan.* Cambridge: Harvard University Asia Center, 1998.

Yokkaichi-shi Kaigisho. *Yokkaichi shōkō kaigisho hyakunenshi.* Yokkaichi: Yokkaichi Shōkō Kaigisho, 1993.

Yokkaichi-shi Kyōikukai. *Yokkaichi kōshi.* Yokkaichi: Yokkaichi-shi Kyōikukai, 1936.

Yokohama Zeikan, ed. *Nagasaki zeikan enkaku.* Vol. 3. Yokohama: Tōkyō Insatsu Kabushiki Gaisha, 1902.

———. *Ōsaka zeikan enkakushi.* Vol. 1. Yokohama: Yokohama Zeikan, 1905.

Yonezu Saburō. *Meiji no Kitakyūshū.* Kitakyūshū: Kokura Kyōdokai, 1964.

Young, Louise. *Japan's Total Empire: Manchuria and the Culture of Wartime Imperialism.* Berkeley: University of California Press, 1998.

Yunesko Higashi Ajia Bunka Kenkyū Sentā, ed. "Treaty of Peace, Amity and Commerce between Great Britain and Japan, Edo, August 26, 1858." In *The Meiji Japan Through Contemporary Sources.* Vol. 1, ed. Yunesko Higashi Ajia Bunka Kenkyū Sentā, 36–44. Tokyo: Centre for East Asian Cultural Studies, 1969.

Index

Page numbers followed by the terms "map" or "table" in italics indicate cross-references to that category of material the text.

Harvard East Asian Monographs
(titles now in print)

69. Eric Widmer, *The Russian Ecclesiastical Mission in Peking during the Eighteenth Century*

73. Jon Sigurdson, *Rural Industrialism in China*

74. Kang Chao, *The Development of Cotton Textile Production in China*

75. Valentin Rabe, *The Home Base of American China Missions, 1880–1920*

78. Meishi Tsai, *Contemporary Chinese Novels and Short Stories, 1949–1974: An Annotated Bibliography*

80. Endymion Wilkinson, *Landlord and Labor in Late Imperial China: Case Studies from Shandong by Jing Su and Luo Lun*

84. J. W. Dower, *Empire and Aftermath: Yoshida Shigeru and the Japanese Experience, 1878–1954*

85. Martin Collcutt, *Five Mountains: The Rinzai Zen Monastic Institution in Medieval Japan*

86. Kwang Suk Kim and Michael Roemer, *Growth and Structural Transformation*

89. Sung Hwan Ban, Pal Yong Moon, and Dwight H. Perkins, *Rural Development*

92. Edward S. Mason, Dwight H. Perkins, Kwang Suk Kim, David C. Cole, Mahn Je Kim et al., *The Economic and Social Modernization of the Republic of Korea*

93. Robert Repetto, Tai Hwan Kwon, Son-Ung Kim, Dae Young Kim, John E. Sloboda, and Peter J. Donaldson, *Economic Development, Population Policy, and Demographic Transition in the Republic of Korea*

94. Parks M. Coble, Jr., *The Shanghai Capitalists and the Nationalist Government, 1927–1937*

96. Richard Wich, *Sino-Soviet Crisis Politics: A Study of Political Change and Communication*

97. Lillian M. Li, *China's Silk Trade: Traditional Industry in the Modern World, 1842–1937*

98. R. David Arkush, *Fei Xiaotong and Sociology in Revolutionary China*

100. James Reeve Pusey, *China and Charles Darwin*

101. Hoyt Cleveland Tillman, *Utilitarian Confucianism: Chen Liang's Challenge to Chu Hsi*

102. Thomas A. Stanley, *Ōsugi Sakae, Anarchist in Taishō Japan: The Creativity of the Ego*

103. Jonathan K. Ocko, *Bureaucratic Reform in Provincial China: Ting Jih-ch'ang in Restoration Kiangsu, 1867–1870*

104. James Reed, *The Missionary Mind and American East Asia Policy, 1911–1915*

105. Neil L. Waters, *Japan's Local Pragmatists: The Transition from Bakumatsu to Meiji in the Kawasaki Region*

106. David C. Cole and Yung Chul Park, *Financial Development in Korea, 1945–1978*

107. Roy Bahl, Chuk Kyo Kim, and Chong Kee Park, *Public Finances during the Korean Modernization Process*

108. William D. Wray, *Mitsubishi and the N.Y.K., 1870–1914: Business Strategy in the Japanese Shipping Industry*

109. Ralph William Huenemann, *The Dragon and the Iron Horse: The Economics of Railroads in China, 1876–1937*

111. Jane Kate Leonard, *Wei Yüan and China's Rediscovery of the Maritime World*

Harvard East Asian Monographs

Harvard East Asian Monographs

Harvard East Asian Monographs

351. Michel Mohr, *Buddhism, Unitarianism, and the Meiji Competition for Universality*
352. J. Keith Vincent, *Two-Timing Modernity: Homosocial Narrative in Modern Japanese Fiction*
354. Chong-Bum An and Barry Bosworth, *Income Inequality in Korea: An Analysis of Trends, Causes, and Answers*
355. Jamie L. Newhard, *Knowing the Amorous Man: A History of Scholarship on* Tales of Ise
356. Sho Konishi, *Anarchist Modernity: Cooperatism and Japanese-Russian Intellectual Relations in Modern Japan*
357. Christopher P. Hanscom, *The Real Modern: Literary Modernism and the Crisis of Representation in Colonial Korea*
358. Michael Wert, *Meiji Restoration Losers: Memory and Tokugawa Supporters in Modern Japan*
359. Garret P. S. Olberding, ed., *Facing the Monarch: Modes of Advice in the Early Chinese Court*
360. Xiaojue Wang, *Modernity with a Cold War Face: Reimagining the Nation in Chinese Literature Across the 1949 Divide*
361. David Spafford, *A Sense of Place: The Political Landscape in Late Medieval Japan*
362. Jongryn Mo and Barry Weingast, *Korean Political and Economic Development: Crisis, Security, and Economic Rebalancing*
363. Melek Ortabasi, *The Undiscovered Country: Text, Translation, and Modernity in the Work of Yanagita Kunio*
364. Hiraku Shimoda, *Lost and Found: Recovering Regional Identity in Imperial Japan*
365. Trent E. Maxey, *The "Greatest Problem": Religion and State Formation in Meiji Japan*
366. Gina Cogan, *The Princess Nun: Bunchi, Buddhist Reform, and Gender in Early Edo Japan*
367. Eric C. Han, *Rise of a Japanese Chinatown: Yokohama, 1894–1972*
368. Natasha Heller, *Illusory Abiding: The Cultural Construction of the Chan Monk Zhongfeng Mingben* 中峰明本 *(1263–1323)*
369. Paize Keulemans, *Sound Rising from the Paper: Nineteenth-Century Martial Arts Fiction and the Chinese Acoustic Imagination*
370. Simon James Bytheway, *Investing Japan: Foreign Capital, Monetary Standards, and Economic Development, 1859–2011*
371. Sukhee Lee, *Negotiated Power: The State, Elites, and Local Governance in Twelfth-Fourteenth China*
372. Ping Foong, *The Efficacious Landscape: On the Authorities of Painting at the Northern Song Court*
373. Catherine L. Phipps, *Empires on the Waterfront: Japan's Ports and Power, 1858–1899*
374. Sunyoung Park, *The Proletarian Wave: Literature and Leftist Culture in Colonial Korea, 1910–1945*
375. Barry Eichengreen, Wonhyuk Lim, Yung Chul Park, and Dwight H. Perkins, *The Korean Economy: From a Miraculous Past to a Sustainable Future*
376. Heather Blair, *Real and Imagined: The Peak of Gold in Heian Japan*

Harvard East Asian Monographs